The ARM RISC Chip
A Programmer's Guide

The ARM RISC Chip
A Programmer's Guide

Alex van Someren

Carol Atack

ADDISON-WESLEY PUBLISHING COMPANY

WOKINGHAM, ENGLAND • READING, MASSACHUSETTS • MENLO PARK, CALIFORNIA • NEW YORK
DON MILLS, ONTARIO • AMSTERDAM • BONN • SYDNEY • SINGAPORE
TOKYO • MADRID • SAN JUAN • MILAN • PARIS • MEXICO CITY • SEOUL • TAIPEI

© 1994 Addison-Wesley Publishers Ltd.
© 1994 Addison-Wesley Publishing Company Inc.

The programs in this book have been included for their instructional value. They have been tested with care but are not guaranteed for any particular purpose. The publisher does not offer any warranties or representations nor does it accept any liabilities with respect to the programs.

Many of the designations used by manufacturers and sellers to distinguish their products are claimed as trademarks. Addison-Wesley has made every attempt to supply trademark information about manufacturers and their products mentioned in this book. A list of the trademark designations and their owners appears on page xviii.

Cover designed by Designers & Partners, Oxford
and printed by The Ethedo Press, High Wycombe, Bucks
Camera-ready copy prepared by the author.
Printed and bound in Great Britain by The University Press, Cambridge.

First printed 1993

ISBN 0–201–62410–9

British Library Cataloguing-in-Publication Data
A catalogue record for this book is available from the British Library.

Library of Congress Cataloging-in-Publication Data is available

In memory of Al Thomas

Foreword

In 1986, Apple established an R&D group called the Advanced Technology Group (ATG). ATG's mission was to explore new technologies that would be important to Apple in the 1990s. We began research and advanced development in areas such as multimedia, object-oriented systems, handheld devices and RISC.

The goal of one early ATG project, code-named Möbius, was to design and prototype a low-cost, high-performance experimental computer. In their search for an appropriate processor, the Möbius engineers discovered Acorn's ARM, the first commercial RISC processor. They found the ARM to be easy to program and to deliver impressive performance for its price.

During the ensuing years, various Apple groups incorporated versions of the ARM into other experimental designs, including a printer controller and a communications controller. The elegant architecture gained a small but devoted following in the company. Yet it still did not make its way into any Apple product.

In the summer of 1990 a small 'skunkworks' group called the Advanced Products Group (APG) was defining a new system architecture called 'Newton'. We sought a microprocessor to power the first product in the line. Given the cost, mobility and performance goals of the project, we specified a fully static part with frugal memory requirements offering a high MIPS-per-watt ratio at a low cost.

We had determined from an earlier ATG analysis of microprocessor architectures that RISC technology covers a wide spectrum of products. The most publicized RISC architectures at that time were those designed for high-end workstations. In the workstation market, top speed is the single most important design criterion. One example of a high-end RISC processor is IBM's Power architecture. Apple and Motorola have worked with IBM to develop Power into PowerPC. The Macintosh computer family will attain new levels of performance through PowerPC.

In 1990, designs for embedded control and other high-volume applications were less well known than those for workstation RISC processors. In these markets, low power consumption, small die size and very low costs are more important factors than absolute speed. While specifying the requirements of a processor for Newton, we noted that our criteria were similar to those for embedded control applications.

That summer, we conducted an assessment of low-cost RISC processors, including designs that our semiconductor vendors had on their drawing boards. We concluded that the simplicity of the ARM bestowed upon it inherent advantages that its competitors would be unlikely to soon surmount. These advantages included die size, cost, power consumption, instruction set efficiency and ease of embedding into ASIC designs.

Although we were impressed by Acorn's processor architecture, we became concerned that their requirements and ours would diverge as years went by. To alleviate that concern, we agreed that an Apple subsidiary, Apple UK would, with VLSI Technology and Acorn, invest in an independent joint venture to develop and market ARM technology.

The founders charged the new company, ARM Ltd, with transforming the ARM from an Acorn standard into an industry standard. The product family would address the nascent market for low-cost, low-power consumption RISC processors. We felt that small, hand-held computing devices would become a significant growth area for our industry and that ARM had the right characteristics to win a significant share of that market.

Because of its CISC-like code density, software for an ARM processor requires less memory than software for RISC architectures targeted at the workstation market. In late 1990 and early 1991, Apple worked with ARM Ltd to enhance this advantage by developing a novel memory management unit with which the Newton Operating System can control page access at a fine grain.

The ARM 610 has fulfilled all the requirements that we established in 1990. ARM Ltd's cycle time, quality and customer orientation have exceeded our expectations. The company's opportunities for technical innovation in the low-power realm are legion.

At the time of writing, the first model of Newton has just been introduced into the market. Since the first public demonstrations of Newton technologies over a year ago, this archetypal PDA has generated widespread interest. As Apple plans future Newton models, we envision that ARM family processors will play an important role in the product line.

RISC assembly programming is generally of interest only to writers of compilers. The ARM is unique in having an instruction set that is not only simple and space-efficient but also straightforward and delightful to use. This factor was important in the development of Newton systems software. Although the ARM C compiler generates impressively tight object code, the Newton developers could not express certain critical inner loops in C and had to code them in assembler.

   Programming the ARM RISC Chip provides a thorough introduction to the art of ARM assembly language programming. It is an essential reference for engineers who need to code to the hardware or who wish to create software development tools. I also recommend it to people who seek an understanding of a unique and elegant processor that is poised to have a significant influence on the electronics industry in the 1990s.

Larry Tesler
Chief Scientist, Apple Computer, Inc.
Member of the Board, ARM Holdings, Ltd
13 Aug 1993

Introduction

I.1   Who should read this book

This book is aimed at a wide range of people who share an interest in microprocessor technology and ARM devices in particular:

- Programmers writing for ARM-based hardware systems.
- Hardware designers looking for an overview of the ARM world.
- Anyone interested in the commercial application of RISC technology.

It provides an introduction to the ARM architecture and to the instruction set, and to the background of ARM Ltd and ARM processors.

I.2   Inside this book

Each chapter of this book focuses on a particular aspect of ARM technology, leading the reader through it and providing real-life examples of instructions and programming to illustrate many of the points made.

Chapter 1 provides an overview of the genesis and early history of the ARM chip, and the foundation of ARM Ltd. It provides the context within which ARM processors were developed, and explains why the ARM was targeted at its particular market sector.

Chapter 2 examines the ARM microprocessor architecture in detail, focusing on the ARM6 processor core, which is the basis of the devices used by Apple and 3DO and is the core of all current generation ARM devices.

Chapter 3 looks at some of the options available to programmers who want to write for ARM-based hardware. It includes a detailed description of the elements of the ARM Cross Development Toolkit. It aims to provide a sufficient introduction to ARM Assembler and C that programmers reading this book can type in and assemble/compile the program examples provided throughout.

Chapter 4 describes the ARM integer instruction set in detail.

Chapter 5 covers aborts, interrupts and exception handling.

Chapter 6 examines the extensions to the ARM architecture. It focuses on the data cache, the write buffer and the memory management unit, all featured in the ARM600.

Chapter 7 describes the possibilities for interfacing ARM processors to other devices, examining the bus interface in detail.

Chapter 8 describes the many variants of ARM processor available, both standalone devices and macrocells which can be combined into new devices. It describes existing devices in detail, and concludes with a look at future directions for the ARM architecture.

Chapter 9 looks at the floating point instruction set.

The appendices provide a page-per-instruction guide to ARM integer and floating point instructions.

▤ I.3   Acknowledgements

This book would not have been possible without the cooperation and support of a large number of people from many companies.

Everyone at ARM Ltd has provided a great deal of assistance. Particular thanks go to Dave Jaggar, David Seal, Jamie Urquhart, Pete Harrod, Robin Saxby, Tudor Brown, Ian Rickards, John Biggs and Simon Segars, for their comments on the manuscript and patience in answering technical queries. Pete Magowan provided invaluable assistance both in kickstarting this project and encouraging it to completion.

The following staff at ARM Ltd's foundries and partners also provided useful comments and assistance:

Sharp: Graham Barker

VLSI: Mike Kaskowitz, Ed Begun, Jamie Smith, Jeff Hendy

GPS: Terry McCloskey, Geoff Callow, Ian Philips

The authors would like to thank: Nicky Jaeger at Addison-Wesley for her patience and encouragement; Professor Steve Furber for his assistance; David Fell, who contributed many of the programming examples; and Venice van Someren for enduring countless technical discussions of no interest to her.

1

The history of the ARM CPU

1.1 Introduction

This chapter outlines the history of the ARM processors from their beginnings as the proprietary solution for a particular set of problems in a particular company to their current status as a highly successful, flexible and customizable set of processors available on the open market.

While some aspects of this story are of purely anecdotal interest, others shed light on some ARM design decisions, which were taken in an unusual set of circumstances to meet specific goals, now seen to meet the demands of an innovative and exciting market place requiring good performance and low power consumption, balanced with low cost.

British readers will probably be familiar with Acorn Computers Ltd, its products and its history of phenomenal success in the UK computer market of the early 1980s. Other readers may not have had access to as much information on the vibrant home computer market in the UK then, or to Acorn's record for technical innovation.

The story starts with the original development of the ARM processor, and ends with the establishment of ARM Ltd as a global force in the microprocessor industry. In between, it sheds some light on various design decisions which were taken in the genesis of the ARM design.

▤ 1.2   The development of the ARM chip at Acorn

The history of the ARM processor family is closely intertwined with that of the British personal computer industry, and reflects differences between the development of the British and American computer industries. A number of different manufacturers achieved prominence in this briefly flowering market, but then never gained a great deal of success beyond the UK and Europe.

The smaller size of the UK market (compared to the US) also ensured that even the most successful companies could not achieve the size of American rivals, affecting their ability to invest in research and development and to ride out the ups and downs of the market for personal and home computers.

1.2.1   Acorn's background

The first ARM chip, the Acorn RISC Machine, was developed between 1983 and 1985 by the advanced research and development team at Acorn Computers, a pioneering developer of microcomputers in the UK. During this time Acorn was one of the leading names in the British personal computer market. Other significant players were Sinclair, another Cambridge start-up, and to a lesser extent the American companies Apple, Commodore and Tandy, along with a host of smaller British developers producing a wide range of machines targeted at the booming home computer market.

Acorn's initial success was sealed when the British Broadcasting Corporation (BBC) commissioned a new home computer model from the company to be sold as the BBC Microcomputer, to tie in with a public computer education programme shown on BBC television in the UK.

The release of the BBC Micro in 1982 caught the crest of the home computer wave in Britain, and the BBC name gave Acorn's design added credibility compared with competing machines from the many other developers in this market. Sales exceeded all expectations: original estimates by the BBC and Acorn were that at best tens of thousands of units would be sold. In fact, to date nearly two million BBC Micro-compatible computers have been sold by Acorn, and it quickly grew from a small company with tens of staff into a medium-sized company employing hundreds with an annual turnover of tens of millions of pounds.

The BBC Micro was based around the 8-bit 6502 processor from Rockwell, the same chip that powered the Apple II. Initial models featured colour graphics and 32 kbyte of random access memory. Data was stored on audio cassettes; hard and floppy disk drive interfaces were also available, and Acorn was an early proponent of local area networking with its Econet system. Another important feature of the BBC Micro was its capacity to accept a second processor attached via an expansion port known as the Tube. Connectivity, interoperability and networking were familiar concepts to many BBC Micro users long before they were established in the rest of the personal computer world, via such options as the Tube. This required a degree of interoperability between host and second processor, as well as Acorn's Econet local area networking standard.

1.2.2   Conceiving the Acorn RISC Machine

Acorn was to continue to release 6502-based variants of the BBC Micro for four more years. Production of the most successful model, the Master, only ceased in May 1993, and these computers form the backbone of computing provision in many British schools. However it was clear to the advanced research and development team that there was no clear step forward to the next generation of processors, no obvious 16-bit processor to use in future Acorn systems. One Acorn model, the Communicator, used a 16-bit 6502 derivative, the 65C816 processor, the same device as used in the Apple IIGS, but Acorn's designers were not convinced that this chip represented the advance they were looking for.

The team tried all of the 16- and 32-bit processors then on the market but found none to be satisfactory for their purposes; in particular, the data bandwidth was not sufficiently greater than that offered by the 6502 to justify basing the next generation of Acorn computers upon them. Processors were tested by building BBC Micro 'second processor' units based upon them, and it became clear that no chip would be found to fit the very precise requirements on which the Acorn design team had settled.

Acorn's processor requirements

Acorn's aim at that time was to produce personal computers which met the needs of the business community by providing office automation facilities. Clearly, more power was needed than was offered by the 6502. In the fine tradition of the computer hobbyist, the design team decided to develop their own processor, which would provide an environment with some similarities to the familiar 6502 instruction set but lead Acorn and its products directly into the world of 32-bit computing.

Acorn has always been renowned for the calibre of its research and development staff. It was able to pick the cream of graduates from Cambridge University, home of a highly regarded computer science faculty, as well as attracting staff from around the world.

To them, designing a processor from scratch to meet their carefully specified criteria was an obvious thing to do. Acorn's phenomenal success with its 8-bit computers had created a research and development environment where staff could afford to pursue advanced projects which would not necessarily result in immediately saleable products, and were actively encouraged to do so.

Genesis of ARM in comparison with other RISC processors

In fact, many of the commercially available RISC processors intended for use as the CPU of a personal computer or workstation were designed or developed in-house by system developers, when microprocessor developers were either concentrating on improving their CISC designs or designing RISC chips for supporting roles or as embedded controllers.

For example, Sun developed the SPARC RISC chip and architecture for its own computer workstations, while notable RISC processors from established chip producers include Intel's i860 graphics processor and AMD's 29000, which has mainly been used as a graphics accelerator or in printers. However, both Sun's and MIPS' efforts were based on earlier research efforts at Stanford and Berkeley universities respectively, while Acorn's project was effectively begun from scratch, although reports on the Berkeley and Stanford research were read by the Acorn team and were part of the inspiration behind designing a RISC processor.

One of the reasons the ARM was designed as a small-scale processor was that the resources to design it were not sufficient to allow the creation of a large and complex device. While this is now presented as (and genuinely is) a technical plus for the ARM processor core, it began as a necessity for a processor designed by a team of talented but inexperienced designers (outside of university projects, most team members were programmers and board-level circuit designers) using new tools, some of which were far from state-of-the-art. With these restrictions on design and testing, it is hardly a surprise that a small device was developed.

While the ARM was developed as a custom device for a highly specific purpose, the team designing it felt that the best way to produce a good custom chip was to produce a chip with good all-round performance.

1.2.3   Designing the first ARM

Work on the development of what was to become the ARM began in 1983. Working samples were received in 1985. The team developing it included Steve Furber, now ICL Professor of Computer Engineering at Manchester University, and Roger Wilson, both of whom had worked on the design of the BBC Micro, as well as Robert Heaton who led the VLSI design group within Acorn.

The design team worked in secret to create a chip which met their requirements. As described earlier, these were for a processor which retained the ethos of the 6502 but in a 32-bit RISC environment, and implemented this in a small device which it would be possible to design and test easily, and to fabricate cheaply.

First the instruction set was specified by Wilson, based on his knowledge gained as the author of much of the original software for the BBC Micro, including its BASIC interpreter. The important initial decisions were to use a fixed instruction length and a load/store model. Other design decisions were taken on an instruction by instruction basis.

Modelling the ARM1 instruction set

The first model of the ARM instruction set was written in BASIC, an approach which made it easy to set everything out and develop a prototype quickly, but proved less flexible when the hardware design needed to be tested and precise timings derived. The subsequent model of the ARM hardware was also written in BASIC. It required a BBC Micro fitted with a 6502 second processor to run, and no further testing was required to verify the design. A team of four people worked on the design, with the two VLSI designers working on the device sharing a single workstation. The actual physical design of the chips was achieved using VLSI Technology's custom design tools.

An event-driven simulator was designed, also in BASIC, which allowed the support chips, the video controller VIDC and memory controller MEMC (which both had slightly more complex timing requirements), and the I/O controller IOC, to be designed and tested. A development of this simulator, since rewritten in Modula-2 and then in C and known as ASIM, is still used by both Acorn and ARM Ltd for design and testing today.

The world's first commercial RISC processor

The first ARM processor, ARM1, yielded working silicon the first time it was fabricated, in April 1985 at VLSI Technology. It bettered the stated design goals while using fewer than 25 000 transistors. These samples were fabricated using a 3 μm process.

There was a great deal of excitement at and confidence in the new chip. The ARM was used internally at Acorn and by Acorn developers when it was made available as a second processor add-on for the BBC Micro; this device used the ARM1 as an additional coprocessor and accelerator for the 6502-based BBC micro. In fact, this second processor was used to improve the performance of the simulation tools the team had designed to finish the support chips and also to develop the next ARM processor.

The second processor add-on also enabled third-party developers to start working with the processor and contemplating the development of software to exploit its advanced features. The purpose of releasing the second processor was to ensure that when a complete ARM-based system was released, potential users and developers had some experience of ARM and were not deterred from developing application software for it by the novelty of the technology and the lack of wide support for it in the market.

Improving on ARM1

The experience of designing ARM1, and of programming the sample chips, showed that there were some areas where the instruction set could be improved in order to maximize the performance of systems based around it. In particular, the Multiply and Multiply and Accumulate instructions were added in order to improve performance by eliminating the use of slow subroutines for this purpose. Without this addition, the ARM could have been 'horribly slow' in some circumstances, according to Furber.

This addition would facilitate real-time digital signal processing, which was to be used to generate sounds, an important feature of home and educational computers.

A coprocessor interface was also added to the ARM at this stage, which would enable a floating point accelerator and other coprocessors to be used with the ARM. Even after all these additions the ARM2 maintained its small die size and low transistor count; the die was 5.4 mm square and the transistor count around 25 000. This second device was also improved by being fabricated in a 2 μm process. That this was an extraordinary achievement, and that the ARM is an unusual processor in terms of size/performance, is shown more clearly in Figure 1.1 which shows the relative die size of the ARM and other processors

1.2.4   The ARM in the market

The ARM arrived into a fast-changing world. By 1985 the computer market looked very different from that of the early 1980s. Then the growth in demand for cheap computers suitable for home use and self-education seemed unlimited. There was room for innumerable start-up companies to grab enough market share to survive, and users bought computers on the basis of their claimed performance.

Now the leading names in the computer market were IBM, producers of clones of its personal computer, and Apple. Compatibility with existing computers, and particularly the IBM standard, was of increasing importance, as was the ability to run market-leading application programs, especially those aimed at the growing business market.

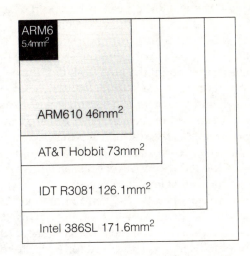

Figure 1.1 Relative die sizes normalized to 0.8 μm process

Unlike Acorn, Apple had adopted an off-the-shelf 32-bit processor, Motorola's 68000, and so it was able to bring a 32-bit computer, the Macintosh, to the market in 1984, although it was some time before it gained full acceptance by the business community. Apple too went through a stage when its technical resources and designs were unsurpassed but not translated into success in the marketplace.

Acorn's problems

Acorn had no replacement computer to offer customers who felt that the BBC Micro and its derivatives were old technology and not as good as the newer machines, which were more clearly aimed at the business market, and much more highly specified than Acorn's models. A technical workstation based on National Semiconductor's 32-bit 32016 was a market flop, and the consumer boom in home computers had evaporated. Acorn had launched a cut-down version of the BBC Micro to be sold into the home market, but it came too late to capitalize on the boom, and Acorn was left with large stocks of unsold machines.

A financial crisis enveloped Acorn, and led to it being taken over by one of Europe's leading computer and office equipment manufacturers, the Italian giant Olivetti Ing et Cie, which apparently bought up Acorn in 1985 for its share of the UK computer market, without knowing that its research labs housed the first samples of a new family of RISC processors.

Delays in bringing ARM-based systems to market

Although the ARM processor had been designed with the clear intention that it was to power the next generation of Acorn personal computers, and it was equally clear that such machines needed to be developed quickly, the design and production of ARM-based systems by Acorn was to be more fraught than the design of the chips themselves. It was to take more than two years from the arrival of working ARM silicon to the launch and shipment of a complete ARM-based system.

Deep within the advanced research and development labs in Cambridge, and at the research lab that Acorn had established in Palo Alto, California, Acorn staff were also designing an office automation system using the ARM processor. This system was a long-term goal of Acorn's co-founder, Dr Hermann Hauser.

A new operating system, known as ARX, was being developed to run on the processor, but progress was slow and Roger Wilson has described it as 'a black hole', at least as far as programming resource was concerned. However, the need for Acorn to release a new product to reach its existing market in education, small businesses and the home meant that this project was abandoned and a home computer, the Archimedes, was launched in 1987 as the first commercial product using the ARM, featuring an 8 MHz version of the ARM2 and the three support chips MEMC, VIDC and IOC, an input/output controller and a simple operating system.

Archimedes: the first ARM-based platform

The Archimedes received a somewhat lukewarm response on its launch. At a time when personal computing appeared to be consolidating behind the IBM PC standard, Acorn had introduced a computer with a new processor, a new operating system, and no base of software to provide users with the applications they needed. Many critics decried the use of RISC technology as a particular failing of the machine, arguing that this commercially unproven technology made any machine based upon it too esoteric for use in schools and businesses.

To answer some of these criticisms, software emulators were launched with the machine, which allowed Archimedes users to run most PC and BBC Micro software, but it took two or three years for a credible amount of application software native to the ARM and Archimedes to be developed.

Since then Acorn has refined and improved its computer models and confirmed its position as a leader in the British home computer and educational computing market. A wide range of software is available to these users, most of it developed by small companies loyal to Acorn since the early 1980s, and including applications intended for home, business and education use. Because of Acorn's dominant position in the UK educational computing market, the range of programs suitable for use in the classroom is probably at least as large as that for any other computer.

1.2.5   Further work on the ARM

The launch of the Archimedes did not signal the end of development of the ARM and its support chips. Acorn continued to support its research and development team in creating improved versions of the chips, offering greater performance.

The purpose of designing the original ARM chips, ARM1 and ARM2, had been to develop a processor capable of offering better-than-acceptable performance in low-cost personal computers. The next step was to expand the design so that it offered the kind of performance expected of a high-end personal computer, or workstation. Intel- and Motorola-based personal computers were already offering performance which perceptibly outstripped that of ARM-based systems.

Acorn's partner in building the chip, VLSI Technology Inc., was to develop further markets for the ARM processor and its support chips, while Acorn continued to develop personal computers based on the chip.

The development of ARM3

To improve the performance of the ARM a 4 kbyte on-chip data and instruction cache was added. This, along with the denser fabrication of the chip using a 1.5 µm process, would allow the new device, dubbed ARM3, to run at a much higher clock rate than its predecessors, thus improving overall performance while using the same support chips and low-cost memory as the ARM2.

The inclusion of the cache and its control circuitry led to a much higher transistor count of around 300 000, but this was still a highly compact device; so much so that problems occurred trying to find an IC package capable of accommodating the tiny ARM3 die.

In 1989 the ARM3 was launched at the significantly increased clock rate of 25 MHz. Acorn's desktop computers using this chip were first launched in 1990, although third parties were selling ARM3 chips on upgrade boards for ARM2-based computers in 1989. The first of these was Aleph One Ltd, a small company based in Bottisham, the next village to ARM Ltd's current home.

VLSI Technology Inc. was having some success in convincing other companies to use the ARM, particularly as an embedded processor. Some companies incorporated ARM into their products; others took samples of the chip to use in their research. One of these was Apple.

▓ 1.3   ARM becomes the Advanced RISC Machine

By 1990 it was clear that although Acorn's financial position had stabilized, an in-house processor design team was an expensive luxury for a small company to support. The ARM development team had now produced a static version of the processor, the ARM2aS, making it even more attractive to potential third-party customers. This new variant added low power consumption to the list of features which made the ARM attractive to developers interested in designing low-cost portable and hand-held devices and electronic personal organizers. It was intended for inclusion in a hand-held personal electronic organizer and communications device, which although developed as far as working prototypes was never actually marketed (the Active Book).

Interest in the ARM family was growing as more designers became interested in RISC, and the ARM's design was seen to match a definite need for high-performance, low power consumption, low-cost RISC processors. In conditions of greatest secrecy an agreement was reached between Acorn, VLSI Technology Inc. and a company which had expressed an interest in the ARM for some time now, Apple.

1.3.1   The foundation of ARM Ltd

A new company was set up with Apple, Acorn and VLSI Technology as founding partners. The Acorn RISC Machine became the Advanced RISC Machine and Advanced RISC Machines Ltd was born. Many of the original designers moved from Acorn to join the new company, with others working in an advisory role. Additional expertise was provided by Apple and new blood was recruited from around the world.

The ARM development team moved out of the building they had long occupied at Acorn's Cambridge headquarters. Newly appointed managing director Robin Saxby, former MD of European Silicon Structures (usually referred to as ES2), chose a converted 18th century barn in the picturesque Fenland village of Swaffham Bulbeck, ten miles outside Cambridge, as ARM's new home.

ARM Ltd was founded with a clear mission to continue the development of the ARM processor and to facilitate its use by system developers, whether as a standalone processor or as a macrocell with custom logic or other ARM components added to it to make a custom chip.

ARM Ltd was also to license its designs to chip foundries who would sell the chips, giving ARM Ltd a royalty, rather than establish its own fabrication facilities. VLSI Technology, which had built all previous ARM chips as well as custom logic devices for both Apple and Acorn, was the first licensee.

ARM's chip numbering system

ARM Ltd adopted a new numbering scheme for its devices. Previously the chips had simply had a single number suffix to denote which generation the design was, such as ARM2 or MEMC1. In the new scheme, a single number is used to represent the processor core macrocell which is the main component of the processor, for example ARM6. This is incremented by 1 from generation to generation, so the next ARM processor core will be ARM7, and so on.

A two-digit number denotes a self-contained chip consisting solely of this device and the minimum necessary interface and test circuitry, for example ARM60 and VIDC20. A three-digit number denotes a device which integrates the processor macrocell with other standard ARM macrocells and/or custom logic, for example ARM250 and ARM610.

1.3.2   Development of ARM6

ARM Ltd's first development was the next step from the ARM3 processor, which was named ARM6 and included full 32-bit addressing and endedness (byte sex) support, one of many changes requested by Apple in order to use the ARM in planned products. An improved video controller, VIDC20, was also developed and a floating point processor was also introduced.

ARM Ltd's first major commission was to design a CPU for Apple suitable for use within a hand-held personal organizer device. This device became known as ARM600, from which the ARM610 used in Newton was later derived. At the same time ARM Ltd's software team developed the ARM Cross Development Toolkit, a suite of software which allowed designers working on a range of platforms to use ARM development tools, assemblers, compilers, and debugging and emulation programs.

Hardware evaluation kits were also produced to enable designers to test the ARM6 processor and to begin to develop operating system and support software for use with their own designs before the availability of finished systems. ARM Ltd developed the PIE (Platform Independent Evaluation) Card, which allowed system designers to test their ideas on an ARM card attached to a host machine running the Cross Development Toolkit.

1.3.3 ARM Ltd creates an identity

A further task for ARM Ltd staff was the establishment of an identity and higher profile for the company and its processors. While the ARM was exclusively Acorn's it was little publicized; magazine articles on RISC processors rarely referred to it, although its sales were in the same league as successful processors such as SPARC and Clipper. Speculation about Apple's interest in ARM Ltd and potential ARM products proved to generate plenty of interest in both the company and the processors, with consequent effects on Acorn's share price, which rose more than ten-fold from early 1992 to early 1993.

ARM Ltd has taken steps to raise its profile within the merchant microprocessor market, with staff making regular presentations at conferences worldwide. A new visual image was adopted (Figure 1.2), with the 'ARM-powered' label to be attached to any systems using ARM processors (Figure 1.3).

1.3.4 ARM develops its markets

The availability of the ARM and foundation of ARM Ltd coincided with a growing potential for its products. While the late 1980s saw the computer market focused tightly on standardized solutions for business users, mostly in the form of IBM PC-compatible hardware, in the early 1990s the increasing saturation of this market combined with the worldwide recession have led computer developers to look for new markets and new types of products to sell.

Figure 1.2 The ARM Ltd logo adopted in 1991

TM

Figure 1.3 The ARM-powered logo

The standards of the 1980s are now themselves starting to look like old technology, and the quest for a new generation of information and leisure technology products has provided immense opportunities for companies like ARM Ltd with timely products.

Leisure and consumer computing

Two types of computer product are believed to have the best chances in this changing market. Many developers have discussed or announced personal information organizers, offering a range of functions to users who would not necessarily have considered using a laptop or desktop computer. Apple's proposed range of Newton personal digital assistants, powered by the ARM, are contenders in this market. The first Newton device, the MessagePad, was launched in summer 1993. Leisure technology is the other growth market, full of companies exploiting the public's demand for escapist entertainment and attempting to emulate the success of Nintendo and Sega, and to use CD-based formats as a means of distributing interactive entertainment.

Late in 1992 a new venture, The 3DO Company, announced that it too had designed the ARM (in this case, ARM60) into its product, a CD-ROM based leisure computing box to be known as the Interactive Multiplayer. 3DO and its licensees plan to ship products, both hardware and software, during 1993. A wide range of leisure and commercial software developers signed up to work with the 3DO format, offering it a good chance of success in a market dependent on both the delivery of technology and the availability of attractive software. 3DO did not plan to manufacture ARM-based hardware itself, but to encourage its hardware licensees to produce a range of products conforming to the standards it defined. Among its licensees are Japanese electronics giant Matsushita.

Both these product types, electronic personal organizers and leisure computing devices, require powerful processors at a cost low enough that the end-product is still competitively priced for a consumer market. Hand-held portable organizers require this computing power to be delivered in a compact form and without heavy power consumption, so that the unit can be small and run from batteries. ARM Ltd's processors are ideal for this and the growth of this market represents a major opportunity for ARM and its customers.

Embedded control

Embedded control forms a large part of the market for microprocessors. The low-cost, high-performance ARM has always been targeted at this market by its original partner, VLSI Technology.

The embedded controller market has traditionally focused on 8-bit microprocessors, but the growing complexity of many control requirements in sophisticated products indicates a need to move to more powerful processors. The ARM and its variants offer manufacturers the opportunity to move directly to 32-bit controllers at low cost and with a great deal of flexibility for designing custom controllers.

Potential applications for custom embedded controllers using ARM macrocells include real-time controllers in the automotive market. Potential applications include engine management systems and entertainment systems controllers.

The ARM has had previous successes as an embedded controller. Cambridge (England) robotics company Microrobotics has used various ARM devices as the basis of its microcontroller system used for applications as diverse as controlling animatronics puppets and complex event lighting systems. British company Rediffusion Simulation uses the ARM in its Commander flight simulator.

Other companies around the world are planning to use the ARM as a controller for arcade computer games, high-speed data communications, videophones, fuzzy logic controllers, and data-logging and test equipment.

1.3.5   Establishing a global presence

As the market for low-cost, low power consumption, high-performance processors expands, ARM Ltd is expanding its global presence by developing relationships with more companies around the world. Since the launch, ARM has developed relationships with more foundries who will license its designs and sell them into different markets.

From its earliest days within Acorn, ARM Ltd has worked closely with VLSI Technology, Inc., its first partner and the first manufacturer of ARM devices.

In the UK, GEC Plessey Semiconductors was signed as an ARM foundry and partner in January 1992. Plessey now produces a range of ARM standard parts. It is also the foundry for the ARM250, a custom processor developed for Acorn out of standard macrocells and a small amount of custom circuitry.

Establishing a relationship with a major Japanese manufacturer was a key component of ARM's strategy, and this was achieved in March 1993 when the Sharp Corporation of Japan signed a deal to manufacture and market ARM processors and associated products. Sharp already has a relationship with Apple which is expected to result in products based on Apple's Newton technology, to which Sharp is contributing.

At around the same time ARM Ltd strengthened its claim to be a truly global company by receiving a significant investment from Japanese investment house NIF. ARM Ltd's investors now include European companies, in the form of Acorn (and through it Olivetti), US companies Apple and VLSI Technology, and NIF in Japan.

Shortly after these agreements were signed, Texas Instruments was added to the list of ARM partners, with the intention of using ARM macrocells as the basis of custom embedded controllers.

ARM Ltd now has offices in California and Japan in order to maintain a close relationship with licensees and their major customers, and to promote existing ARM devices and the company's ability to produce new ones to future customers. It is likely that ARM will continue to establish relationships with new partners around the world.

1.4   ARM design objectives

The original objective of the ARM design team was to produce a processor which provided a logical advance from the 6502 processor, and was suitable for use as the central processor of a business or home computer. It was not intended to produce the most powerful processor on the market, but to produce a processor which harnessed the latest techniques to provide computing power at a price which meant that it could be included in a low-cost personal computer system.

As the market for ARM devices has grown and the requirements of potential customers have developed and become more sharply defined, so too have ARM Ltd's design objectives. The ability to develop custom processors and controllers quickly from its library of standard macrocells has always been there, but this is now being formalized in the Quick-Design system, which was launched at the COMDEX exhibition in November 1992. As the name implies, the purpose of QuickDesign is to create a custom part from standard parts as quickly as possible, and to show how these can be interfaced with custom technology developed by ARM Ltd or the customer working in partnership to produce a timely and low-cost product.

ARM Ltd's design objectives are now clearly stated as developing processors which use RISC design principles to meet the following goals.

1.4.1   High performance for low price

The original ARM1 device was intended to power an Acorn computer, a personal computer rather than the workstations which other RISC processors such as the MIPS and the SPARC were designed for. Rather than use the advantages of RISC to make a large chip, more powerful than its CISC equivalent, the Acorn chip used RISC techniques to make a smaller chip of equivalent power to those used in other personal computers.

The ARM processor has always differed from other commercially available RISC processors in that it is intended to meet a price/performance ratio rather than to be the most powerful processor available. Acorn's computers have always been aimed at the middle of the market, so the processor designed to power them was too. ARM processors are not the most powerful, but offer an extremely good price/performance ratio compared to other processors, at about a dollar per million instructions per second (MIPS) in the case of ARM6.

1.4.2   Short design time

One of ARM Ltd's stated goals is to provide a quick and effective design service to produce custom processors based on ARM macrocells. This has been formalised as the QuickDesign process, which offers customers the following benefits:

- A partnership approach to product development, ensuring that products meet the customers' requirements.
- Access to ARM Ltd's library of macrocells, and design tools and services.
- Help in designing any custom parts of the processor design, bringing together ARM Ltd's design expertise with the customer's own knowledge of the application and market being developed for.

Because of the simplicity and small size of ARM devices, custom chips can be developed and fabricated to meet specific customer requirements, and resulting products can reach the market quickly. The ARM610 was developed from initial specification to the delivery of working silicon in less than four months. Short development times are critical for custom products intended to form part of systems entering a market which is likely to be hotly contested from the start, such as that for hand-held computer devices.

It also provides some measure of confidence that future developments of the ARM processor family will appear on schedule, so that system designers need not worry that their new designs will be held up while vital components are developed and debugged. ARM Ltd's own mythology is that virtually all the chips they have designed have worked first time; a row of champagne bottles, each opened to celebrate the arrival of working silicon, lines the staircase at ARM Ltd's barn to bear witness to this.

1.4.3   High performance for low power consumption

A further advantage of the small size of ARM devices is that they do not consume as much power as other, larger processors.

This has proved a critical key to the success of ARM processors. Unlike many other processor designs, the ARM was easily re-implemented in static form rather than the usual dynamic CMOS. This, along with the small die size, reduced power consumption, making ARM processors ideally suited for power consumption-critical products such as portable computers. Furthermore, it allows the clock to be stopped, a useful power saver in portable designs.

1.4.4   Easily customized designs

The above factors combine to make the ARM product range extremely flexible. The small size of the ARM processor means that it can easily be combined with its support chips, cache memory, or custom circuitry to make self-contained custom chips. All ARM devices are designed as macrocells, building blocks which can be combined within a single chip.

The ARM610, commissioned by Apple, is one example based on macrocells, which includes the 32-bit ARM6 processor core, a 4 kbyte cache, a write buffer and a memory management unit. Even with all these additional components, the end result is a much smaller package than familiar processors such as the 80386.

Acorn Computers has also enjoyed the fruits of commissioning a custom chip from ARM which effectively combined the original ARM2 four chip set on to a single device, the ARM250. This process was carried out from the original concept to volume production in 12 months, resulting in a single device with a sixth of the footprint, one third the power consumption and half the cost of the devices it replaced.

1.5   RISC versus CISC processor design

How does the adoption of RISC technology help ARM Ltd. to reach its goals in the design and production of microprocessors, and what led Acorn's design team to choose the RISC route in the early 1980s when it was commercially unproven?

The term Reduced Instruction Set is applied to a great many processors and it is not obvious that at the extremes of the category they have much more in common with each other than they do with CISC devices. RISC techniques are often employed in extremely large and complex devices such as the i860, where the size and complexity of the chip means that advantages it gains from using RISC techniques are very different from those gained by the ARM processor.

Why was the ARM from its inception designed as a reduced instruction set processor? At the time the first ARM chip was being designed, RISC was a relatively new concept and CISC processors were still being developed which offered growing performance.

RISC's advantages were originally propounded as being:

■ Smaller die size, because a RISC chip is simpler and requires fewer transistors to implement its smaller instruction set.
■ Shorter design process; smaller chips and fewer instructions mean the design will be less complicated, and hence will take less time to complete and debug.
■ Improved performance; smaller chips with shorter signal paths mean that each instruction cycle is shorter and thus quicker.

As shown in this chapter, all three of these advantages of RISC design have been apparent in the design history of the ARM processor. Choosing to design a RISC chip meant that Acorn's designers could design a small chip with few resources, and yet reasonably expect that it would deliver the required performance within the available time-scale.

The 6502, to which Acorn's designers looked when designing the original ARM, had a short and simple instruction set which lent itself well to RISC. RISC was a sensible option for the design team to consider; all three of the above points suggested it as a suitable choice when designing the chip. The team's resources in terms of staff, time and development tools were limited, and the requirement was for a processor which would be cheap to make and sell but still offered sufficiently high performance that computers based on it would perform as well as or better than comparable personal computers.

The advantages of RISC that have attracted further users to the ARM chip set appear mainly to be its delivery of high performance for low cost, in a compact package which takes up little space and consumes little power. While processors fulfilling this set of requirements may have been a small market niche a few years ago, it is now a highly competitive and fast-growing area of the computer market, and ARM Ltd and its processors are placed well to compete within it.

▤ 1.6   Summary

The ARM processor, unlike many other processors, was designed within a single company to meet its particular requirements for product development. RISC technology was adopted partly because of its perceived technological benefits, partly because it seemed appropriate to the design goals, and partly because it offered a way of producing a powerful processor using limited resources.

While at its launch the ARM and systems based on it were seen as being ahead of their time, the current vogue for all things RISC has led to an increased interest in the ARM. This, combined with changing market conditions influencing Acorn, led to the ARM design team being established as ARM Ltd, with investment from other partners including Apple Computer, and to the redesign of the ARM itself to exploit its benefits still further.

From being a single design aimed at a particular project the ARM is now a set of highly customizable processors and supporting macrocells suitable for use in a wide range of applications but targeted at systems requiring high performance from a compact device with low power consumption.

2

The ARM6 CPU core architecture

2.1 Introduction

This chapter describes the architecture of the ARM6 CPU core, the 32-bit RISC processor macrocell upon which the current generation of ARM processors is based. ARM6 is the first processor core to be developed by ARM Ltd from the original Acorn RISC design; it has been modernized and adapted to take account of the requirements of the global computer market in the 1990s.

The ARM6 CPU differs significantly from the earlier Acorn design in its adoption of a 32-bit program counter/address space and its ability to operate on external data buses of either byte sex. Both of these changes came about as a result of input from Apple Computer. At the same time the CPU core was revised to use only 'static' logic as first introduced in the ARM2aS, lowering the power consumption of the processor and allowing it to operate at reduced clock frequencies for even greater power savings.

From a programming perspective the ARM6 CPU core presents a programming model which is simple and consistent. The small register set and minimalist instructions combine to give very high program density (that is a low average number of bytes per instruction) while maintaining a high degree of functionality.

▓ 2.2   The ARM6 data path

The ARM6 CPU has a 32-bit address bus, 32-bit internal data paths and a single 32-bit external data interface through which both instructions and data pass during program execution. This traditional design approach, known as a 'von Neumann' architecture, imposes limits on the processor performance but was adopted for the ARM due to its simplicity and low cost of implementation (Furber, 1989).

As a result, instructions which load data from or store data to memory must take at least two clock cycles to execute (the first one for the instruction, the second for the load or store itself). Although it is possible to reduce instruction execution time by using separate instruction and data paths (the so-called Harvard architecture) the ARM approach has the counter-advantage that it allows multi-stage addressing operations such as indexing or stack operations to be implemented without increasing the complexity of the CPU. ARM6 exploits this valuable side-effect by providing many instruction formats which can exploit these addressing styles.

2.2.1   Pipelining

To reduce the bottleneck at the data bus interface the ARM6 uses a multistage 'pipeline' to allow many parts of the processor to operate concurrently and continuously under most circumstances (Figure 2.1). The ARM6 arithmetic logic unit (ALU) itself is not pipelined because it doesn't need to be: a single clock cycle can encompass a register read, a shift on one operand, the ALU operation itself and writing the result back to a register again.

However, the instruction fetch and decode units are pipelined in three stages so that while the ALU is executing an instruction its successor is being decoded and the one after that is being fetched from memory. This allows the ARM to complete an instruction every clock cycle under most circumstances, that is when it doesn't have to perform a data memory access.

Data load and store operations take additional cycles to perform the data transfer itself. Branches to new addresses take three cycles because they break the pipeline (since instruction flow is not sequential) and it must refill before the next instruction can be executed. To reduce the need for branches the instruction set allows all instructions to execute conditionally, since spending a single cycle not executing a conditional instruction is clearly quicker than a three-cycle pipeline refill.

The memory interface exploits pipelining by bringing internal sig-

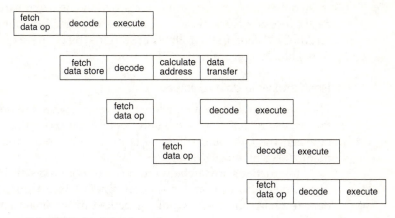

Figure 2.1 ARM pipelining in action

nals off-chip which 'look ahead' to forthcoming memory accesses and allow the use of fast local access modes offered by standard dynamic RAM. Again, the ability of every instruction to execute conditionally increases the chance that the program address references will run sequentially, thereby allowing the memory sub-system to make predictions about the next address required.

2.2.2   ARM6 CPU core functional blocks

The major functional blocks within the ARM6 core, seen in Figure 2.2, are:

- The read and write data register blocks (bottom left and right)
- The instruction decoder and control logic (right-hand side)
- The multi-port register bank (centre top)
- The Booth's multiplier (centre)
- The barrel shifter (centre)
- The Arithmetic Logic Unit 'ALU' (centre bottom)
- The address register (top) and address incrementer (just below)

Three internal 32-bit data paths exist, each of them associated with one of the register bank ports. The register bank has two read ports and one write port. The PC has an extra read port and an extra write port dedicated to it. This arrangement allows the ARM to do many things in a single execution cycle. The main internal buses are:

- The A bus (first instruction operand)
- The B bus (second instruction operand, read/write memory data)
- The ALU bus (ALU result)

These buses join the functional blocks together in a limited way: the interconnections in turn impose restrictions on what can be achieved in each processor clock cycle. Figure 2.2 shows the internal structure of the ARM6 CPU core. In the following sections the purpose of each of its functional blocks is examined in turn.

Read and write data registers

The read and write data registers hold instructions and data (data only in the write register) immediately before and/or after data transfers between the CPU and other parts of the processor (for example cache memory) or memory system.

Instructions are latched into the read data register during the 'fetch' phase, passed on to the instruction pipeline (see Figure 2.1) during the decode phase and then actually executed in the final phase of the three-stage pipeline.

Data to be written off-chip comes from the register bank on the B-bus and is latched in the write data register before being output. When a byte is to be written the data output block replicates it four times across the 32-bit width of the data bus so that external byte-wide memory may be wired directly to the data bus and the 'not Byte/Word' (nB/W) signal and address bits A[1..0] used to select which byte is to be written; Table 2.1 summarizes this.

Table 2.1 Address encoding for byte and word access (Little-endian)

Access	nBW	A1	A0
Word access	1	x	x
Least significant byte	0	0	0
Next least significant byte	0	0	1
Next least significant byte	0	1	0
Most significant byte	0	1	1

Instruction decoder and control logic

The instruction decoder and control logic block is responsible for managing the flow of instructions through the pipeline, their decoding and execution, the loading and storing of data to and from memory, receiving interrupts and asserting the relevant control signals to indicate the state of the CPU to the rest of the system.

Central to the instruction decoder is the 'instruction pipeline', which holds the current instruction and any instructions already fetched that are

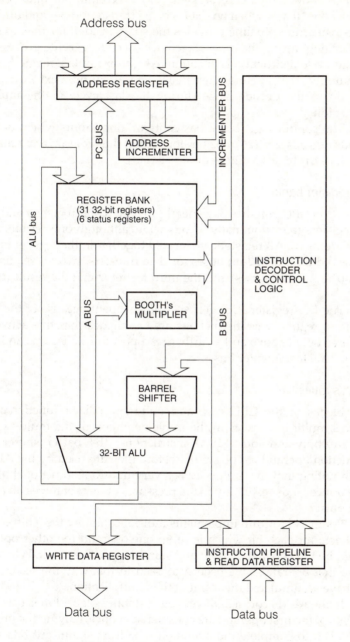

Figure 2.2 ARM6 block diagram

awaiting execution. ARM pre-fetches instructions into the pipeline in order to allow the CPU to be kept busy on continuous data processing instructions (that is when no data is being transferred on- and off-chip). A three-instruction pipeline provides the space needed for this, to support pre-fetching during the three-stage fetch/decode/execute process. When a multi-cycle instruction is encountered (for example a memory transfer or multiply) the pipeline must freeze and allow the next instruction to pass on to the decode stage during the last cycle of the multi-cycle instruction.

The control logic block has configuration inputs which determine the address bus size (26 or 32 bit) for each of the program and data spaces as well as the byte sex (little- or big-endian).

The register bank

The ARM6 CPU core has 31 general-purpose 32-bit registers and six status registers (also nominally 32 bits wide, although only 11 bits are currently defined). All registers are located together in the register bank and are served by three 32-bit buses for data transfers: two for reading operands (the A and B buses) and the third for returning the result (the ALU bus).

The PC (register R15) gets special treatment because of the need to update it regularly as instructions are executed: it has five active ports, the three noted above and a further read port for the PC bus and a write port for the Incrementer bus.

Booth's multiplier

Two blocks of the CPU core add quite specialized functionality: the Booth's multiplier assists in the implementation of the multiply (MUL) and multiply-and-add (MLA) instructions; the barrel shifter allows instruction operands to be shifted before they are used by the ALU. It is worth noting that the multiplier is a very non-RISC functional block. Its appearance lends testimony to the pressures of market forces on architectural purity.

Booth's algorithm implements multiplication by the 'shift-and-add' approach: for each bit which is set in one operand the other operand is shifted by the relevant amount and summed into the result. When all bits in the first operand have been processed in this way the result register will have accumulated the result of the multiplication.

In the ARM6 core a 2-bit version of Booth's algorithm is used, that is two bits of the first operand are considered at once, halving the maximum time taken to complete the operation. The least significant bits are processed first, working through to finish with the most significant bits. This operation time is further decreased by 'early termination' which occurs when no further bits are set in the first operand. The Booth's multiplier receives one of the operands for the multiplication from a register along the A bus and outputs two bits of the operand at a time to the multiply control logic. A third output indicates when all remaining bits of the operand are zero, signalling early termination of the multiply operation.

Barrel shifter

A barrel shifter is a form of shift logic which can shift or rotate its input by any number of bits to produce an output within a fixed period: that is the degree of shifting has no impact on the time taken. The ARM6 CPU core includes a 32-bit barrel shifter which also has associated logic to allow values to be arithmetic shifted (that is to preserve the sign bit) or rotated through the carry bit (to give a 33-bit shift register). In ARM processors the use of a shifted operand *never* increases the time taken to execute an instruction, a fact which can be exploited very effectively by compilers to execute small constant integer multiplications and divisions.

Arithmetic Logic Unit

The ALU performs all arithmetic, logical and comparison operations on two input operands, often the contents of two registers in the register bank. It consists of 32 duplicate 'bit slices', that is the logic for a single bit of the ALU, along with carry generation circuitry. All operations are performed on the full 32-bit width of the input data: Figure 2.3 shows a single bit slice of the ALU logic from the earlier ARM2 core.

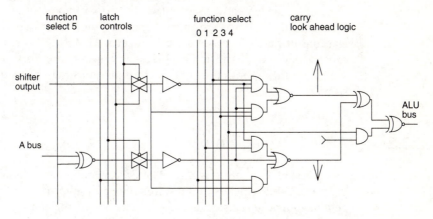

Figure 2.3 ARM ALU logic for one bit (after Furber, 1989)

It is interesting to note in passing that the ALU does not actually implement a subtract function; instead it always adds the two operands but may invert one first to achieve a subtraction.

Address register and address incrementer

The address register and its associated incrementer are used to select the address to be used for the next memory access cycle. There are four possible sources of the address: the current PC value, the output of the ALU (for example for loads and stores), an address from the output of the incrementer or an exception address generated by the control logic. Whichever of these sources is selected the resulting address is then latched in a register under external control of the 'address latch enable' (ALE) signal.

The address incrementer output is the most common source of addresses: it simply generates a new address which is four bytes (one word) greater than the previous one. Whenever this occurs the incremented value is copied back into the program counter (R15) every cycle to ensure that the register value is kept up to date.

2.3 The ARM6 programming model

2.3.1 Introduction

The CPU can directly manipulate two data types: Bytes (8 bits) and Words (32 bits); words are aligned on four-byte boundaries where the two least significant address bits are both zero. All ARM6 instructions occupy exactly one word, and internal data operations are performed only on word quantities. Both byte and word data types may be loaded from and stored to memory

2.3.2 ARM CPU registers

The ARM6 CPU core has a total of 37 registers, comprising 31 general-purpose 32-bit registers and 6 status registers (Figure 2.4). At any time 16 general-purpose registers and one or two status registers are accessible to the programmer, the remaining registers being switched in by the CPU as required. Exactly which registers are visible depends on the processor mode. ARM6 supports six CPU 'modes' which reflect the privilege level and facilities available to the program under execution. The modes are as follows:

- User mode (normal program execution)
- FIQ mode (entered in response to a Fast Interrupt reQuest)

- IRQ mode (entered in response to an Interrupt ReQuest)
- Supervisor mode (a privileged and protected mode for the operating system)
- Abort mode (entered after a data or instruction prefetch abort)
- Undefined mode (entered when an undefined instruction is executed)

Mode changes may be brought about under program control, as a result of an external interrupt, or as a result of a processing exception (for example Abort/Undefined). Most programs are expected to execute in User mode, with excursions into the other modes as interrupts and operating system calls dictate.

In any CPU mode 16 registers are directly accessible by the programmer (see Figure 2.4). All except R15 are general purpose and may be used to hold data or address values. Register R15 stores the Program Counter (PC) which points to the next instruction to be executed in memory. Since ARM instructions are word-aligned, the PC contains zeros in its bottom two bits and a word address in bits [31:2]. Because the program counter is accessible to programmers, it can be included in standard instructions, and as a base for load and store instructions. This permits the easy generation of position-independent code, an important benefit for many modern operating systems where dynamic or run-time linking is available.

A further register, the Current Program Status Register (CPSR) is also accessible to programmers in all modes. This register stores the condition code flags and the CPU mode bits. Several further Stored Program Status Registers (SPSRs) exist for each of the non-User modes; the CPSR is saved into the relevant SPSR whenever a mode change occurs.

General-purpose register R14 is hard-wired within the CPU to act as a link register (LR) used to save the PC when a Branch and Link instruction is executed. It can be treated as a general-purpose register at all other times.

By convention, but not hard-wiring, register R13 is used as the Stack Pointer (SP) during program execution. Although this is not mandatory, special facilities exists to support this technique (see below).

For each of the non-User CPU modes either three or eight further registers are switched in when a mode change occurs, to obviate the need to save registers to memory (see Table 2,2). In FIQ (Fast Interrupt) mode registers R8_fiq through R14_fiq and SPSR_fiq are switched in; in other modes registers R13_mode, R14_mode and SPSR_mode are available.

In a RISC CPU such as ARM the overhead associated with saving the critical CPU context state (PC, flags, stack pointer) to memory is large enough for these switched register banks to give significant performance improvements.

The extra-large set of registers in FIQ mode allows the interrupt

General registers and program counter

User32 mode	FIQ32 mode	Supervisor32 mode	Abort32 mode	IRQ32 mode	Undefined32 mode
R0	R0	R0	R0	R0	R0
R1	R1	R1	R1	R1	R1
R2	R2	R2	R2	R2	R2
R3	R3	R3	R3	R3	R3
R4	R4	R4	R4	R4	R4
R5	R5	R5	R5	R5	R5
R6	R6	R6	R6	R6	R6
R7	R7	R7	R7	R7	R7
R8	R8_fiq	R8	R8	R8	R8
R9	R9_fiq	R9	R9	R9	R9
R10	R10_fiq	R10	R10	R10	R10
R11	R11_fiq	R11	R11	R11	R11
R12	R12_fiq	R12	R12	R12	R12
R13	R13_fiq	R13_svc	R13_abt	R13_irq	R13_undef
R14	R14_fiq	R14_svc	R14_abt	R14_irq	R14_undef
R15 (PC)	R15 (PC)	R15 (PC)	R15 (PC)	R15 (PC)	R15 (PC)

Program status registers

CPSR	CPSR	CPSR	CPSR	CPSR	CPSR
	SPSR_fiq	SPSR_svc	SPSR_abt	SPSR_irq	SPSR_undef

Figure 2.4 Register organization

service routine to operate directly from private registers, usually without the need to save any state at all. In other CPU modes the link register LK and stack pointer SP (R13) are shadowed by banked registers to minimize the amount of context which must be saved. If registers R0 through R12 are required by Supervisor, IRQ, Abort or Undefined mode programs then their current contents should be saved on the stack and restored on return to User mode.

Table 2.2 The CPU mode bits

M[4:0]	Mode	Accessible register set	
10000	usr_32	PC,R14..R0	CPSR
10001	fiq_32	PC, R14_fiq..R8_fiq,R7..R0	CPSR, SPSR_fiq
10010	irq_32	PC, R14_irq..R13_irq, R12..R0	CPSR, SPSR_irq
10011	svc_32	PC, R14_svc..R13_svc, R12..R0	CPSR, SPSR_svc
10111	abt_32	PC, R14_abt..R13_abt, R12..R0	CPSR, SPSR_abt
11011	und_32	PC, R14_und..R13_und, R12..R0	CPSR, SPSR_und

2.3.3   Program Status Registers

The format of the Program Status Registers is shown in Figure 2.5.

The N, Z, C and V bits are the condition code flags, which may be changed as a result of arithmetic, logical and comparison operations in the CPU and which may be tested by all instructions to determine whether execution is to take place.

The I and F bits are interrupt disable bits, disabling IRQ and FIQ interrupts respectively when set.

The M4..M0 bits are the CPU mode bits which determine (when written) and indicate (when read) the mode in which the CPU operates. Not all combinations of these bits are meaningful: see Table 2.2 for more information.

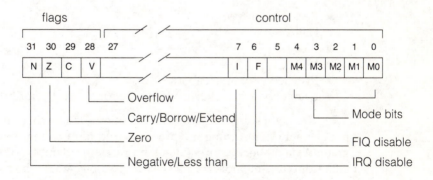

Figure 2.5 Format of the program status registers (PSRs)

2.3.4   CPU modes and exception handling

Normal program execution takes place in the ARM CPU's User mode. In User mode programs operate within the confines of the system memory management strategy and are prevented from executing privileged instructions and from altering the processor mode bits in the PSR. When the normal flow of the program is broken by an exception, perhaps because of a memory management fault or an external interrupt, the CPU mode changes according to the type of exception, and the PC is forced to a new value. The new PC value is read from a table of 'exception vectors' stored at fixed addresses in memory, causing a branch to an exception handling routine whose address has been initialized there by the operating system.

Interrupts cause a change to the relevant interrupt mode (IRQ or FIQ). The Software Interrupt (SWI) instruction causes a change to Supervisor mode. Memory management exceptions cause a change to Abort mode and undefined instructions cause a change to Undefined mode.

When any kind of exception occurs the CPU state prior to handling the exception must be preserved, so that the original program can be resumed when exception handling is completed. The ARM CPU uses the banked registers to hold the previous CPU state and provide fresh registers for the exception handler. The previous contents of the PC and CPSR are copied into the appropriate R14 and SPSR and the PC and mode bits in the CPSR are then forced to the relevant value. The interrupt disable flags are automatically set where required to prevent recursive nesting of exceptions.

Several exceptions can occur at the same time, so exceptions are assigned priorities and serviced in a fixed order according to priority. The exception priorities are:

- Reset (highest priority)
- Data abort
- FIQ
- IRQ
- Instruction prefetch abort
- Undefined instruction, SWI instruction (lowest priority)

The highest priority form of exception occurs when the CPU Reset pin is asserted, restarting the processor and terminating the current program. A data abort occurs when the processor attempts to read or write data from/to a memory location which is protected by the memory management unit; the instruction prefetch abort occurs when an instruction fetch refers to a protected address.

Exceptions are discussed in more detail in Chapter 5.

2.3.5   Instruction execution and timing

Execution of instructions within the ARM6 core results in memory access cycles which fall into one of four categories:

- Non-sequential cycle (N cycle). The CPU is requesting a transfer at an address which in unrelated to the address used in the previous cycle.
- Sequential cycle (S cycle). The CPU is requesting a transfer at an address which is either the same as or one word greater than the address used in the previous cycle.
- Internal cycle (I cycle). The CPU is performing an internal operation and no memory transfer is required.
- Coprocessor cycle (C cycle). The CPU wishes to use the data bus to communicate with a coprocessor and no memory transfer is required.

The CPU core generates a pair of signals, known as nMREQ and SEQ, which encode the current cycle as in Table 2.3.

Table 2.3   CPU cycle encoding

nMREQ	SEQ	Cycle type
0	0	Non-sequential (N)
0	1	Sequential (S)/Active (A)
1	0	Internal (I)/Latent (L)
1	1	Coprocessor (C)

The exact duration of each type of cycle is determined by the memory system logic used in each implementation. The ARM2, ARM6 and ARM60 processors output the signals shown above directly; the ARM3 ARM600 and ARM610, on the other hand, only ever perform S or I cycles to the memory system because of their caches, and these cycles are known as Active (A) and Latent (L) respectively on these processors.

Because of the pipelining employed in the ARM's control logic instruction execution overlaps considerably. Typically, one instruction is using the internal data paths while the next instruction is decoded and the one after that is being fetched. Instructions that are *not* executed take one sequential cycle; those that are executed take various numbers of cycles (summarized in Table 2.4, below) expressed in terms of the N, S, I and C cycles described above. The elapsed time in cycles may therefore be calculated if care is taken to consider pipelining.

Table 2.4 ARM instruction speeds

Instruction	Cycle count	Additional
Data processing (ALU operations)	1 S	+1 S for shift by register +1 S + 1 N if R15 updated
MSR, MRS	1 S	
LDR	1 S + 1 N + 1 I	+ 1 S + 1 N if R15 updated
STR	2 N	
LDM	n S + 1 N + 1 I	+ 1 S + 1 N if R15 updated
STM	(n-1) S + 2 N	
SWP	1 S + 2 N + 1 I	
B, BL	2 S + 1 N	
SWI, trap	2 S + 1 N	
MUL, MLA	1 S + m I	
CDP	1 S + b I	
LDC, STC	(n-1) S + 2 N + b I	
MRC	1 S + b I + 1 C	
MCR	1 S + (b+1) I + 1 C	

Table 2.4 expresses the instruction cycle timings in terms of the four cycle types. In the table the following abbreviations are used to represent various important parameters:

■ n is the number of words transferred
■ m is the number of cycles required by the multiplier
■ b is the number of cycles spent busy-waiting for the coprocessor, and is determined by the coprocessor itself

These timing figures can only be converted into 'real' time when the speed of the host memory system for each of the N and S cycles is known —these parameters vary from design to design. This process is discussed in more detail in Chapter 6.

▤ 2.4   Summary

The ARM6 CPU core is a 32-bit processor with 32-bit data and address buses. It includes 31 general-purpose registers and six status registers. Sixteen general-purpose registers are accessible to the programmer at any time, the remainder being switched in and out of visibility according to the current processor mode. There are six 32-bit CPU modes, of which User mode is intended for normal program execution but others are selected following hardware and software interrupts and memory management aborts.

Pipelining is employed to speed the execution of instructions. Three stages of pipelining: fetch, decode and execute are employed. Because branches break the pipeline it is usual to employ the ARM's conditional execution facility instead wherever possible.

Some parts of the CPU core are devoted to specialized functions. The barrel shifter performs shifts and rotations, and the Booth's multiplier assists in multiplication instructions along with the arithmetic logic unit (ALU).

The length of time instructions take to execute is determined by the type of instruction and the number of component memory or coprocessor accesses involved. Four distinct types of cycle are identified by the core for consideration by the memory subsystem. Integrated processors with on-chip caches present only a subset of these cycle types off-chip.

3

The ARM development environment

3.1 Introduction

RISC processors are particularly dependent on their support software. Good high-level language compilers and/or experienced assembly language programmers are needed to make the most of the economies provided by a RISC system. It is no use having a concise instruction set if compilers do not produce optimized, high-density output.

ARM Ltd has developed a set of tools to enable system designers and developers to write and test software for ARM-based systems, and also to provide a guideline to the performance of these systems before the hardware is available. These tools are usually supplied to developers in the form of the ARM Software Development Toolkit. This chapter provides an overview of the contents of the ARM Software Development Toolkit and how they can be used.

Issues affecting all components of the toolkit are discussed first, followed by a look at each component in turn, discussing its uses and the facilities it provides.

Many examples of ARM Assembler code and ARM C are given throughout the later chapters of this book. This chapter aims to introduce the Assembler and C compiler in sufficient detail that the reader is able to understand the examples and also to enter them, and assemble or compile them.

▓ 3.2   ARM Software Development Toolkit (SDT)

The ARM Software Development Toolkit (SDT) is available for a number of commonly used operating systems, including DOS and variants of Unix; a version of the Toolkit is also available for the Apple Macintosh. The Toolkit is supplied by ARM Ltd's foundry partners as part of their support for their customers, but is developed and maintained by ARM Ltd.

The Toolkit consists of several components:

- the Assembler: `armasm`
- the C compiler: `armcc`
- the Linker: `armlink`
- and the Debugger: `armsd`

Each of these tools is discussed extensively in this chapter. For a full technical specification of these programs and standards the reader should refer to the ARM Software Development Toolkit documentation.

Toolkit configuration

The ARM6 CPU cores support several different configurations of program counter size, data address space size, byte sex and cache, write buffer and memory management hardware. The Toolkit supports all possible combinations of these configurations, although programmers need to ensure that the target system hardware is also correctly set up for the configuration they intend to use. Programmers using the Toolkit will find that they need to customize some parts of the toolkit, such as the C libraries, so that they can be used on their particular ARM platform.

Some possible CPU configurations cannot be mixed, such as programs compiled to use hardware memory management with those compiled not to. The ARM Linker will either refuse to link or warn against impossible combinations.

3.2.1   Address space support

Current ARM processors (ARM6 and variants) support either 32-bit or 26-bit program and data address spaces. Earlier versions (ARM2, ARM3 and variants) support only 26-bit address spaces; it is possible that future ARM variants will not support 26-bit address spaces. The Toolkit supports 32-bit modes by default but can be requested to produce 26-bit code if this is required by the target processor. To do this, it is necessary to ensure that the correct C library and ARM emulation tools are installed; consult the Toolkit documentation for further details.

3.2.2   Byte sex/endianness support

ARM processors from ARM6 onwards can be configured to have either big-endian or little-endian byte sex. The Toolkit is shipped supporting the byte sex of its host system, so versions for SunOS are preconfigured to be big-endian, and versions for DOS are preconfigured to be little-endian. Again, this can be altered using the `config` utility supplied with the toolkit, and again it is necessary to install the correct libraries and emulation tools for the combination of program counter mode and byte sex required.

3.2.3   Memory management support

Some ARM processors (for example ARM600/610) include memory management hardware which, when initialized and enabled by the operating system, obviates the need for software protection such as stack-limit checking on function entry. All the ARM tools are configured to assume software stack-limit checking, but the `config` tool can be used to remove this from the C compiler and Assembler. The ARM library, ARMulator and symbolic debugger all have to be rebuilt to support the chosen hardware memory management module .

3.2.4   Using the Toolkit components together

The elements of the Toolkit are designed to work together. For example, programmers may prefer to generate some parts of a project in C and some in assembly language. All object code, however it was created, must be passed through the ARM Linker before it can be used as run-time executable code.

A single project might pass through all the parts of the Toolkit. It could start by being programmed in C to prove the general principles. The ARM C compiler would then be used to compile the C source into assembly language. This could then be hand-tuned for optimum performance, using the ARM Symbolic Debugger. If the program needed to be tested on actual ARM hardware, a device such as the Platform Independent Evaluation (PIE) card could be used, as a slot card in an IBM PC-compatible or via a serial link. Finally, the Linker would be used to link the finished code and produce run-time object code.

▤ 3.3   The ARM Assembler

For programmers wishing to produce code of the highest possible density, written to work with the processor as closely as possible for maximum performance, there is no substitute for the Assembler. Writing ARM Assembler requires some skill to achieve efficient results, but is simpler than other RISC processor assemblers. However, hand-writing assembly language makes it possible to produce extremely dense code which exploits ARM-specific hardware features such as conditional execution of instructions or the barrel shifter.

The ARM Assembler `armasm` is a key component of the Software Development Toolkit. It simplifies the development of software which needs to be closely fitted to ARM processor hardware and allows hand optimization to achieve the maximum performance in speed- or throughput-critical applications.

3.3.1   Format and organization of ARM assembly language

The instructions and directives that are understood by the ARM Assembler are listed in Appendices A to C. The CPU instructions summarized in the appendices are the subject of the next chapter.

Lines of input to the ARM Assembler generally take the following form:

```
label                   instruction     ; comment
```

The significant issue is that each of the three components must be separated by at least one white space character (eg space, tab). Empty lines are allowed and ignored by the Assembler.

The program listings throughout this book are presented as an example of good practice in laying out and organizing assembly language so that it is easy to read and maintain. Ideally, Assembler input should be laid out in three columns separated by tabs, so that routine labels, instructions and comments are all easily identifiable at a glance.

Labels

Labels are tags given to sections of code to allow the address of the label to be referred to by the program. The Assembler is case-sensitive, so programmers should take care to ensure that label and macro names are used with consistent capitalization to avoid errors.

If a label is used it must appear at the start of the line; if no label is used the line must begin with a space or a tab. Labels are treated as symbols (see below) and obey similar rules; they must start with an upper- or lower-case letter or an underscore character, and should ideally not use the same name as instruction mnemonics or directives to avoid confusion. Labels generated by the Assembler are given names beginning with an underscore.

Local labels

The Assembler supports a 'local label' facility, allowing sub-labels within a parent label; a local label is simply a two-digit number that is 00..99. Local labels are useful when many labels or macro-generated labels are required, since they may be redefined several times; the Assembler uses the definition closest to the point of refernce. Local label areas are declared using the 'routine' directive ROUT in the following way:

```
MyRoutine    ROUT              ; define start of routine
             ...
01           ...               ; local label 01
             ...
02           ...               ; local label 02
             ...
             BNE    %01        ; reference to label 01
             ...
```

Local labels are distinguished by their initial two-digit number, which may optionally be followed by the parent label name, for example 06MyRoutine.

References to local labels must begin with the per cent character %, optionally followed by B or F to tell the assembler to search *backwards* or *forwards* for the label, and A or T to look at *all* macro levels or only *this* one for the label. If there is no B or F, searching occurs in all directions. If there is no A or T, searching occurs at this macro level and all levels closer to the original source than this one, but not at more deeply nested macro levels.

The letters refer to the local label, not to the parent routine label. For example, in the following:

```
MyRoutine    ROUT
             ...
             B      %01MyRoutine
             ...
01MyRoutine
```

%F01MyRoutine would work in place of %01MyRoutine, but %B01My-Routine wouldn't.

So a reference to a local label might look like the following:

```
BAL          %BT25fred         ; branch to sub-
                               ; label 25 of routine 'fred'

B            %A19              ; branch to #19
```

```
        B            %67print_char  ; branch to #67 of 'print_char'
```

The following example demonstrates the use of the A and T suffixes in nested macros. Macro B is defined:

```
        MACRO
        MacroB
01

        ...
        MEND
```

Macro A is defined:

```
        MACRO
        MacroA
        ...                ;Code, not including
        ...                ; 01 definition
        B       %01
        MacroB
        MEND
```

The following code appears in the main source file:

```
01

        MacroA
```

The %01 in MacroA will find the label in the main source file—it is further away than the one in MacroB, but more deeply nested macros are not searched:

- %T01 would produce an error
- %A01 would find 01 in macro B

Instructions

The instruction field of the source file is expected to include a valid ARM instruction or Assembler directive followed by any arguments required. A space or tab character must separate the label or beginning of the line and the instruction or directive itself, if one is included in the line. Refer to Appendices A to C for details on the syntax of Assembler instructions and directives.

Comments

All text and numbers appearing after a semicolon are treated as a comment, that is ignored by the Assembler. The only exception to this is if the semicolon is contained within a string constant.

Blank lines may also be included to make the code easier to read; they are ignored by the Assembler.

3.3.2   Areas

AREAs are the independent, named, indivisible chunks of program source which are then taken and manipulated by the Linker. All programs will consist of one or more areas; complex programs may be written in several self-contained pieces which are linked together. The syntax of the AREA directive is:

```
AREA name{,attr}{,attr}...{,ALIGN=expression}
```

Each assembled or compiled program will normally consist of two areas, a writable area for data and a read-only area for code; re-entrant code will have a third area, marked 'BASED sb', which contains relocatable address constants.

Areas can be given one or more attributes which determine the way they are handled by the Linker and provide information about memory management in the run-time environment. The attributes shown in Table 3.1 can be used.

Table 3.1 AREA directive attributes

Attribute	Effect
ABS	Area has an absolute address and is not relocatable.
REL	Area is relocatable by the Linker. This is the default setting.
PIC	Position-independent code.
CODE	Area contains machine instructions.
DATA	Area contains data.
READONLY	Area cannot be written to.
COMDEF	Common area definition.
COMMON	Common area.
NOINIT	Data area initialized to zero and containing only space reservation directives.
REENTRANT	Re-entrant area (apply only to code areas).
BASED Rn	Static base data area, containing tables of address constants locating static data items. Labels defined in this area are treated as register-relative expressions for the purposes of load and store instructions.
ALIGN{=exp}	Adjust program counter to be address aligned (see text).

The ALIGN sub-directive can also be used to force the start of the area with a 2^n byte address boundary. The default is a 4-byte word boundary but any number between two and 12 can be used; for example, ALIGN=3 aligns to an 8-byte boundary.

The example below declares a relocatable, reentrant code area called IRQ_Service:

```
AREA IRQ_Service, CODE, REENTRANT
```

while this example declares a data area called Despatch_Table aligned to a four byte boundary:

```
AREA Despatch_Table, DATA, ALIGN=2
```

3.3.3   Constants

Constants may be used as arguments to any instruction; three types of constant are supported: numeric, string and Boolean.

Numeric constants

Numeric constants are allowed in several forms: decimal, hexadecimal (either 'C' style or Acorn style), or any number base between two and nine entered in the form n_xxx where n is the number of the base and xxx a number in that base. For example:

```
123                     decimal
0xffe3                  hexadecimal 'C' style
&65FF                   hexadecimal Acorn style
7_350                   base seven
```

String constants

String constants should be enclosed by double quotes. To use the double quote or dollar characters within a string, enter a pair of the character required. For example:

```
"Value is $$"                        ; =="Value is $"
"A Christmas Carol"
```

Boolean constants

The Boolean constants True and False should be written as {TRUE} and {FALSE}.

3.3.4   Symbols, labels and variables

Symbols can represent numeric, logical and string values or addresses. Labels are a special form of symbol distinguished by their position at the start of lines. The address is not explicitly stated but is resolved during assembly.

Symbol names

Symbols must start with a letter in either case; the Assembler is case-sensitive and treats the two forms as distinct. Symbols may contain alpha-numeric characters and the underscore character, and may be up to up to 255 characters in length (all characters are significant). Further characters, such as punctuation marks and symbols, can be used if the symbol name is enclosed by vertical bar characters, for example |fish$$@|. Example valid symbol names are:

```
TimeCounter
Time_0800
|"time"_@03|
```

Symbols should not use the same name as instruction mnemonics or directives; although the Assembler can tell them apart, a programmer may not always be able to.

Equational directives

The Assembler supports several directives to give symbolic names to numeric expressions and registers, both integer and coprocessor.

Number equating directives

```
label EQU expression
```

```
label *   expression
```

These two synonymous directives associate the symbol label supplied with the result of the expression. Here are some typical examples:

```
|Two^Ten|                 EQU     32 * 32
Kilo                      EQU     |Two^Ten|
Mega                      EQU     Kilo * Kilo
BaseAddress               *       0x007f01c0
```

Register equating directives

```
label RN numeric-expression
```

```
label FN numeric-expression
```

The RN directive defines register names; registers may only be referred to by name: the names R0–R15, r0–r15, PC, pc, LR and lr are pre-defined.

The FN directive defines floating-point register names; the names F0–F7 and f0–f7 are pre-defined.

Typically, register equates are used at the start of assembly language source files to establish aliases for registers within that file, for example:

```
Base            RN    0        ; Define integer
                               ; register aliases

Index           RN    1

Stride          RN    2

Result          FN    6        ; Define floating-point
                               ; aliases

Amplitude       FN    7

Phase           FN    8
```

Coprocessor equating directives

```
label CP numeric-expression

label CN numeric-expression
```

The CP directive defines coprocessor names, which must be in the range 0 to 15. The names p0–p15 are pre-defined.

The CN directive defines a name for a coprocessor register number; c0–c15 are pre-defined.

```
ARM600_Sys  CP    15       ; System control coprocessor #15

ARM_ID      CN    0        ; p15, c0 - ARM ID

Control     CN    1        ; p15, c1 - Control

TT_Base     CN    2        ; p15, c2 - Transl. Table Base

Domain_Ctrl CN    3        ; p15, c3 - Domain Access Control
```

Symbols as variables

Symbols can be used as variables to represent numbers, logical values and string values. They are declared using the GBL (global) and LCL (local) directives and values assigned to them using the directives SETA, SETL or SETS according to whether the symbol is typed Arithmetic, Logical or String.

Scope of variables

The scope of global variables extends across the entire source file while that of local variables is restricted to a particular instantiation of a macro. Addresses can also be represented by symbols, but in this case the value is only assigned during assembly or when the file is linked.

Built-in variables

There are several special variables built into the assembler. They are shown in Table 3.2.

Table 3.2 Built-in variables in ARM Assembler

Variable	Purpose
{PC} or '.'	Current program location counter
{VAR} or '@'	Current storage area location counter
{TRUE}	Logical constant true
{FALSE}	Logical constant false
{OPT}	Current assembly listing option (see Appendix C)
{CONFIG}	Has the value 32 or 26 according to PC address size

Declaring and assigning to variables

The variable declaration and assignment directives have a syntax which is slightly different from the ARM instruction syntax. Below are some example variable declarations:

```
GBLA        MemorySize              ; global arithmetic
                                    ; symbol

MemorySize  SETA    32*1024*1024    ; set MemorySize to
                                    ; 32Mbyte

GBLL        Big_Switch              ; global logical symbol
Big_Switch  SETL    {TRUE}          ; set Big_Switch to TRUE

GBLS        Message                 ; global string symbol
Message     SETS    "Hello world";  ; set Message to quoted
                                    ; string
```

3.3.5   Conditional and repetitive assembly

IF...ELSE...ENDIF

ARM Assembler source can be assembled conditionally using the IF, ELSE and ENDIF directives. If the logical expression given is true, the code between IF and ELSE is assembled; if it is false, the code between

ELSE and ENDIF is assembled instead.

The syntax of the IF...ELSE...ENDIF directives is:

```
    IF logical-expression
code section 1...
    ELSE
code section 2...
    ENDIF
```

A space or tab character must precede the directives, as otherwise they would be mistaken for labels.

The characters [, | and] may be used as alternatives for IF, ELSE and ENDIF respectively. For example:

```
    [       a=b     ; IF (a==b) THEN
    ...             ; do this...
    |               ; ELSE
    ...             ; do that...
    ]               ; ENDIF
```

WHILE...WEND

A further conditional Assembly construct is available in the form of the WHILE and WEND directives. As long as the expression following the WHILE directive is true, the code between the WHILE and WEND directives will be assembled; if the expression is false to start with, this code will not be assembled.

The syntax here is:

```
    WHILE logical-expression
code....
    WEND
```

3.3.6   Macros

The Assembler provides a macro facility which can be used to insert a frequently used group of instructions or directives with one line of code. The code represented by a macro can use another macro, with up to 255 levels of nested macros. Using macros makes code easier to change, because the change need only be entered once, and also makes code easier to read and understand. Macros are typically used to define more complex instructions which can then be entered quickly as a single line of Assembler.

The MACRO and MEND directives are used to enclose macro definitions and to show the Assembler that the code enclosed between them will be called as a macro.

The first line of the macro is a template of the line that invokes it. Macros are invoked by a name which is supplied here, along with any parameters the macro takes.

Macros should not contain any unclosed WHILE/WEND loops or IF/ENDIF constructions. If they do, they should be terminated with the MEXIT directive as well as MEND, to ensure that further expansion does not take place within these constructions.

If you wish to label a macro, the label must be specified as an argument to the MACRO directive.

A macro example

Below is an example macro called 'TABLE' which takes two parameters, a starting value and a decrement, and emits a table of values arrived at by repeatedly decrementing the starting value:

```
                AREA Example, DATA      ; defined area as data
                MACRO                   ; start macro
                                        ; definition
$label          TABLE   $start, $dec    ; macro name and
                                        ; parameters
                LCLA    counter         ;  declare local
                                        ; variable
$label
counter         SETA    $start          ; assign parameter to
                                        ; local
                DCB     counter         ; First table entry
                WHILE   counter >= $dec
counter         SETA    counter - $dec
                DCB     counter         ; Subsequent table
                                        ; entries
                WEND
                ALIGN                   ; force word alignment
                MEND                    ; end of macro
                                        ; definition
```

To invoke the macro simply requires it to be called by name along with any parameters, as follows:

```
a_table         TABLE   10, 3
```

Miscellaneous directives

The following directives are also important in understanding the programming examples which appear in this book. The ARM Assembler supports a wide range of directives, not all of which are relevant here: consult Appendix C or the ARM Software Development Toolkit documentation for an exhaustive and up-to-date list.

Alignment directive

```
ALIGN {power-of-two{, offset-expression}}
```

This directive forces the program location counter to a word-aligned address (that is address divisible by four) or optionally to be aligned to some other power of two with a further optional byte offset.

End of source file directive

```
END
```

Every source file for the Assembler *must* end with this directive on a line by itself.

Storage reservation directives

```
{label} DCB expression-list
```

```
{label} DCW expression-list
```

```
{label} DCD expression-list
```

```
{label} % numeric-expression
```

These directives define byte, half-word or word quantities in memory, optionally associating a label. The expression list can consist of any series of numeric or string expressions separated by commas; note that strings must have an explicit terminating zero added manually if required, for example:

```
    My_String         DCB     "Venice in peril",0
```

The per cent % directive initializes the specified number of bytes to zeros.

Store layout directives

```
^ expression{,base-register}{label}
```

```
# expression
```

These directives allow 'storage maps' to be set up and optionally associated with a base register and a label.

The ^ directive sets the origin of a storage map at the address given by the expression. A storage map location counter, referred to as '@', is also set to the same address. Each ^ directive resets @ to allow many storage maps.

The # directive describes the space within a storage map. Each time # is used its label (if any) is given the value of @ and then incremented by the number of bytes following the #.

Where a base register is specified with the ^ directive, that register then becomes implicit in all symbols subsequently defined by # until cancelled by a subsequent ^ directive. These register-relative symbols can later be used in LDR/STR instructions. For example:

```
                        ^        0, r9
                        #        4
        Label           #        4
                        . . .
                        LDR      r0, Label; load 'register-relative'
```

where the LDR instruction is equivalent to:

```
                        LDR      r0, [r9, #4]; explicit register-relative
```

Refer to Chapter 4 for further information on the use of storage maps (see LDR/STR).

Literal table origin directive

```
LTORG numeric-expression
```

The LTORG directive forces the literal pool, used to store program constants, to be placed immediately after the directive. A default LTORG is obeyed at every END directive which is not part of a nested assembly, but larger programs may require several LTORGs to avoid violating the ±4 Kbyte offset limit imposed by the LDR/STR instruction.

3.3.7   Running armasm

ARM Assembler is invoked from the command line using the following command:

```
armasm {options} sourcefile objectfile
```

The sourcefile is the name of the file containing the code to be assembled and the objectfile is the name by which the assembled code is to be stored. A number of command-line options are supported by the Assembler to allow the selection of various modes; they are discussed in the next section.

The following example command assembles the file source to the file object, including debugging tables and a listing to be stored in the file listing:

```
    armasm -g -list listing source object
```

The following example assembles the file source to the file object, including debugging code and specifying the ARM Procedure Call Standard version 3 and that the code supports re-entrancy:

```
    armasm -g -apcs 3/REENTRANT source object
```

Command-line switches

The command-line switches shown in Table 3.3 can be used when invoking the Assembler. All switches should be preceded by a hyphen. Capital letters indicate abbreviated forms of the switches that can be used. If the switch is not explicitly entered the default setting indicated in the table is assumed.

Table 3.3 Assembler command-line switches

Switch	Purpose
-Help	Displays a summary of command-line options.
-Depend *depend-file*	Saves make source file dependencies in the file named
-I*dir{,dir}*	Adds directories to the source file search path so that the full path name need not be entered when files are named as arguments to the GET and INCLUDE directives.
-PreDefine *directive*	Pre-executes a SETx (and associated GBLx) directive.
-NOCache	Turns off source caching between passes one and two of the Assembler to save memory. The default is caching on.
-MaxCache *n*	Sets the maximum source cache size in megabytes. The default is 8 Mbyte.
-NOEsc	Ignore C-style escape sequences.
-NOWar	Turn off warning messages. The default is on.
-g	Output ARM Symbolic Debugger debugging tables.
-LIttleend	Little-endian byte order (the default).
-BIgend	Big-endian byte order.
-Apcs *option* {*/qualifier*}{*/qualifier...*}	Selects a procedure call standard (APCS). An APCS option need only be entered if you need to use a setting different from that to which your copy of the SDT is configured.

Listing options

Listing options (Table 3.4) can be set within the source code by using the OPT directive. A listing will only be produced if listing is explicitly turned on using the -list command-line switch. The default setting is to produce a listing which includes the declaration of variables, the expansion and invocation of macros, conditional and MEND directives, on the second pass of the Assembler. Different settings can be achieved using the OPT options listed in Appendix C.

If the listing is being produced as pages, titles and subtitles can be added from within the code using the TTL and SUBT directives respectively.

Table 3.4 Assembler listing options

Listing option	Purpose
-list *listingfile*	This option produces an additional listing file, saved in the file *listingfile*. The contents of the file can be changed from the default with the use of the following sub-options:
-NOTerse	Turns the terse flag off, allowing conditional code not assembled to be listed anyway.
-WIdth *n*	Sets the page width for listings; the default is 79.
-Length *n*	Sets listing page length. The default is 66; setting length to zero will produce output with no page breaks.
-Xref	Lists cross-reference information on symbols, that is where they are defined and where they are used, by line numbers.

3.4   The ARM C compiler

The ARM C compiler, `armcc`, is a mature compiler which conforms to the 1990 ANSI C language standard. It also supports the pcc dialect of C (usually associated with Berkeley Unix) and is based upon Norcroft C.

Libraries

Two libraries are provided with the SDT which support cross-compiled C. Both are supplied in two forms: as source which needs to be re-targeted to work with particular hardware, and as binaries which will work immediately with the ARMulator ARM software emulator.

The first library is a minimal standalone run-time library, which contains division and remainder functions, stack-limit checking functions, lowest-level memory management functions (stack and heap), program start-up and simple I/O functions. It is provided as an ARM Assembler file.

The second library is a full ANSI C library and contains:

■ Target-independent modules in ANSI C
■ Target-independent modules written in ARM assembler
■ Target-dependent modules in ANSI C
■ Target-dependent modules in ARM Assembler

The target-dependent modules are supplied by ARM in versions which will work immediately on the ARMulator, and as an additional example, on Acorn computers running the RISC OS operating system. They are also supplied as source files which need to be targeted towards the ARM hardware which is being developed.

3.4.1 Using the ARM C compiler

The ARM C compiler uses the following file naming conventions to identify different classes of file it uses and produces. In most operating systems these appear as filename extensions in the form 'filename.x'; in others which do not support filename extensions files should be placed in a directory named after the file type, or are placed there by the compiler. The filename types are:

program.c	C source file
program.h	C header file
program.o	ARM object file
program.s	ARM assembly language
program.ls t	Output listing file

Command-line options

Several command-line options are available and should be entered when invoking armcc. armcc is invoked in the following way:

```
armcc {options} -c filenames
```

So, for example,

```
armcc -list -c cprog.c
```

will compile the file cprog.c to a file cprog.o and generate a listing file cprog.lst.

Any combination of the options in Table 3.5 can be used.

Table 3.5 ARM C compiler options

Option	Purpose
-help	Prints on-screen a summary of the command line options available.
-pcc	Instructs the compiler to produce pcc dialect C.
-fussy	A synonym for 'strict': see below
-strict	Be extra strict about forcing conformance to the C standard selected (that is ANSI or pcc).
-list	Create a listing file. This includes lines of object code along with any error messages or warnings generated by the compiler.
-LIttleend	Compile code in little-endian byte order.
-BIgend	Compile code in big-endian byte order.

≡ 3.5   The ARM Linker

The ARM Linker combines object files with object libraries and resolves address references to create an executable program. All object files generated by the ARM Assembler and the ARM C compiler must be linked before they can be run as standalone programs.

The Linker requires at least one pre-compiled or assembled object file in ARM Object Format (AOF), that is standard output from the ARM C Compiler or the ARM Assembler. In addition it can accept one or more object libraries in ARM Object Library format.

The Linker performs the following functions:

- Resolves symbolic references between object files
- Extracts from object libraries any object modules referred to in the object files it is linking
- Sorts object fragments (AOF areas) according to their attributes
- Consolidates fragments with similar attributes into contiguous chunks of code

So, for example, CODE areas scattered across several assembled object files will be placed together. The Linker further resolves relocatable addresses and finally generates an output image which is the executable program.

3.5.1   Using the Linker

Table 3.6 ARM Linker command-line options

Option	Purpose
-Help	Prints a list of command-line options available to the Linker
-Output *name*	Give a name for the Linker's output (usually the image file)
-Debug	Include ARM Symbolic Debugger tables in the output image, that is preserves symbol information. Low-level debugging information generated by the Linker is also included.
-VIA *filename*	Read the list of file names contained in the file *filename*. As many -VIA options as required can be used. Files contained in the list must be in a linkable format, that is AOF or libraries.
-Verbose	Print on-screen messages indicating the Linker's progress. A stronger option, -VV, provides even more information.
-MAP	This option creates a map of the base and size of each area being linked.
-Xref	Lists references between input areas.
-Symbols *filename*	Stores a list of symbols used in the link step in the file *filename*.
-Base *address*	Sets the Linker output to load at the specified address.
-Entry *address*	If no entry point is included in the program image, an entry address must be specified on the Linker command-line.
-Case	Matches symbol names regardless of their case.
-Unresolved symbol	Any references to an undefined symbol are matched to the symbol specified here. Symbol must therefore be a defined global symbol or the link will fail.

The Linker is invoked from the command line using the following form:

```
armlink {options} input-file-list
```

The following example links the files named, producing debugging tables and printing on-screen messages about the progress of the linking operation:

```
armlink -D -v fred1.o fred2.o fred3.o
```

Command-line options

The options in Table 3.6 are available at the command line and should be entered as described. Capital letters show minimum abbreviations which can be used.

3.5.2   Linker output options

Linker output can take one of several forms: each Toolkit is supplied configured for a particular output format. Other Linker output formats are available by means of command-line options. Refer to the ARM SDT documentation for further information.

Further formats include overlaid images and RISC OS modules for use with Acorn Computers' RISC OS operating system.

3.6   The ARM Symbolic Debugger

3.6.1   Introduction to the ARM debugger

The ARM Software Development Toolkit includes the ARM Symbolic Debugger armsd.

The armsd debugger

armsd contains the ARM processor emulation package ARMulator and enables ARM code to be executed on the Toolkit host computer without any ARM hardware being required. The ARMulator is described more fully in the next section.

armsd also debugs code running under the ARM debug monitor on an evaluation card with an RS232 serial connection to the Toolkit host, such as the ARM PIE card.

These two forms of the debugger enable system developers to start producing and debugging code for their target ARM hardware using the software ARMulator, and later either one of ARM or their chip supplier's evaluation cards or their own ARM-based hardware.

■ armsd is set up by default to use the ARM6 architecture and the

SDT host's byte ordering. However, it can be configured to include the 26-bit ARMulator and to support the opposite endianness to the host. A set of C libraries to handle all four possible combinations of program counter size and byte sex is provided in the SDT.

3.6.2   Remote debug options

There are two options which are combined for remote debugging with `armsd`: the Remote Debug Protocol and the Remote Debug Interface.

The Remote Debug Interface provides the ARM symbolic debugger with a uniform way to communicate with the debug monitor in three different situations: first, when `armsd` is being run on the ARMulator, or in the self-hosted version designed for use with Acorn Computers' RISC OS operating system; second, when `armsd` and the ARMulator are being run in separate Unix processes; and third, when `armsd` is driving a debug monitor and debuggee on ARM-based hardware connected to the host via a serial or SCSI connection.

The Remote Debug Protocol contains a set of C functions which simplify the calling of debugging procedures such as starting and ending sessions, reading and writing memory addresses and CPU and coprocessor states, setting and clearing break- and watch-points, and stepping through the program being debugged.

3.6.3   Debugging using `armsd`

The `armsd` debugger enable both low-level and high-level debugging to be carried out. Commands for high-level debugging include commands for accessing and, where relevant, changing the contents of variables, symbols, constants, arguments and memory locations. Programs can be executed using the Go command, or stepped through until break- or watch-points set using the debugger are reached. Program context can be displayed and commands allow quick movement between contexts and procedures.

Low-level debugging commands permit the display of contents of the registers, and of floating-point registers. The contents of memory can be examined and listed in hexadecimal, ASCII and instruction formats. Low-level symbols (for example register names) can be defined and used in debugging; the standard ARM register names are predefined.

In both forms of debugging log files of activity can be stored.

▤ 3.7   The ARMulator

The ARMulator is a software ARM6 processor emulator supplied as part of the SDT. Two variants are available; the standard one emulates the ARM6/60/600 environment with its 32-bit address space, while the second version emulates the 26-bit program counter of the ARM2/3/61 if required.

The ARMulator is intended to assist developers create and test ARM-hosted software on non-ARM systems. Such software can be accurately benchmarked and the performance of the hardware and software under development predicted. Working with ARMsd via the Remote Debug Interface the ARMulator can be used to test and debug ARM-based programs before the hardware on which they will be run is ready.

The ARMulator also provides an emulation of the ARM processor suitable for integration into more complex hardware simulations.

The ARMulator operates in two different modes, each suitable for different tasks. The instruction-based mode executes an instruction at a time, either singly or in sequence. The clock-cycle mode executes either one tick of the ARM's master clock, or alternate phases of the master clock. In both cases inputs are read from the ARMulator's model of the ARM processor's pins, and outputs are written back to them.

The ARMulator includes its model of the ARM processor core and models of memory and coprocessor interfaces, as well as an operating system interface. Examples of all of these are provided with the SDT, representing an ARM evaluation card, but users of the SDT are expected to want to construct their own memory model to meet their own requirements. A library of functions to assist in this process is included with the SDT.

ARMulator models can be built either to emphasize rapid prototype development or to provide the fastest possible ARM emulation.

▤ 3.8   Summary

The ARM Software Development Toolkit provides a range of choices for programmers wishing to develop for the platform.

The Assembler and C compiler both allow code to be written which can be tightly optimized to extract the best performance from the ARM.

A range of debugging facilities are provided. Programmers can test their work using software or hardware simulation products, and use these in conjunction with the debugger.

The Linker takes assembled or compiled source files and produces object code for the specified ARM environment.

4

The ARM6 integer instruction set

4.1 Introduction

The ARM instruction set is a good target for high-level language compilers; there are few interdependencies between instructions, so assembly language programming is also straightforward. Not many programmers wish to work at the binary instruction level, so in this chapter we concentrate on the assembly language syntax for ARM integer instructions, with some of the examples being illustrated in both C and Assembler. Details of the binary format of each instruction may be found in Appendix A.

This chapter describes the syntax and meaning of each of the instructions understood by the ARM6 CPU core; instruction set extensions for floating-point operations and other architecture extensions are discussed in their respective chapters.

The first part of the chapter describes those aspects of the instruction set that are common to all instruction types, for example the syntax conventions and major architectural issues. Subsequent sections detail each of the instruction classes and demonstrate their applications. Finally, the last section discusses restrictions and limitations imposed on ARM programming, notably those to do with the Program Counter (r15).

4.2   Syntax conventions

Throughout this chapter and the rest of the book a number of conventions are used to allow instruction syntax and function to be concisely described; examples of these conventions are shown below:

```
Text like this
```

is used to represent commands, instructions or syntax definitions.

```
items in italics
```

represent fields which must be completed before a command or instruction may be issued.

```
{items in braces}
```

are *optional* and so only need to appear if the optional feature is desired.

```
Square brackets, for example: CPSR[31:28]
```

mean bits 31 to 28 inclusive of the register or bus in question, here the CPSR.

4.3   Conditional execution

All ARM instructions are conditionally executed according to the state of the CPSR flags and the condition field within the instruction. This is one of the most significant features of the ARM instruction set, since it allows very dense in-line code (without branches) to be written. Instructions that are not executed take a single clock cycle, so the time penalty of not executing several conditional instructions is frequently less than the overhead of the branch instruction or subroutine call that would otherwise be required.

Every ARM instruction contains a four-bit field, always instruction word bits [31..28] in the ARM6 instruction set, which encodes the circumstances under which the instruction will actually be executed. The sixteen possible conditions are represented by two-character mnemonics which are appended to the instruction itself, so Branch (B in assembly language) becomes BEQ for Branch if Equal.

The 'AL'ways condition code

Most instructions are assembled with the default condition field always (mnemonic AL) which ignores the state of the condition flags and executes the instruction anyway. The Assembler assumes the always condition unless specifically instructed otherwise. Where truly conditional execution is actually required another value for the condition field must be used. Table 4.1 summarizes the possible instruction condition mnemonics.

4.3.1   ARM instruction condition fields

Table 4.1 lists the full set of ARM condition codes which can be appended to instructions.

Table 4.1 Instruction condition mnemonics

Code	Mnemonic	Flags	Meaning
0000	EQ	Z set	equal
0001	NE	Z clear	not equal
0010	CS or HS	C set	unsigned higher or same
0011	CC or LO	C clear	unsigned lower
0100	MI	N set	negative
0101	PL	N clear	positive or zero
0110	VS	V set	overflow
0111	VC	V clear	no overflow
1000	HI	C set and Z clear	unsigned higher
1001	LS	C clear or Z set	unsigned lower or same
1010	GE	N==V	greater or equal
1011	LT	N!=V	less than
1100	GT	Z clear AND (N==V)	greater than
1101	LE	Z set OR (N!=V)	less than or equal
1110	AL	Don't care	always

4.3.2 Byte ordering (little-endian versus big-endian)

ARM integer instructions operate on data sizes of either a byte (8 bits) or a word (32 bits). ARM addresses refer to bytes, so the address of an aligned word always has the bottom two bits clear. No other data types are directly supported by the instruction set, but of course arbitrary data types such as bit fields or half words may be manipulated using sequences of ARM instructions.

The ARM6 CPU can be configured to operate with either of the two different conventions for byte ordering, known as 'little-endian' or 'big-endian' byte ordering. The byte which is reached by an address whose bottom two bits are both zero, that is XXXXXX00, can be either the least significant in the addressed word (little-endian) or the most significant (big-endian).

Various computer manufacturers have adopted each strategy: the IBM360, MIPS, Motorola and SPARC architectures are all big-endian, whilst the DEC VAX & DEC Alpha, Intel 80x86 and default ARM architectures are all little-endian (Hennessy and Patterson, 1990).

Table 4.2 summarizes the effects of byte ordering on the byte referenced by particular addresses; here the ARM's bus interface signal 'not-Byte/Word' and the two least significant address bus bits are considered.

Table 4.2 Byte ordering

Big-endian	Little-endian	nByte /Word	A0	A1
Word	Word	1	X	X
Most significant byte	Least significant byte	0	0	0
Second most significant byte	Second least significant byte	0	0	1
Second least significant byte	Second most significant byte	0	1	0
Least significant byte	Most significant byte	0	1	1

The configuration of byte ordering is achieved through manipulation of the CPU core's control signals, usually through the execution of coprocessor instructions. Refer to Chapter 9 for further information.

▤ 4.4   Data processing instructions

4.4.1   Introduction to data processing instructions

The largest group of ARM instructions is the data processing instructions. Data transfers between registers, arithmetic and logical operations, and comparisons all fall into this category. All data processing instructions accept one or more registers as their operands and always return the result to a register, optionally setting the condition code flags according to the result. See Figure 4.1 for a full list of instructions.

First operand

The first source operand of a data processing instruction (except for MOV and MVN) is always a register and is known in syntax definitions as 'Rn'. Any register may be specified, including the program counter (r15), allowing various flavours of PC-relative addressing to be synthesized.

Second operand

The second operand (or the only operand of MOV and MVN) may be either a register, known as Rm and optionally shifted before use, or an 8-bit immediate constant, optionally rotated before use. The shifted register forms allow one of the following types of multi-bit shift:

- Logical Shift Left (LSL)
- Logical Shift Right (LSR)
- Arithmetic Shift Right (ASR)
- Rotate Right (ROR)

In each case the number of bits to shift by is supplied either as a constant or by another register.

One further shift type is available: Rotate Right Extended (RRX) performs a single bit rotation of the operand through the Carry flag.

Results: data

Any register may be specified as the destination for the result of a data processing instruction. This leaves open the possibility of using the Program counter (r15) as the destination, in which case the flow of instruction execution is likely to change to a new address. In a very few circumstances this might be attractive (for example calculated branches) but it is fraught with complexities: a discussion of the pitfalls of using the PC as a destination is included in Pitfalls, quirks and restrictions on page 102.

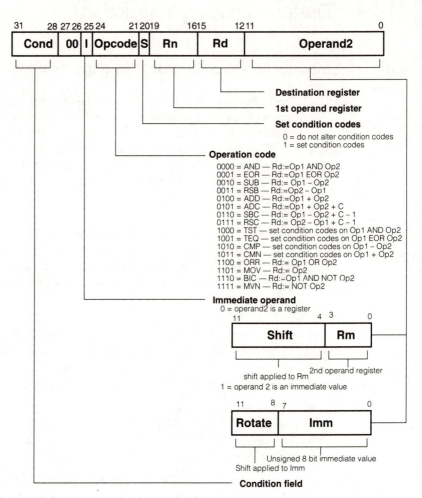

Figure 4.1 Data processing instructions

Results: condition code flags

The PSR condition code flags N, Z, C, V may be optionally updated by these instructions according to whether or not the S suffix is appended to the instruction mnemonic.

The comparison instructions CMN, CMP, TST, and TEQ *always* update the condition codes, so no S suffix is needed, and they return no other result.

4.4.2   Shifted operands: instruction-specified shift amounts

When the shift amount is specified by the instruction it is contained in a 5-bit field and may therefore take any value in the range 0..31. The shift amount determines how many bits are shifted in the manner specified by the shift type field.

The shift type field selects between LSL, LSR, ASR, ROR and RRX. A detailed description of the action of each type of shift follows; a figure provides a diagrammatic explanation of each.

LSL—logical shift left

The contents of the register Rm are moved by the number of bits specified by the shift amount to more significant bit positions. The least significant bits thus revealed are filled with zeros; the most significant bits are discarded except that the least significant discarded bit becomes the shifter carry output (which may later set the C flag in the CPSR) (Figure 4.2).

An LSL with a shift amount of zero is treated as a special case: the shifter carry output is simply the old value of the C flag. The contents of the operand register Rm are passed through un-shifted.

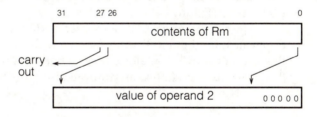

Figure 4.2 Logical shift left by five bits

LSR—logical shift right

The contents of the register Rm are moved by the number of bits specified by the shift amount to less significant bit positions. The most significant bits thus revealed are filled with zeros; the least significant bits are discarded except that the most significant discarded bit becomes the shifter carry output (which may later set the C flag in the CPSR) (Figure 4.3).

Since the shift form LSR #0 is redundant (because it would duplicate the effect of LSL #0) its instruction format is reserved and used to encode LSR #32. This yields a result of zero, but makes the shifter carry output become bit 31 of the source register.

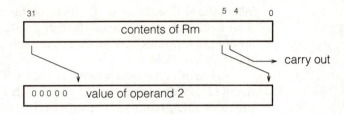

Figure 4.3 Logical shift right

ASR—arithmetic shift right

The contents of the register Rm are moved by the number of bits specified by the shift amount to less significant bit positions. The most significant bits thus revealed are filled with copies of bit 31 of Rm (the sign bit) thereby preserving 2's complement signed values through the shift. The remaining less significant bits are discarded, with the exception that the most significant discarded bit becomes the shifter carry output, which may later set the C flag in the CPSR (if the S suffix was present in the instruction) (Figure 4.4).

The shift form ASR #0 is reserved and used to encode ASR #32; this duplicates the sign bit 31 of the source register throughout the result (ie the result only ever contains either all ones, that is –1, or all zeros, that is 0). In this case the shifter carry output also takes the value of bit 31.

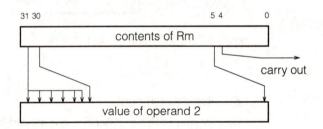

Figure 4.4 Arithmetic shift right

ROR—rotate right

The contents of the register Rm are moved by the number of bits specified by the shift amount to less significant bit positions (like LSR) and those bits which are rotated beyond bit zero are re-inserted at the high end of the result (in place of the zeros inserted here by LSR) (Figure 4.5).

The shifter carry out takes the value of the bit in Rm which ends up as bit 31 of the result, except when ROR #0 is specified.

ROR #0 encodes the special case which performs Rotate Right Extended (RRX); see below.

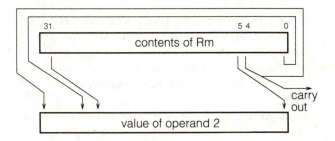

Figure 4.5 Rotate right

RRX — rotate right extended

The contents of the 33-bit shift register formed by concatenating the C flag and Rm (see Figure 4.6) is rotated by a single bit to less significant bit positions and the new shifter carry out becomes the original bit zero. Note that only a single bit shift ever occurs.

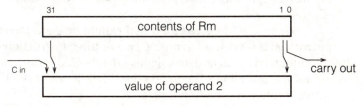

Figure 4.6 Rotate right extended

4.4.3   Shifted operands: register-specified shift amounts

When register-specified shifts are used the least significant byte of the shift amount register Rs is used to determine the shift amount. Rs may be any register other than r15 (PC). One of the following behaviours will occur according to the value of this byte.

If the shift amount is zero the contents of Rm will be passed on unchanged and the previous C flag will be returned as the shifter carry output.

If the shift amount is between 1 and 31 the result will be the same as that produced by the same kind of shift instruction but with a fixed shift amount.

If the shift amount is 32 or more the result will be as expected from the behaviours described above, namely:

- LSL by 32 has the result zero and carry out of bit zero of Rm
- LSL by >32 has result zero, carry out zero
- LSR by 32 has result zero and carry out of bit 31 of Rm
- LSR by >32 has result zero, carry out zero
- ASR by 32 or more has result filled with and carry out of bit 31 of Rm
- ROR by 32 has result equal to Rm, carry out equal to bit 31 of Rm
- ROR by >32 is scaled to fit the range 1..32

4.4.4 Immediate operands

The alternative to a shifted operand in data processing instructions is an (optionally rotated) constant. An 8-bit immediate value is rotated by twice the amount specified by a 4-bit unsigned 'shift amount' field to give a result which is used as the operand. This allows many typical constants, notably including all powers of two, to be generated from a small field in the instruction. Note that a shift amount of zero, that is no rotation, is allowed.

Where a value is required that cannot be generated by this form of instruction it is typical to employ two or three instructions, for example a shift followed by an add, to calculate the desired result into a register. The assembler also allows the instruction LDR (see Section 3.3.8) as an alternative solution for loading constants.

If the assembler has the option of using a shift amount of 0, it always will. For example, #1 could be encoded as:

```
 1 ROR 0
 4 ROR 2
16 ROR 4
64 ROR 6
```

The assembler will always choose the first option. This affects what the shifter carry out becomes.

4.4.5 Data movement data processing instructions

```
MOV{cond}{S} Rd,Op2                 Rd:=Operand2

MVN{cond}{S} Rd,Op2                 Rd:=NOT Operand2
```

The data movement instructions are logical operations which work on 32-

bit operands.

- MOV yields a copy of the operand at the destination
- MVN yields the bitwise logical inverse of the operand

In both cases, using the S suffix causes the condition code flags to be set according to the result:

- N is set equal to bit 31 of the result
- Z is set to 1 if the result is zero and 0 if the result is non-zero
- C is set to the shifter carry out
- V is unchanged

Typical uses of the MOV/MVN instructions include:

- Loading constants into registers (but note that some constants cannot be generated in this way)
- Copying the contents of one register to another
- Applying a shift or rotation to a register
- Logically inverting a whole register

Instruction examples

Below are some examples of the data movement instructions in use. First some simple examples, copying register contents and loading them with constants:

```
MOV         r0, r1          ; r0 := r1

MVN         r0, #0          ; r0 := -1

MOV         r0, #0          ; clear r0

MOV         r2, #10         ; r2 := 10 (decimal 10)

MOV         r3, #0xa        ; r3 := 10 (hexadecimal a)

MOV         r3, #&a         ; r3 := 10 (hexadecimal a)
```

The second example above is always substituted by the assembler if you write MOV r0, #-1; other small negative constants are treated similarly.

Because of the limited size of the immediate operand field (8 bits) the shifting options are important in allowing larger constants to be loaded than can be fitted in 8 bits. An 8-bit immediate value is rotated right by a 4-bit shift amount according to the following rule:

```
result := 8-bit value ROR (2 * shift amount)
```

In fact, all immediate values are affected in this way: those that don't need to be shifted are given a shift amount of zero. Here are some examples of values which can only be loaded by shifting the immediate field:

```
MOV         r4, #0x1000;  r4 := 0x00001000

MOV         r5, #0xf000000f;  r5 := 0xf000000f

MOV         r5, #0xfc000003;  r5 := 0xfc000003
```

Note that in the latter two cases the fact that a *rotate* is being performed when shifting is exploited to allow the eight significant bits to be placed at opposite ends of the result; this is rather contrived, but demonstrates the flexibility of the technique.

Another regular use of MOV is to copy the link register (r14) to the program counter at the end of a subroutine which has been entered using the BL instruction (see later). In this case it is enough to issue the following instruction to resume execution at the instruction after the subroutine call:

```
MOV         r15, r14        ;copy return address to pc
```

This instruction is often written using the Assembler's register naming facility as follows:

```
MOV         pc, lr          ; as above but with
                            ; 'named' regs
```

The explicit shifting options allow obvious simple effects such as power-of-two multiplications and divisions, and sign extension to be performed. Here are some examples:

```
MOV         r0, r1, LSL #1;  r0 := r1 << 1 (in C
                            ; notation)
                            ; that is r0 := r1 * 2

MOV         r0, r1, ASR #2;  r0 := r1 >> 2 (in C
                            ; notation)
                            ; that is r0 := r1 / 4,
                            ; rounded down

MOV         r1, r2, LSL #4;  r1 := r2 * 16

MOV         r1, r2, ASL #4;  as above, that is
                            ; ASL==LSL

MOV         r0, r0, LSL #16; sign extend a 16-bit
                            ; value
MOV         r0, r0, ASR #16

MOV         r0, r0, LSL #24;  sign extend an
                            ; 8-bit value
```

```
MOV         r0, r0, ASR #24

MOV         r0, r1, LSL r2; r0 := r1 << r2 (C
                          ; notation)
                          ; shift by register option
```

We can also use the shift options to select a bit within a word, perhaps to test its state and act accordingly. In the examples below we use the notation r0[n] to mean bit n of r0, and r0[n:m] to mean bits n through m inclusive:

```
MOVS        r0, r1, LSR #1;  C (flag) := r1[0]
MOVCC       r0, #10       ; if C=0 then r0 := 10
MOVCS       r0, #11       ; if C=1 then r0 := 11

MOVS        r0, r4        ; if r4 == 0 then r0 := 0
MOVNE       r0, #1        ; else r0 := 1
```

We can use MVN to generate logical inverses, or to move negative constants:

```
MVN         r3, r3        ; logically invert r3

MVN         r0, #0        ; r0 := -1 (since NOT 0 =
                          ; FFFFFFFF)

MVN         r0, #0xF      ; r0 := 0xFFFFFFF0

MOVS        r0, r4        ; if r4 == 0 then r0 := 0
MVNNE       r0, #0        ; else r0 := -1
```

NOP: No operation (pseudo-instruction)

The pseudo-instruction NOP is supported by the Assembler and generates a preferred instruction which has no effect on the registers or flags other than increasing PC by 4 but takes one S-cycle to complete. The instruction is typically:

```
MOV         R0, R0
```

No condition is allowed: a conditional no-op is just the same as an unconditional one. Of course, it is possible to write a conditional NOP directly, for example:

```
MOVEQ       R0, R0
```

4.4.6 Arithmetic data processing instructions

Add and Add with carry

```
ADD{cond}{S} Rd, Rn, Op2          Rd:=Rn+Op2

ADC{cond}{S} Rd, Rn, Op2          Rd:=Rn+Op2+Carry
```

The add instructions perform 32-bit addition on unsigned or 2's complement 32-bit values. ADD performs the addition without considering the carry bit, while ADC adds in the carry bit before yielding the result.

Presence of the S suffix causes the condition code flags to be set on the result, its absence leaves the flags unaffected. All ARM arithmetic and comparison instructions treat each operand as a 32-bit integer, either unsigned or 2's complement signed (it makes no difference). The flags reflect the result when S is present in the following way:

- The V (overflow) flag is set if signed overflow occurs into bit 31 (the sign bit) of the result. This may be ignored for unsigned operands, but signals a possible error if the operands were signed 2's complement.
- The C (carry) flag is set to the carry out of bit 31 of the ALU. This indicates a possible overflow error if the operands were considered unsigned.
- The Z (zero) flag is set if and only if the result was zero.
- The N (negative) flag is set to bit 31 of the result, indicating that the result is negative where the operands were considered signed.

Here are some typical ADD instruction examples:

```
ADD         r0, r0, #1; r0 := r0 + 1

ADD         r0, r1, r2; r0 := r1 + r2

ADDS        r0, r1, r1, LSL #2; r0 ; r1 * 5 and set
                                ; flags
```

The ADC instruction is often used in conjunction with ADD to allow multi-precision calculations on integers. It works like this:

```
ADC         r0, r1, r2; r0 ; r1+r2+Carry flag
```

Another use of ADC is to bring the C flag into a register:

```
ADC         r0, r0, r0; shift r0 left one, r0[0] :=
                        ; Carry
```

Here is the classic implementation of a 64-bit addition which adds r0,r1 to r2,r3 giving r4,r5 (where r0, r2 & r4 hold the least significant words):

```
ADDS            r4, r0, r2; add LS words and generate
                                    carry
ADC             r5, r1, r3; add MS words and carry
```

The example below uses the `armcc` compiler to demonstrate the efficient compilation of a minimal leaf function involving the use of an ADD. Here is the source listing in C:

```
int addints(int a, int b)
        {
                int c ;
                c = a + b;
                return c;

        }
```

which compiles to:

```
ADD             r0, r0, r1; r0:=r0+r1
MOV             pc, lr ; return
```

Subtract and reverse subtract

```
SUB{cond}{S} Rd, Rn, Op2              Rd:=Rn-Op2

SBC{cond}{S} Rd, Rn, Op2>             Rd:=Rn-Op2+Carry-1

RSB{cond}{S} Rd, Rn, Op2              Rd:=Op2-Rn

RSC{cond}{S} Rd, Rn, Op2              Rd:=Op2-Rn+Carry-1
```

The subtraction instructions perform 32-bit subtraction of unsigned or 2's complement operands. SUB simply subtracts the second operand from the first, while SBC does the same but deals with the carry (really a NOT Borrow). The presence of the S suffix causes the condition code flags to be set according to the result, just as for the ADD and ADC instructions.

The reverse subtraction instructions RSB and RSC mimic the normal subtractions but reverse the order of subtraction of the operands. This allows the flexible shifted operands available only for Operand2 to be applied to the other operand; their behaviour is otherwise identical.

The Carry flag is set by these instructions if no borrow is needed from the next word in a multi-word subtraction. The SBC and RSC instructions would normally follow to implement the borrow if required.

Here are some typical uses of the SUB and SBC instructions:

```
SUB             r0, r1, r2; r0 := r1 - r2

SUB             r0, r1, #1; r0 := r1 - 1

SBC             r0, r1, r2; r0 := r1-r2 + Carry flag - 1
```

```
SUB              r0, r1, r2, ASR #16; r0 := r1 - (r2 ASR
                                                  #16)


SUBS             r4, r0, r2; 64-bit subtraction, stage one
SBC              r5, r1, r3; r4,r5 := r0,r1 - r2,r3
```

The reverse subtract instructions are important when we want to subtract something *from* a constant, rather than the other way around; for example:

```
RSB              r0, r1, #42; r0 := 42 - r1


RSC              r0, r1, r2; r0 := r2 - r1 + Carry flag -
                                                  1
```

A special case of this, subtracting from zero, is useful because it allows a signed value to have its sign reversed, leading to the following implementation of the 'absolute value' function:

```
MOVS             r0, r0          ; set the flags
                                 ; (particularly N)
RSBMI            r0, r0, #0      ; if negative, r0 := 0 - r0
```

The reverse subtractions are also useful when it is necessary to shift the first operand of the subtraction, for example:

```
RSB              r2, r1, r1, LSL #3; r2 := (8 * r1) - r1,
                                 ; that is 7 * r1
```

4.4.7   Logical data processing instructions

AND, EXCLUSIVE OR, OR

AND{*cond*}{S} Rd, Rn, *Op2*   Rd:=Rn AND Op2

EOR{*cond*}{S} Rd, Rn, *Op2*   Rd:=Rn EOR Op2

ORR{*cond*}{S} Rd, Rn, *Op2*   Rd:=Rn OR Op2

The binary logical operator instructions perform bitwise logical operations on (unsigned) 32-bit values. The Boolean operators AND, OR and EXCLUSIVE OR (EOR) are supported. The presence of the S suffix causes the condition code flags to be updated by the result, but note that the overflow flag V is never affected by logical instructions. The Carry flag C is set to the carry out of the shifter, so it is unaffected if the second operand is an unshifted register or a constant in the range 0–0xFF.

The AND, EOR and ORR instructions are frequently used to mask, invert and set bits respectively. These instructions have wide-ranging applications, as the following examples demonstrate:

```
AND          r0, r0, #0xFF; mask off most
                          ; significant 24 bits

ANDCSS       r0, r1, r2, ASR r3; if Carry flag set
                          ; then
                          ; r0 := r1 AND (r2 ASR r3)
                          ; followed by setting
                          ; NZC flags

MOV          r0, #0x55     ; r0 := 55 hex
MOV          r1, #0xaa     ; r1 := aa hex
ANDS         r2, r0, r1    ; r2 := 0, N := 0, Z := 1
```

Applying the EOR operation to the same argument twice clears every bit, so this is another way of zeroing a register:

```
EORS         r0, r0, r0    ; r0 := 0, N := 0, Z := 1
```

We can also construct difficult constants (those which are too big for the 8-bit immediate field) by combining bits using ORR:

```
MOV          r0, #0xff     ; r0 := 0xff
ORR          r0, r0, #0xff00; r0 := 0xffff
```

Bit clear

```
BIC{cond}{S} Rd, Rn, Op2          Rd:=Rn AND NOT Op2
```

The Bit Clear (BIC) instruction performs the composite logical function 'a AND (NOT b)' which is useful for clearing bits: for each bit set in Rm the corresponding bit in Rn will be cleared. The presence of the S suffix causes the condition code flags to be set on the result, but remember that the overflow flag V is never affected by logical instructions. The Carry flag is again set to the carry output from the shifter, so it is unaffected if the second operand is an unshifted register or a constant in the range 0–0xFF.

We might write:

```
BIC          r0, r1, #3     ; r0 := r1 AND NOT 3
                            ; that is r0 := r1 AND
                            ; 0xFFFFFFFC
```

The Assembler will convert BICs into ANDs during assembly where appropriate, for example AND r0, r1, #xFFFFFF will assemble to BIC r0, r1, #xFF000000. Similarly, the ARM C compiler correctly optimizes expressions which perform the 'AND NOT' function to a single BIC instruction, rather than generating two separate instructions. Here is an example which demonstrates this:

```
int andnot(int a)
    {
                        int c;
                        c=a & ~0x80;
                        return c;

    }
```

which compiles to:

```
        BIC         r0, r0, #128
        MOV         pc, lr
```

4.4.8   Arithmetic and logical comparison data processing instructions

Compare and Compare negative

CMP{*cond*} Rn, *Op2*   Flags:=Rn SUB Op2

CMN{*cond*} Rn, *Op2*   Flags:=Rn ADD Op2

The arithmetic compare instructions are functionally equivalent to the ADD and SUB instructions but do not write the result; they merely set the flags on the basis of the result and then discard it. The S suffix is not required because it is always implied for these instructions (they would do nothing at all otherwise). The flags are set on the result of comparison operations in the same way as for arithmetic instructions (see ADD).

Although comparisons are central to many programming tasks the need for them is somewhat reduced when programming the ARM because of the conditional features of all instructions. In particular, comparisons against zero are cheap since setting the S bit of a data processing instruction and then making the following instruction EQ conditional requires no discrete comparison.

It is even possible to perform a comparison conditionally.

Comparison examples in Assembler

Here are some examples of typical comparisons:

```
            CMP         r2, #23         ; r2==23?
            MOVEQ       r2, #45         ; if so, make r2:=45
```

```
        CMP         r0, #0          ; test r0..r3 == 0
        CMPEQ       r1, #0
        CMPEQ       r2, #0
        CMPEQ       r3, #0
        MOVEQ       r4, #12         ; r4 := 12 if all
                                    ; r0..r3 held 0
        MOVNE       r4, #23         ; r4 := 23 if any were
                                    ; non-zero

        ORRS        r4, r0, r1      ; faster version of
                                    ; the above
        ORREQS      r4, r2, r3
        MOVEQ       r4, #12         ; r4 := 12 if all r0..r3
                                    ; held 0
        MOVNE       r4, #23         ; r4 := 23 if any were
                                    ; non-zero

        CMN         r1, r2          ; if (r1 + r2) == 0
        MOVEQ       r0, #0          ; then r0 := 0
        MVNNE       r0, #0          ; else r0 := -1
```

Conditional execution example: Euclid's GCD algorithm

The following C code fragment is taken from an implementation of Euclid's GCD algorithm in the ARM Software Development Toolkit Cookbook:

```
while (a != b)
{ if (a > b) a -= b;
  else        b -= a;
}
```

Without the use of conditional instruction execution this might be naively coded as follows:

```
gcd         CMP         a, b    ;
            BEQ         end
            BLT         less_than
            SUB         a, a, b
            B           gcd
less_than   SUB         b, b, a
            B           gcd
end         ...
```

A considerably more compact implementation may be achieved using conditional instruction execution, for example as follows:

```
gcd           CMP         a, b
              SUBGT       a, a, b
              SUBLT       b, b, a
              BNE         gcd
```

Compiler optimization using conditional instructions

Below is a simple comparison example written in C which demonstrates the compiler's use of in-line conditional instructions:

```
int cmptst(int a, int b)
        {
                int c ;
                c=(a==b);
                return c;

        }
```

This compiles under `armcc` to the following sequence of Assembler instructions:

```
        CMP         r0, r1      ; test
        MOVNE       r0, #0      ; not equal, return false
        MOVEQ       r0, #1      ; equal, return true
        MOV         pc, lr      ; return
```

This sort of optimization of simple conditional choices is widely used by the compiler.

Logical compare instructions

```
TEQ{cond}Rn, Op2                        Flags:=Rn EOR Op2

TST{cond}Rn, Op2                        Flags:=Rn AND Op2
```

The logical compare instructions are derived from the AND and EOR instructions in just the same way as the arithmetic compares are derived from ADD and SUB; they perform the relevant operation and set the flags on the result, discarding the result itself. The S suffix is not required because it is always implied for these instructions (they would do nothing at all otherwise).

The V flag is unaffected by logical compare instructions; the C flag is preserved unless a shift is used, in which case it is set to the shifter carry output. The Z and N flags are set if the result is all zeros or the top bit is set, respectively.

Below is an example which uses a CMP, which sets all flags, followed by a TEQ, which only sets some, to perform a fairly common function: it replaces non-printable ASCII characters with a period:

```
CMP         r0, #31       ; test r0 <= 31?
TEQ         r0, #127      ; test r0 == 127?
MOVLS       r0, #"."      ; if either then r0 := "."
```

This is a particularly compact example; overlapping of comparison results can often trim a few instructions from a complex series of tests.

To demonstrate TST, here is an example which checks the alignment of an address and returns a logical result:

```
TST         r1, #3        ; is r1 word aligned?
MOVEQ       r0, #1        ; r0 := 1 if so
MOVNE       r0, #0        ; otherwise r0 := 0
```

Multiplication instructions

```
MLA{cond}{S} Rd, Rm, Rs, Rn       Rd:=(Rm*Rs)+Rn

MUL{cond}{S} Rd, Rs, Rm           Rd:=Rm*Rs
```

The multiply instruction MUL performs a 32-bit integer multiplication on unsigned or 2's complement operands; it yields the least significant 32 bits of the product of the two operands. MLA adds in a third operand to the product before returning the result; this saves a cycle which would otherwise be needed for a separate ADD instruction. In both cases the N and Z flags are set on the result and the C and V flags are set to *meaningless values*.

There are some restrictions on combinations of registers which may be used with this instruction, notably that Rd and Rm may not be the same and Rd may not be r15 (the program counter): consult MUL in Appendix A for more information.

Here are some multiplication examples:

```
MUL         r0, r1, r2    ; r0 := r1 * r2

MUL         r0, r1, r0    ; r0 := r1 * r0 (valid)
MUL         r0, r0, r1    ; INVALID, Rd=Rm=r0
```

The second of these shows the restrictions on register use quite graphically, since it ought to give the same result. In fact only the first form is allowed.

The MLA instruction allows an addition to be performed at the same time very efficiently:

```
MLA         r0, r1, r2, r3 ; r0 := (r1 * r2) + r3
```

In fact this function is particularly useful when indexing through arrays, where we might instead write the following to make it a little clearer:

```
MLA             ptr, index, stride, base; ptr := (index *
                                      ; stride) + base
```

This is a very general and potentially rather time-intensive solution; for small strides the same effect can be achieved more efficiently using shifts.

A multiplication followed by an addition is a sufficiently common requirement that the armcc compiler optimizes for it specifically, as can be seen in the example below:

```
int mulints(int a, int b, int c)
        {
                int d;
                d=(a*b)+c;
                return d;
        }
```

which compiles to:

```
MLA         r0, r1, r0, r2 ; perform r0:=r1*r0+r2
MOVS        pc, lr         ; return, setting flags
```

Notice that the compiler orders the MLA parameters rather counter-intuitively; this is to overcome the restrictions on the destination register noted above, since the compiler wants to return the result in R0; fortunately the multiplication stage is commutative.

4.4.9   Data movement instructions

Address

```
ADR{cond}{L} Rd, expression      Rd:=expression

                                 (pseudo instruction)
```

ADR allows address constants to be loaded into registers for use in refer-ring to register-based variables (that is those which are referred to using 'base+index' addressing modes: see LDR/STR, below). Two variants are supported; ADR for short (that is local) references, and ADRL for long references; they are assembled to one or two instructions respectively, chosen by the Assembler from ADD, SUB, MOV and MVN.

The ADR (load address to register) instruction is a pseudo-instruc-tion provided by the Assembler rather than a true ARM instruction; it is frequently used both in real ARM programming and in the examples in this book.

For example, we might write the following to load the address of 'BasePtr' into r3:

```
BasePtr     DCD          0
            . . .
            ADR          r3, BasePtr
            . . .
```

Here ADR is used to address a table in a code fragment from a decimal numeric display routine:

```
            ADR      r0, table             ; load pointer to
                                           ; table in r0
            ADD      r0, r0, r1, LSL #2 ; r0 := (table + (r1 * 4))
            . . .
table       DCD      1                     ; table of decimal
                                           ; constants
            DCD      10
            DCD      100
```

4.4.10   Single register data movement instructions

Load register and store register: basic forms

```
LDR{cond}{B} Rd, address{!}        Rd:=contents of
                                   address

LDR{cond}{B} Rd,=expression        Rd:=expression

STR{cond}{B} Rd, address{!}        contents of
                                   address:=Rd
```

The LDR and STR instructions load and store the contents of single registers to and from memory. Along with the multiple register data movement instructions LDM/STM and swap SWP these are the only ARM instructions which interact with main memory. All other instructions use values in registers.

Either a whole 32-bit word or a single byte may be addressed using these instructions according to the presence or absence of the B suffix. Because ARM addresses are specified in bytes the address used for word operations must be word aligned, that is have its two least significant bits both zero; for byte operations the little-/big-endian status of the CPU affects which byte is addressed.

Many different addressing modes are available for these instructions: they fall broadly into three groups: pre-indexed, post-indexed and relative (discussed in the next section). Table 4.3 presents a summary of the different forms for pre- and post-indexed addressing.

■ Rn is any register number 0..15 and holds the base address
■ Rm is any other register except R15 and holds a signed address

Table 4.3 Pre-and post-indexed addressing

Mode	Effective address	Indexing
[Rn]	Rn	none
[Rn, ± *expression*]	Rn ± *expression*	Pre-indexed
[Rn, ± Rm]	Rn ± Rm	Pre-indexed
[Rn, ± Rm, *shift count*]	Rn ± (Rm shifted by *count*)	Pre-indexed
[Rn], ± *expression*	Rn	Post-indexed
[Rn], ± Rm	Rn	Post-indexed
[Rn], ± Rm, *shift count*	Rn	Post-indexed

increment or offset
- *expression* is an expression evaluating to a result in the range –4095 to +4095 (ie sign plus 12 bits)
- *shift* is one of LSL, LSR, ASR, ROR or RRX
- *count* is a constant in the range 1..31 representing the shift count, which may *not* come from a register. RRX takes no count; it always shifts one bit only

Pre-indexed addressing modes

In the pre-indexed addressing modes a register Rn must be specified for use as a base during indexing. This register may then be used in one of several ways:

- To reference the variable without modification: the [Rn] form
- With an added offset: the [Rn, ± expression] form
- With a second index register added in: the [Rn, ± Rm] form
- Or with the index register scaled by shifting before use: the [Rn, ± Rm shift count] form.

Here are some examples of the basic addressing modes:

```
        LDR       r0, [r1]        ; r0 := value at address
                                  ; in r1

        LDR       r0, [r1, #132] ; r0 := value at (r1 + 132)

        STR       r0, [r1, r2]    ; contents of (r1 + r2)
                                  ; := r0
```

```
LDR           r0, [r1, r2, LSL#2]; r0 := value at
                                  ; (r1 + (r2 * 4))
```

The fourth example above demonstrates the use of a shifted index register: in this instance r2 is shifted left two places, multiplying it by four, before being added to the base address in r1 to form the final address. This calculation might be used to access the r2th component of a string of words based at r1.

Base register write-back

The pre-indexed addressing modes allow the base register to be optionally updated after use with the new value just calculated; this is known as 'writing back' the base. The syntax for base write-back is to append an exclamation mark '!' to the instruction. Subsequent uses of the same instruction will employ the updated value of the base, thereby maintaining the continuity of a sequence of references. This is a frequent requirement where, say, the data being manipulated is a table of values.

Below is a slightly contrived example which exploits some of these features. This routine initializes a table backwards, placing 0 in the last entry, 1 in the previous and so on.

```
wackbirds   ADR         r0, table_end ; load r0 with table_end
            ADR         r1, table     ; load r1 with table
                                      ; (start)
            MOV         r2, #0        ; initialize loop counter
loop        STR         r2, [r0, #-4]!; store r2 at current
                                      ; position
            ADD         r2, r2, #1    ; increment loop counter
            CMP         r0, r1        ; got to the end?
            BNE         loop          ; no, go round again
            ...
            ALIGN
table       %           table_length*4
table_end
```

Post-indexed addressing modes

Post-indexed addressing modes allow essentially the same variations on how the base and optional index are used, but always perform the calculation *after* the operation and *always* write back the result (so no exclamation mark is required). Syntactically these instructions are distinguished by placing the base register *alone* within square brackets and then appending any index offset calculations after a comma. Here are some examples:

```
LDR           r0, [r1], r2  ; r0:=[r1], then
                            ; r1:= r1 + r2
```

```
                STR             r0, [r1], #20  ; [r1]:=r0, then
                                               ; r1:= r1 + 20

                ADR             r0, table      ; Subtly different from
                ADR             r1, table_end  ; the routine shown in the
                MOV             r2, #0         ; previous section.
loop            STR             r2, [r0], #4
                ADD             r2, r2, #1
                CMP             r0, r1
                BNE             loop
                ...
                ALIGN
table           %               table_length*4
                ...
table_end
```

The third example shown above is modified from an earlier example to show the use of post-indexed addressing modes; this version fills its table in the natural order, placing a zero in the first table entry, a one in the next and so on.

Load register and store register: relative addressing forms

To assist with the addressing of literals the Assembler supports a number of syntactical short cuts which save time and improve legibility. They all exploit the ability of the ARM to support PC-relative addressing. Table 4.4 summarizes the various relative addressing modes.

Table 4.4 Relative addressing modes

Mode	Effective address	Indexing
Rn, PC-relative expression	Result of expression	PC-relative
Rn, Register-relative expression	Rn ± field_offset	Rn-relative
Rd, =expression	PC ± literal_offset	PC-relative

For example, a symbol may be invoked by name leaving the Assembler to resolve the addressing, for example:

```
                LDR             r5, ThreeCubed ; load r5 with symbol
                ...
ThreeCubed  DCD     27                         ; constant placed here
```

In this case an instruction of the form LDR r5, [PC, #constant] is generated, or an error is generated if the symbol definition is out of range.

The Assembler provides two directives, the characters ^ and #, which may be used to establish data structures which are 'based on', that is are addressed relative to, a particular register; the example below illustrates this:

```
                    ^              0, r1          ; define 3D point
                                                  ; structure
XCoord      #              4                      ; XCoord at r1+0
YCoord      #              4                      ; YCoord at r1+4
ZCoord      #              4                      ; ZCoord at r1+8
            ...
            ADR            r1, Point1             ; initialize r1 to Point1
            B              Common_Code
            ...
            ADR            r1, Point2             ; initialize r1 to Point2
Common_Code LDR            r2, YCoord             ; r2 := YCoord, that is r2
                                                  ; := [r1+4]
```

Here a data structure suitable for representing three-dimensional points is defined as a structure based on register r1. Subsequent references to components of the data structure may then be made using LDR. In other words, the Assembler translates the reference to YCoord into LDR r2, [r1, #4] automatically.

LDR literal syntax

A special case of LDR syntax is supported to allow literals to be loaded directly. The form of LDR with the syntax LDR Rn, =expression is used and the Assembler generates an LDR with a PC-relative address. This address points to the literal result of evaluating the expression which is stored in a nearby 'literal pool' generated by the Assembler.

```
        LDR            r0, =0x12345678; r0 loaded from
                                       ; literal pool
```

Comparative example: block copying

We can use the LDR and STR instructions to develop a simple example program which copies a four-word block of data from the address in r7 to the address in r8. Here it is:

```
        LDR            r1, [r7, #0]
        LDR            r2, [r7, #4]
        LDR            r3, [r7, #8]
        LDR            r4, [r7, #12]
        STR            r1, [r8], #4
        STR            r2, [r8], #4
        STR            r3, [r8], #4
        STR            r4, [r8], #4
```

This brute force approach to block copying exploits four registers which it first loads and then stores, taking advantage of both pre-indexing and post-indexing. The routine has the unusual property that r8 is left pointing beyond the destination and r7 remains unaltered. The routine appears here mainly to allow it to be contrasted with the implementation using the LDM/STM multiple-register instructions to be described below.

4.4.11   Swap

```
SWP{cond}{B} Rd, Rn, [Rbase]      Rd:=[address],
                                  [address]:=Rn
```

The data swap instruction swaps a byte or word between a register and memory, locking the memory bus in the process to preserve the atomicity of the operation (where supported by external hardware). This operation is useful in multiprocessor hardware environments where it forms the basis of 'semaphore' functions required by most multi-tasking operating systems.

The source Rn and destination Rd are both registers, the memory address is given by the contents of the third register Rbase. The SWP instruction then writes the contents of Rn to the address given by Rbase and the previous value at that address is placed in Rd. For example:

```
ADR        r2, &8000FFE3 ; initialize r2
SWP        r0, r0, [r2]  ; swap R0 with memory
                         ; at address in r2

SWP        r0, r1, [r2]  ; swap R1 to memory &
                         ; return old value in R0
```

4.4.12   Multiple-register data movement instructions

```
LDM{cond}mode Rn{!},{reg_list}{^} reg_list:=[addresses]

STM{cond}mode Rn{!},{reg_list}{^} [addresses]:=reg_list
```

The multiple-register data movement instructions are a powerful extension of the single-register instructions. They transfer a set of registers, anywhere between one and all 16 of them, between the CPU register bank and memory. To cater for the need to specify up to sixteen registers the register set is expressed by 16 bits of the instruction word, one bit per register. The register list *must* be enclosed in braces (that is the braces do not signify optional parameters as they do elsewhere in this book) except where the Assembler's 'register list' feature is exploited: see Chapter 3.

These instructions can automatically build data structures in memory from a set of registers, for example to push and pop groups of registers to and from a stack. Even apparently complex problems such as dealing with discontinuous lists of registers are supported by these instructions, by virtue of the 'one-bit-per-register' format of the instruction word; registers are always loaded and stored in the same order, regardless of which registers are involved. Multiple-register instructions are executed more quickly than the equivalent sequence of single-register instructions on most ARM-based hardware through reduced overheads and the use of fast 'paged mode' access to Dynamic RAMs.

How the multiple-register instructions are used

For any multiple-register instruction the memory area to be used must be addressed by a base register, Rn, just like the single-register (LDR/STR) instructions. The differences are in the treatment of registers other than the first in the set: the base address can be incremented or decremented automatically for each register in the list according to the particular instruction syntax used. The presence of an exclamation mark '!' suffix to the instruction causes the base address to be written back to Rn after updating, to allow it to be re-used subsequently.

The choices in using these instructions are to decide whether the data structure in memory is going to grow *upwards* by memory address or *downwards* and whether the base address is going to be adjusted *before* or *after* the load or store operation occurs. It is worth noting that mismatching these instructions can result in catastrophic 'out-by-one' programming problems; two alternative syntaxes are supported by the Assembler in an effort to minimize the scope for confusion.

Using multiple-register transfer instructions to implement stacks

A data stack which is frequently used in ARM programming grows downwards in memory, that is the 'top' of the stack is the lowest address occupied by a stacked value. To add a new value (push) we must decrement the stack pointer to address the next vacant location and then store the value at that address. To retrieve (pop) the top value we load it from the address given by the stack pointer and then increment the stack pointer to point to the next value.

The ARM multiple-register instructions support this kind of stack directly; they also support the alternative style where the stack pointer points to the first *vacant* location rather than the last *occupied* one. These differences correspond to the difference between adjusting the offset before or after the load or store, as noted above. These instructions can also support stacks which climb upwards in memory rather than downwards, similarly noted above.

A two-letter suffix is used to tell the Assembler which form of indexing is required and two alternative syntaxes are allowed:

- FD, ED, FA and EA stand for Full Descending, Empty Descending, Full Ascending and Empty Ascending. 'Full' corresponds to the 'last occupied' style described above, whilst 'Empty' corresponds to the 'first vacant' style.
- IA, IB, DA and DB stand for Increment After, Increment Before, Decrement After and Decrement Before.

The first syntax is designed to be used when stacks are being implemented and describe the type of stack and its direction; the second syntax represents the functionality of the instruction directly and so is suitable when not using these instructions for stacks.

The effects of these instruction mnemonics are summarized in Table 4.5.

Table 4.5 Possible load and store multiple combinations

Name	Stack	Other	L bit	P bit	U bit
pre-increment load	LDMED	LDMIB	1	1	1
post-increment load	LDMFD	LDMIA	1	0	1
pre-decrement load	LDMEA	LDMDB	1	1	0
post-decrement load	LDMFA	LDMDA	1	0	0
pre-increment store	STMFA	STMIB	0	1	1
post-increment store	STMEA	STMIA	0	0	1
pre-decrement store	STMFD	STMDB	0	1	0
post-decrement store	STMED	STMDA	0	0	0

Register load/store order in LDM/STM instructions

It is important to appreciate that registers are always placed in memory so that the lowest numbered register always appears at the lowest address, regardless of the addressing style used. This presents no difficulty if the same registers are unstacked as had previously been stacked. However, to stack multiple registers and then unstack them one at a time requires some care; consider these two examples:

```
push_two_EA STMEA      r2!, {r0,r1}   ; push r0,r1 "empty
                                      ; ascending"
        . . .
pop_one     LDMEA      r2!, {r1}      ; r1 pops first
pop_another LDMEA      r2!, {r0}      ; and r0 second

push_two_FD STMFD      r2!, {r0,r1}   ; push r0,r1 "full
                                      ; descending"
        . . .
pop_one     LDMFD      r2!, {r0}      ; r0 pops first
pop_another LDMFD      r2!, {r1}      ; and r1 second
```

In the first case the two registers unstack in one order, and in the second they unstack in the opposite order; these two cases are not inconsistent: the first stack is growing downwards and the second upwards. The most important thing to remember is that using the same instruction syntax on the same registers for both LDM and STM will ensure success.

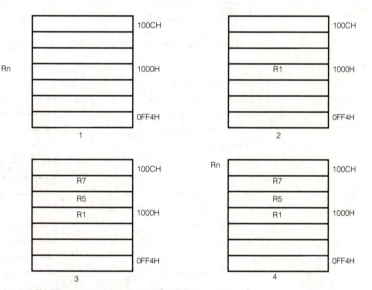

Figure 4.7(a) Post-incremented addressing

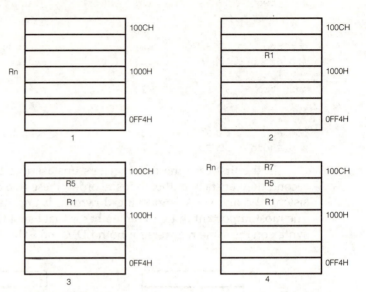

Figure 4.7(b) Pre-increment addressing

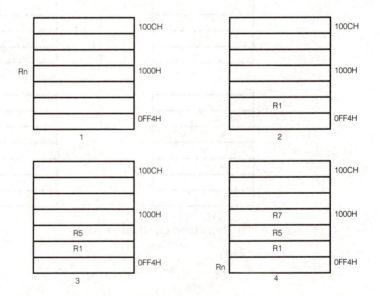

Figure 4.7(c) Post-decrement addressing

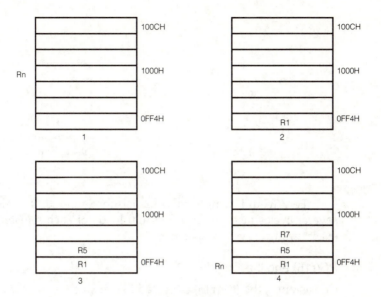

Figure 4.7(d) Pre-decrement addressing

Multiple-register instruction examples

Here are some of the possible ways in which the LDM and STM instructions might be used in real programs. First, let us consider the implementation of the four-word block copy which we introduced in the previous section on LDR/STR; here is the new version using multiple-register instructions:

```
LDMIA       r7, {r1-r4}     ; load r1-r4 from [r7]
STMIA       r8!, {r1-r4}    ; store r1-r4 at [r8],
                            ; writing
                            ; back r8 to reflect
                            ; final address
```

This implementation is both six instructions shorter and nine cycles faster than the previous version, clearly demonstrating the benefits of the multiple-register instructions.

We can also re-visit the 3D data point which we used in an earlier example. Instead of loading each of the three parts of the point's coordinates in using individual LDR instructions we can simply use a single multiple-register load, as follows:

```
                    ^           0, r1          ; define 3D point
                                               ; structure
XCoord      #       4                          ; XCoord at r1+0
YCoord      #       4                          ; YCoord at r1+4
ZCoord      #       4                          ; ZCoord at r1+8
            ...
            ADR             r1, Point1         ; initialize r1 to Point1
            ...
            ...                                ; hopefully Point1
            ...                                ; gets assigned
            ...                                ; before doing this:
            ...
            LDMIA           r1,{r3, r4, r5}; load r3-r5 with x, y, z
```

Few would dispute that this is more concise; it is also likely to be several cycles faster than individual loads of each register, although the exact timing is system-specific.

PC(r15) and the '^' suffix

Consistently, the PC (r15) is treated like any other register by the multiple register transfer instructions and this has some important implications. Registers included in the list are always transferred in the order lowest first, highest last. This ensures that if r15 is included in the list it is always the last register to be transferred. Note that the value in r15 will be advanced by +12 from the address of the instruction causing the transfer.

The ^ suffix can be employed with these instructions but only if the instruction will be executed in a non-user CPU mode. If it is included then its interpretation depends on whether r15 is included in the register list:

- LDM with r15 included and ^ present
  SPSR_*mode* is transferred to CPSR at the same time as r15 is loaded.
- STM with r15 included and ^ present
  The User mode registers specified by the instruction are transferred, rather than those for the privileged mode in which the instruction is executed. This is useful when an operating system wishes to save the user state, for example when process switching. Base write-back must not be used in this circumstance.
- LDM or STM with r15 not included but ^ present
  In both cases the User Mode registers are used instead of the current mode registers, just as above. Note that a banked register must not be accessed in the cycle after this instruction, so it is best followed by a NOP for safety.

Base register restrictions

The PC (r15) must not be used as the base register with these instructions;

it is difficult to imagine a use for this instruction even if it were allowed.

If the base register is included in the register list then LDM will overwrite it; STM will store the 'wrong' (unmodified) base value if it is the first register in the list. Otherwise it will store the correct value.

4.4.13   Program Counter and Program Status Register instructions

Branch and Branch with link

```
B{cond} label                          PC := address of label

BL{cond} label                         r14:= PC-4, then PC:=
                                       address of label
```

The Branch instruction B and the related Branch with Link BL are used to divert the flow of instruction execution from its normal sequential progress through increasing addresses. Like all other ARM instructions the branches are conditional, so all 15 different conditional branches are available to these instructions. The default condition, as for other instructions, is 'always' so as to reduce unnecessary typing.

Both variants of branch instruction include a 24-bit signed 2's complement offset which is shifted left two bits (that is multiplied by 4), sign extended to 32 bits and added to the PC. The field therefore gives a word-multiple relative address to which execution will be transferred.

The 24-bit size of the offset field means that branches are restricted to a ±32 Mbyte range. It is therefore possible for some addresses to be out of range of a single branch instruction, although this is unlikely in reality. If a very long (that is >32 Mbyte) branch is required the following instruction syntax allows long branches:

```
        LDR         PC, =long_target; branch by loading PC
                                    ; with a literal
```

Because the ARM CPU pre-fetches instructions the branch offset must take into account the fact that the PC is 2 words (8 bytes) ahead of the current instruction. The Assembler adjusts the offset accordingly, but it is still potentially confusing when reading the raw object code; any good Disassembler would resolve such address corrections.

Here are some examples of the branch instructions:

```
        B           elsewhere       ; (always) goto
                                        'elsewhere'

        CMP         r1, #0          ; if r1==0 then
        BEQ         fred            ; goto label 'fred'
```

```
here        BAL         here            ; endless loop

            ADDS        r1, r1, #1      ; r1 := r1 + 1, set flags
            BLCC        somewhere       ; call 'somewhere' if
                                        ; r1 was not &FFFFFFFF
```

It is important to keep in mind that branches may also be achieved using data processing instructions which update r15 directly by using it as the destination register, for example MOV, ADD etc. For example, the following instruction sequence has superior functionality to BL, but requires two separate instructions:

```
            MOV         LR, PC          ; copy PC to LR (r14)
            ADD         PC, ...         ; adjust PC to new address
```

Returning to an earlier issue, here is an example of how a mutually exclusive 'semaphore' interlock using the SWP instruction might be programmed:

```
            ADR    r0, semaphore    ; make r0 point at
                                    ; semaphore
            MVN    r1, #0           ; non zero to claim it
                                    ; (once only)
loop        SWP    r1, r1, [r0]     ; attempt acquisition
            TEQ    r1, #0           ; see if we got control
            BNE    loop             ; no, spin once more (r1
                                    ; will still not be zero)

            ...                     ; these operations
            ...                     ; are atomic as far
            ...                     ; as the rest of the
            ...                     ; system is concerned
            MOV    r1, #0           ; release: zero means
                                    ; not claimed
            STR    r1, [r0]    ;
            ...                     ; semaphore now
                                    ; claimable again
```

Branch with link

The BL instruction saves the PC (r15) in the Link register (r14) of the current register bank to allow a branch to a subroutine to return to the instruction after it upon completion. The CPU adjusts the PC value saved in r14 to take account of pre-fetching and so stores the correct address of the following instruction. Note that the CPSR (containing the flags) is *not* saved by this instruction, so a separate MRS instruction (see Move program status register on page 97) would be needed if this is required.

Here are some example subroutine branches:

```
BL           Subroutine      ; call 'subroutine'
...                          ; return here using
                             ; MOV pc, lr

ADDS         r1, r1, #1      ; r1 := r1 + 1, set flags
BLCS         was_minus_one   ; call 'was_minus_one'
                             ; if C=0
                             ; ie if r1 was 0xFFFFFFFF
                             ; beforethe ADDS
```

4.4.14   Program Status Register transfer instructions

Move program status register

MRS{*cond*} Rd, *psr*   Rd:=*psr*

MSR{*cond*} *psr*,Rm   *psr*:=Rm

MSR{*cond*} *psrf*,Rm   *psr_flags*:=Rm

MSR{*cond*} *psrf*,#*expression*   *psr_flags*:=*expression*

These instructions allow the contents of the Current or Stored Program Status Register (CPSR/SPSR) to be transferred between the status register in question and a general register. The format of the CPSR/SPSR is shown in Figure 4.8.

The symbols CPSR or CPSR_all, and SPSR or SPSR_all are used to indicate that *all* data bits of the current or stored PSR are to be transferred; these options are shown as *psr* in the syntax definitions above.

Similarly, CPSR_flg or SPSR_flg are used to indicate the *flags alone* are to be transferred; these options are shown as *psrf* in the syntax definitions above.

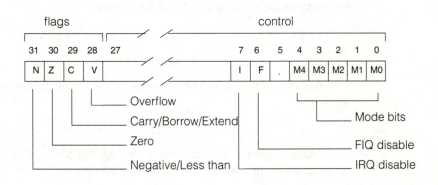

Figure 4.8 Format of the program status registers (PSRs)

In the ARM6 CPU the PSRs are organized as three groups of bits: the flags (bits [31..28]), the interrupt masks (bits [7, 6]) and the mode bits ([4..0]). Future ARM CPUs may use the remaining reserved bits [27..8] and bit [5], so it is important to observe two rules when using these instructions:

- All currently reserved bits must be preserved when altering the PSR.
- The value returned by currently reserved bits must not be relied upon when testing other bits.

In User mode all PSR bits may be read but only the four flag bits N, Z, C and V may be written; in privileged modes all bits may be read and written.

The following code fragment demonstrates the correct 'read–modify–write technique which should be employed; in this example to perform a mode change:

```
MRS         Rtmp, CPSR; Rtemp := CPSR
BIC         Rtmp, Rtmp, #&1F; clear mode bits
ORR         Rtmp, Rtmp, #new_mode; OR in new_mode
MSR         CPSR, Rtmp; CPSR := Rtemp
```

Here are some examples of PSR transfer instructions which may be executed in User mode:

```
MSR         CPSR_all, R3   ; CPSR[31:28] := r3[31:28]

MSR         CPSR_flg, R3   ; CPSR[31:28] := r3[31:28]

MSR         CPSR_flg, #&A0000000
                           ; set Z,V and clear N, C
```

The following examples demonstrate the difference in effect when instructions are executed in privileged modes:

```
MSR         CPSR_all, R3   ; CPSR[31:0] := r3[31:0]

MSR         CPSR_flg, R3   ; CPSR[31:28] := r3[31:28]
```

We can *always* read the contents of the CPSR, in any mode, as follows:

```
MRS         r0, CPSR       ; r0[31:0] := CPSR[31:0]
```

Status transfer instructions involving the SPSRs may *only* be executed in privileged modes, such as the following:

```
MSR         SPSR_all, r0   ; SPSR<mode>[31:0] :=
                           ; r0[31:0]
```

```
MSR           SPSR_flg, r0   ; SPSR<mode>[31:28] :=
                             ; r0[31:28]

MRS           r0, SPSR       ; r0[31:0] :=
                             ; SPSR<mode>[31:0]
```

4.4.15   Coprocessor instructions

Coprocessor data operations

CDP{*cond*} p#, *exp_1*, cD, cN, cM{,*exp_2*} ;cD:=Op(cN,cM)

The coprocessor data operation instructions cause the opcode encoded in the two expressions to be passed to the given coprocessor number p# to cause it to perform the operation specified by the two expressions exp_1, exp_2 on coprocessor registers cN, cM and store the result in coprocessor register cD.

This class of instructions is the coprocessor equivalent of the ARM data processing instructions. Coprocessors may have up to 16 registers of their own which are addressable by the ARM (4-bit fields are used) and these instructions specify three coprocessor registers to allow dyadic (two-operand) instructions to give a result in a third register.

Floating-point instructions which perform dyadic operations, such as ADF (Add floating), are assembled to one of these instructions automatically. Here is a typical CDP instruction in its undisguised form:

```
CDPEQ        p2, 5, c1, c2, c3, 2; If EQ then
                            ; coprocessor 2 to do
                            ; operation #5 variant 2
                            ; on cr2 and cr3 giving cr1
```

Load and store from coprocessor

LDC{*cond*}{L} p#, cD, *address*   Load CP regs

STC{*cond*}{L} p#, cD, *address*   Store CP regs

The coprocessor load/store instructions cause coprocessor number p# to transfer data between the single register crD and memory at the address specified. The optional L suffix selects between 'long' and 'short' transfers; the meaning of this field is coprocessor-specific.

This class of instruction is the coprocessor equivalent of the ARM single-register data transfer instructions. A limited set of basic addressing modes are available to coprocessor load/store instructions; they are summarized in Table 4.6.

The first of these addressing modes is a special Assembler syntax for the pre-indexed mode properly written as '...[PC, #expression]'. The

Table 4.6 Basic addressing modes for coprocessor load/store instructions

Mode	Effective address	Indexing
expression	Result of *expression*	PC-relative
[Rn]	Rn	None
[Rn, #*expression*]{!}	Rn ± *expression*	Pre-indexed
[Rn],#*expression*	Rn ± *expression*	Post-indexed

expression is limited to the range –1020 to +1020 and must be word-aligned, that is divisible by four. Refer to the section concerning the LDR/STR instructions for further information on these addressing modes.

The floating-point load/store instructions, such as LDF (Load floating), are assembled to one of these instructions automatically. Here are some typical raw LDC and STC instructions:

```
LDC          p1, c2, table ; load c2 of coprocessor
                           ; #1 from 'table'
                           ; (PC-relative)

STCEQL       p2, c3, [r5, #24]!; conditionally store
                           ; c3 of coprocessor #2
                           ; at [r5]+24 and
                           ; update r5; long
                           ; transfer mode
```

Coprocessor register transfer instructions

```
MCR{cond} p#, exp_1, Rd, cN, cM{,exp_2}cX := Op(Rd)

MRC{cond} p#, exp_1, Rd, cN, cM{,exp_2}Rd := Op(cX)
```

The coprocessor register transfer instructions allow coprocessor registers and ARM registers to be transferred freely, optionally performing some operation before the transfer. Coprocessor number p# is instructed to perform an operation by the two expressions exp_1, exp_2 before transferring the result if the transfer is coprocessor to ARM, or afterwards if the transfer is from ARM register Rd to coprocessor registers cN and cM.

An important use of these instructions is to communicate the coprocessor status back to the ARM CPSR flags. When r15 is used as the destination of an MRC instruction, bits 31..28 of the result overwrite the CPSR N, Z, C and V flags respectively; all other CPSR bits are unaffected, as is r15 itself.

Examples of this type of coprocessor instruction include:

■ The floating-point instruction FLT, which converts an integer in an ARM register into a floating-point value of specified precision and stores it in the floating-point register specified.
■ The floating-point compare instruction CMF which compares two floating-point values and sets the integer CPU flags according the result.

Here are some typical examples of raw MCR and MRC instructions:

```
MCR          p6, 0, r4, c6; perform operation #0 of
                         ; coprocessor 6 on r4
                         ; and store result in cr6

MRC          p3, 9, r3, c5, c6, 2;
                                 ; perform operation #9
                                 ; variant 2 of
                                 ; coprocessor 3 on cr5
                                 ; and cr6 giving r3
```

4.4.16   Miscellaneous instructions

Software interrupt

```
SWI{cond} expression                 Enter Supervisor mode
```

The software interrupt instruction causes the CPU to switch to Supervisor mode by causing a Software Interrupt trap, as follows: the PC is saved in r14_svc, the CPSR is saved in SPSR_svc and then the PC is forced to &00000008. This address will normally have been initialized by the operating system to be an unconditional branch to a service routine.

The result of the expression is truncated to 24 bits and passed in the instruction but ignored by the CPU. Typically, the operating system service routine will follow back the saved PC value in r14_svc and decode the expression to perform some service for the user program. A standard convention in current ARM operating systems is to print the ASCII character in the bottom byte of r0 in response to SWI #0. This convention is followed in some examples appearing within the book, as well as by the ARM Software Development Toolkit described in Chapter 3.

4.4.17   Specific coprocessors

ARM also supports general-purpose instructions for passing commands to, and data to and from, coprocessor devices. Such coprocessors can extend the instruction set to deal efficiently with data manipulations that are not part of the integer instruction set. An example of this is the floating-point instruction set.

The ARM floating-point instruction set operates on a variety of data types which conform to the IEEE 754-1985 standard; increased precision is the attraction of using a larger data type, but small low-precision data types are included. The floating-point data types are:

- IEEE single-precision (32 bits)
- IEEE double-precision (64 bits)
- double-extended precision (80 bits)
- packed (binary coded) decimal (96 bits)
- expanded packed decimal (128 bits).

Floating-point instruction mnemonics are provided by the ARM Assembler for clarity; these in turn generate general-purpose coprocessor instructions when assembled.

Other coprocessors have also been implemented: the ARM600 and its derivative the ARM610 have their memory management unit, instruction and data cache and write buffer all controlled through the use of coprocessor instructions. The ARM floating-point instruction set is discussed in detail in Chapter 9, and summarized in Appendix B.

4.4.18 Pitfalls, quirks and restrictions

Data processing instructions: writing to r15

It is legitimate to use the program counter (r15) as the destination for these instructions, which has the effect of changing the flow of instruction execution in the same way as a branch instruction (see section Branch and Branch with link on page 95).

When r15 is the destination but the S suffix is not present, the result overwrites the contents of r15 without affecting the CPSR. The next instruction is fetched from the new address in r15 and program execution continues from there: this allows calculated branches, suitable for switch or case constructs.

When r15 is the destination and the S suffix *is* present the result overwrites r15 and the CPSR is overwritten with the SPSR for the current mode. This form of the instruction may only be used in non-User modes.

Data processing instructions reading r15

You may use r15 as either of the normal operand registers in a data processing instruction, but not to specify a register-specified shift amount. When using r15 as an operand, remember that it normally contains an address advanced by 8 from the address of the current instruction. However, if the instruction uses a register-specified amount, it will be advanced by 12 bytes rather than 8.

Use of r15 (PC) in load/store instructions

r15 (PC) must never be used as Rm, nor as Rn if write-back is specified. When using r15 as the base (Rn) remember that it contains an address advanced by 8 from the address of the current instruction.

Effect of CPU endian configuration on byte load/stores

The action of the LDR{B} and STR{B} instructions on the data bus is affected by the ARM6 CPU byte sex or endianness control signal. The two possible states, little-endian and big-endian, are discussed in turn below:

- **Little-endian configuration:**
  For byte loads (LDRB) the CPU expects data on data bus bits D[7..0] for word addresses, data bus bits 15..8 for word addresses plus one etc. The selected byte is placed in the bottom 8 bits of the destination register and the high order bits filled with zeros.
  For word loads (LDR) plus 1, bits 15..8 of the data from memory will be placed in bits 7..0 of the register. Bits 31..8 of the register are left in an undefined state.
  For word addresses plus 2, bits 31..16 go to register bits 15..0; register bits 31..16 are undefined.
  For word addresses plus 3, bits 31..24 go to register bits 7..0; register bits 31..8 are undefined.
  For byte stores (STRB) the data is replicated by the CPU four times across all data bits D[31..0].
  For word stores (STR) a word-aligned address should be used; the whole word is presented on the data bus D[31..0] and is *unaffected* even if the address is not word-aligned.
- **Big-endian configuration:**
  For byte loads (LDRB) the CPU expects data on data bus bits 31..24 for word addresses, data bus bits 23..16 for word addresses plus one etc. The selected byte is placed in the bottom 8 bits of the destination register and the high order bits filled with zeros.
  For word loads (LDR) a word-aligned address should be used. For addresses offset from a word address by 0 or 2 the data will be rotated into the register so the addressed byte occupies bits 31..24; addresses offset by 1 or 3 must not be used.
  For byte stores (STRB) the data is replicated by the CPU four times across all data bits D[31..0].
  For word stores (STR) a word-aligned address should be used; the whole word is presented on the data bus D[31..0] and is *unaffected* even if the address is not word-aligned.

Effect of configured Abort type on load/stores

The CPU state after these instruction is affected by the CPU's early/late abort configuration. When configured for early aborts any base register write-back is prevented if an abort occurs. When configured for late aborts the write-back is allowed and the abort handler must correct for this before re-executing the instruction.

When configured for late aborts, the pre-indexed and post-indexed forms of this instruction, where, unusually, Rm and Rn are the same, must not be used, otherwise the abort handler may not be able to unwind the instruction.

Data aborts during LDM/STM

Refer to Chapter 5 on aborts and exceptions for information on the behaviour of and recoverability from aborted multiple-register transfer instructions.

4.5 Programming examples

Now that we have considered all of the different ARM instructions it is possible to examine 'real' ARM program examples. The SWI encoding described above is used extensively in these examples: ARM Ltd's development system supports this convention too, so these examples may be used directly by most readers.

To begin with, here is a routine which calls SWI 0 to help display the contents of register r0 in binary:

```
printbin    MOV       r1, #31          ; number of bits-1
            MOV       r2, #1
loop        TST       r0, r2, LSL r1 ; extract a bit
            MOVEQ     r0, #"0"         ; zero?, load ASCII zero
            MOVNE     r0, #"1"         ; one?, load ASCII one
            SWI       0                ; SWI 0 - print char in r0
            SUBS      r1, r1, #1       ; decrement number
                                       ; of bits to go
            BPL       loop             ; some left?, go round
                                       ; again
            MOV       pc, lr           ; return.
```

Similarly, here is an example routine which generates the contents of r0 in hexadecimal as a sequence of eight ASCII bytes stored starting at the address in r1:

```
memhex     STMFD      sp!, {r0-r2, r14}; save registers to
                                    ; be corrupted
           MOV        r2, #8          ; number of bytes
                                    ; resulting
loop2      MOV        r14, r0, LSR #28; capture some bits
           CMP        r14, #9
           ADDGT      r14, r14, #"A" - 10; get ASCII
                                    ; alphabetic base
           ADDLE      r14, r14, #"0"; get ASCII numeric base
           STRB       r14, [r1], #1 ; store byte and increment
           MOV        r0, r0, LSL #4 ; shift up a nibble
           SUBS       r2, r2, #1      ; decrement number of
                                    ; bytes
           BNE        loop2          ; some left?, go round
                                    ; again
           LDMFD      sp!, {r0-r2, pc}; return (pc:=r14) & old
                                    ; r0-r2
```

4.6 Summary

The ARM integer instruction set contains 10 instruction formats, plus the undefined instructions. The combination of instruction types and conditional execution of instructions means that there is a great flexibility within the instruction set, despite its relatively small size.

5

Aborts, exceptions and interrupts

▤ 5.1 Introduction

This chapter examines the way the ARM processors deal with unusual events which occur during program execution, known as 'exceptions'. Possible sources of exceptions include:

- the processor's 'Reset' input
- software interrupts (using the SWI instruction)
- external interrupts (FIQ/IRQ)
- undefined instructions
- memory management protection faults
- floating-point arithmetic faults

Each kind of exception is considered in turn, giving special attention to the hardware interrupts FIQ and IRQ.

Floating-point exceptions are discussed along with the floating point instructions in Chapter 9.

▤ 5.2   ARM processor exceptions

The normal flow of program execution is sequential through increasing addresses, perhaps with the occasional branch to a nearby label or a sub-routine branch-with-link. Exceptions occur when the normal flow of execution is broken, perhaps because of a software interrupt, an illegal memory reference or to service an interrupt from a peripheral.

If program execution is to resume at the point it was disturbed by the exception the state of the CPU must be preserved while the exception is dealt with. Furthermore, it is possible for several exceptions to occur simultaneously, in which case the processor must reliably be able to deal with each exception in some well-defined order of priorities. Needless to say, the ARM CPU cores deal with these issues in an efficient way.

Flexible management of exceptions is provided in ARM processors through the use of 'exception vectors' located at the start of the memory address space (that is at address 0x00000000). The first eight words of the address space are reserved for the vectors of each of the eight possible types of exception.

Table 5.1 summarizes the exception vectors at the start of the ARM address space.

Table 5.1 Exception vectors summary

Address	Exception	Mode on entry
&00000000	Reset	Supervisor
&00000004	Undefined instruction	Undefined
&00000008	Software interrupt	Supervisor
&0000000C	Abort (prefetch)	Abort
&00000010	Abort (data)	Abort
&00000014	(Reserved)	
&00000018	IRQ	IRQ
&0000001C	FIQ	FIQ

Each exception vector is a single 32-bit word and is placed without any further addresses between it and its neighbour. Because only a single word is allowed per exception vector it is normal practice to place an unconditional branch instruction (B) at each address with its branch offset field pointing to the relevant exception service routine.

In the special case of FIQ, which uses the last vector, the exception handler can run on sequentially from its vector address, removing the need for a branch and its associated delays.

5.2.1   Servicing an exception

Most exceptions are usually accompanied by a change of processor mode. The CPU automatically selects a mode according to the nature of the exception, so, for example, a FIQ interrupt causes the CPU to change to FIQ_32 mode.

All variants of the ARM processors contain 'banked' registers to allow the CPU state to be efficiently preserved when an exception arises; banked registers ensure that little or no state information will need to be written to memory, providing working register space to the exception handler without the need to save User Mode state. Figure 5.1 summarizes the register set available and is repeated from Chapter 2.

Whenever an exception occurs the following things happen within the CPU, in this order:

- The PC (r15) is saved in the banked r14 of the new mode
- The CPSR is saved in the banked SPSR of the new mode
- The PC (r15) is loaded with the relevant vector for the exception (see below)
- The CPSR mode flags are forced to the relevant value for the new mode (see below)
- The CPSR interrupt mask bits may also be set to prevent nesting of interrupts

Notice that the general effect is rather as if a 'branch-with-link' instruction (BL) had been executed; the combination of saving the CPU state (PC and CPSR) followed by a branch (caused by loading a new value into the PC) is certainly similar. The significant difference between an exception and a BL instruction is that a change of processor mode *also* occurs, so the software executed as a result of branching through the vector can deal with the exception free of the normal constraints of User mode (for example memory management or instruction restrictions).

All non-user modes have at least r13, r14 and the CPSR bank switched when the mode change occurs. r14 contains the previous PC (r15) address while r13 is traditionally used as a stack pointer. FIQ mode has a further five registers available, r8–r12, to allow more room for the FIQ handler to work in.

Special treatment of the FIQ exception vector
The FIQ vector is the last in the exception vector table so that the instruc-

General registers and program counter

User32 mode	FIQ32 mode	Supervisor32 mode	Abort32 mode	IRQ32 mode	Undefined32 mode
R0	R0	R0	R0	R0	R0
R1	R1	R1	R1	R1	R1
R2	R2	R2	R2	R2	R2
R3	R3	R3	R3	R3	R3
R4	R4	R4	R4	R4	R4
R5	R5	R5	R5	R5	R5
R6	R6	R6	R6	R6	R6
R7	R7	R7	R7	R7	R7
R8	R8_fiq	R8	R8	R8	R8
R9	R9_fiq	R9	R9	R9	R9
R10	R10_fiq	R10	R10	R10	R10
R11	R11_fiq	R11	R11	R11	R11
R12	R12_fiq	R12	R12	R12	R12
R13	R13_fiq	R13_svc	R13_abt	R13_irq	R13_undef
R14	R14_fiq	R14_svc	R14_abt	R14_irq	R14_undef
R15 (PC)	R15 (PC)	R15 (PC)	R15 (PC)	R15 (PC)	R15 (PC)

Program status registers

CPSR	CPSR	CPSR	CPSR	CPSR	CPSR
	SPSR_fiq	SPSR_svc	SPSR_abt	SPSR_irq	SPSR_undef

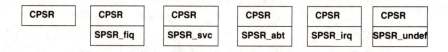

Figure 5.1 Register organization

tions for its service routine can follow it directly if desired, thereby removing the overhead of several cycles which results from branching.

Exception priorities

When several exceptions occur simultaneously they are resolved in order of priority and then each serviced in turn before execution of the interrupted program resumes. ARM6 services exceptions in the following order:

- Reset (highest priority)
- Data abort
- FIQ
- IRQ
- Instruction prefetch abort
- Undefined instruction, SWI instruction (lowest priority)

Note that not all exceptions can occur at once: 'undefined instruction' and 'SWI instruction' are mutually exclusive since they each correspond to particular decodings of the current instruction.

5.3   Types of ARM exception

Each of the different types of exception supported by the ARM6 core are outlined in the next few sections. Interrupts and memory aborts are examined in more detail in later sections.

5.3.1   Reset

The Reset input is expected to be used only for signalling 'power-up' when a system is first switched on, or for re-starting a system *as if* it had just been powered-up, perhaps as a result of user intervention such as pressing a Reset button. The fact that a program interrupted by a Reset cannot be restarted limits the usefulness of the Reset exception for other purposes.

When the processor's external 'nReset' input is asserted, ARM6 abandons the current instruction and continuously executes no-operations (NOPs) whilst presenting incrementing addresses on the address bus.

Once 'nReset' is de-asserted again ARM6 then:

- Overwrites r14_svc and SPSR_svc with the (undefined) contents of PC and CPSR
- Forces CPSR mode bits M[4:0] to %10011, switching the CPU to Supervisor mode, then sets the I and F flags to disable both kinds of interrupt
- Forces the PC to address 0x00000000 to fetch the next instruction

Since undefined (meaningless) values for PC and CPSR are saved in the banked registers it is not possible to resume execution of the previous program after a Reset.

5.3.2   Undefined instruction exception

Whenever the ARM6 core executes *any* coprocessor instruction or certain undefined instructions then the instruction is broadcast to all coprocessors attached to the CPU. If there are no coprocessors attached or none of them responds to the instruction in question then an 'Undefined instruction' exception occurs and the ARM6 then:

- Saves the address of the aborting instruction plus 4 in r14_und and saves CPSR in SPSR_und
- Forces CPSR mode bits M[4:0] to %11011, switching the CPU to Undefined mode, then sets the I flag in the CPSR
- Forces the PC to address 0x00000004 to fetch the next instruction

This mechanism allows the ARM instruction set to be expanded either through the addition of coprocessor devices and/or by providing software which intercepts the address vector for this exception and interprets the 'new' instruction in question. Refer to Chapters 2 and 9 for more information on coprocessor instructions.

5.3.3   Software Interrupt (SWI)

The software interrupt instruction SWI causes the CPU to switch to Supervisor mode and contains within the instruction word a 24-bit parameter field which can be retrieved later. The purpose of this instruction is to allow User mode programs to request privileged services from the operating system, for example input/output operations, which many operating systems will only allow in Supervisor mode. When a SWI instruction is executed ARM6:

- Saves the address of the SWI instruction plus 4 in r14_svc and saves CPSR in SPSR_svc
- Forces CPSR mode bits M[4:0] to %10011, switching the CPU to Supervisor mode, then sets the I flag to disable IRQs
- Forces the PC to address 0x00000008 to fetch the next instruction

The value of the 24-bit parameter can be readily accessed using r14_svc and it is typically interpreted as an index to a list of possible services provided by the operating system.

In some of the examples in this book we have followed the *de facto* standard in the ARM world that SWI 0x00000000 will cause the ASCII character in bits [7..0] of r0 to be printed to the standard output stream by the operating system. The ARM SDT environment discussed in Chapter 3 supports this standard.

5.3.4 Data and Prefetch abort exceptions

The ARM processors distinguish between two different kinds of abort exception:

- Prefetch aborts occur when the CPU attempts to execute an instruction which has been prefetched from an 'illegal' address.
- Data aborts occur when a data transfer instruction attempts to load or store data at an 'illegal' address.

In each case 'illegal' addresses are those which have been determined by the memory management subsystem as not being accessible to the processor in its current mode. Both data and prefetch aborts may be caused either by an on-chip MMU (where present, for example in ARM600/610) or by assertion of the processor's 'Abort' input. If the external 'Abort' input is asserted during an external memory access that memory access is flagged as illegal. The memory management subsystem, which is totally separate from the CPU core, is solely responsible for deciding whether a memory access is allowable and causing the abort if necessary.

When an abort of either kind occurs, the ARM6:

- Saves the address of the aborted instruction plus 4 (for prefetch aborts) of plus 8 (for data aborts) in r14_abt and saves the CPSR in SPSR_abt
- Forces CPSR mode bits M[4:0] to %10111, switching the CPU to Abort mode, then sets the I flag in the CPSR
- Forces the PC to address 0x0000000C (prefetch aborts) or 0x00000010 (data aborts) to fetch the next instruction

Refer to the section on memory management in Chapter 6 for more information about possible sources of data and prefetch aborts.

5.3.5 External IRQ interrupt

When the CPU's external Interrupt Request IRQ input is asserted (low) and the I bit in the CPSR is clear the current instruction is completed and the ARM6 then:

- Saves the address of the next instruction plus 4 in r14_irq and saves CPSR in SPSR_irq

- Forces CPSR mode bits M[4:0] to %10010, switching the CPU to IRQ mode, then sets the I flag to disable further IRQ interrupts
- Forces the PC to address 0x00000018 to fetch the next instruction

Interrupts are discussed in more detail in the next few sections of this chapter.

5.3.6   External FIQ interrupt

When the CPU's external Fast Interrupt Request 'FIQ' input is asserted (low) and the F bit in the CPSR is clear the current instruction is completed and the ARM6 then:

- Saves the address of the next instruction plus 4 in r14_fiq and saves CPSR in SPSR_fiq
- Forces CPSR modes bits M[4:0] to %10001, switching the CPU to FIQ mode, then sets both the I and F flags to disable both kinds of interrupt
- Forces the PC to address 0x0000001C to fetch the next instruction

FIQs have a higher priority than IRQs in two respects: firstly they are serviced first when multiple exceptions arise, and secondly servicing them in turn disables IRQs (as noted above), thus preventing any IRQs from being serviced until after the FIQ handler has re-enabled them.

5.4   An example interrupt handler

In order to illustrate the process of despatching interrupts the following extract from the IRQ handler for the DEMON debugger is included. This routine demonstrates good practice in several ways, notably its versatile 26-bit or 32-bit address space option and its model register context saving.

Since this routine is only an extract from a much larger source file its header, where all the definitions appear, is not included – good choices for label and constant names ensure that its legibility is not diminished.

```
; (C) Advanced RISC Machines Ltd. 1993

; Author: Dave Jaggar

;

; This routine is the Serial chip interrupt handler. When an
```

```
; interrupt occurs, one of three things has happened
; 1) the timer has started another period
; 2) an error happened (character or break)
; 3) a character has been received
;


SerialIntSTR        r14, [r14,-r14] ; store lr at zero
        LDR         r14, =SavedRegs  ; re-base r14
        STMIA       r14!, {r0-r13}   ; save them
        LDR         r0, [r0,-r0]     ; get old r14 into r0
        SUB         r0, r0, #4       ; adjust ready for
                                     ; the return
IF {CONFIG} = 26
        STMIA       r14!, {r0}       ; store them too
ELSE
        MRS         r1, SPSR         ; get the old CPSR
        STMIA       r14!, {r0,r1}    ; store them too
ENDIF
        LDR         r0, =ResetVectorCopy; restore location
                                     ; zero
        LDR         r0, [r0]
        STR         r0, [r0,-r0]     ; store it


        MOV         r3, #SerialChipBase
        LDR         r0, [r3, #ISR]   ; get the interrupt
                                     ; status register
        TST         r0, #ISRTimerTicked; Timer Interrupt ?
        BEQ         IntNoTick


        LDR         r2, =TimerVal
        LDR         r1, [r2]         ; load the current value
        ADD         r1, r1, #1       ; increment it
```

```
              STR         r1, [r2]         ; store it back
              MOV         r1, #ResetTimer  ; clear the interrupt
              STR         r1, [r3, #CR]


IntNoTickLDR              r0, [r3, #SR]    ; get the status
                                           ; register
              TST         r0, #SRNastyError; any errors ?
              BLNE        ROMReset         ; Hard Reset


              MOV         r3, #SerialChipBase
              LDR         r0, [r3, #SR]    ; get the status
                                           ; register
              TST         r0, #SRRxReady   ; character arrived
              BLNE        NewMessage


              LDR         r14, =SavedRegs
IF {CONFIG} = 32
              LDR         r0, [r14, #60]   ; pick up the CPSR
              MSR         SPSR, r0         ; ready to restore
ENDIF
              LDR         r0, =NextIntHandler; pass the interrupt
                                           ; on?
              LDR         r0, [r0]         ; pass the interrupt
                                           ; on?
              CMP         r0, #0


              STRNE       r0, [r14, #60]   ; fake the PC
              LDMNEIA r14, {r0-lr,pc}      ; restore registers


              LDMEQIA r14, {r0-lr}         ; restore registers
              MOVEQS      pc, lr           ; and resume
```

▥ 5.5   Interrupt latency

Although interrupts are *in principle* capable of very rapidly bringing asynchronous events to the attention of the application or operating system, their usefulness can be tempered by the time taken to get around to actually servicing the interrupts, a period known as the 'interrupt latency'.

The ARM's two interrupt inputs differ in the hardware support present to help minimize interrupt latency. As well as having a higher priority than IRQ the FIQ interrupt service handler has a private register bank which is much larger than that for IRQ mode and also has its exception vector strategically placed last in the vector table, in the expectation that these concessions will minimize the FIQ latency.

Clearly, FIQ interrupts stand a considerably better chance of being serviced quickly than IRQs, which must wait until any pending FIQs have been serviced before they stand any chance of being serviced themselves. Nevertheless, some other issues can contribute to degrading the latency of FIQs, in particular long instructions and the presence of the cache.

Interrupts are only considered by the processor at the end of execution of each instruction. Some instructions can take many cycles to execute in their most complicated cases: MUL and MLA can both potentially take up to $1 S + 16 I$ cycles, and the multiple register transfer instructions LDM and STM can take up to $17 S + 2 N + 1 I$ cycles when all 16 registers are being transferred. Any interrupt which is unfortunate enough to come along at the start of execution of either of these instructions is doomed to have a long wait before any consideration is given to it.

Because the current ARM cache design *randomly* replaces lines of four words when a new cache slot is required it is quite possible that the service routine for an interrupt will be thrown out of the cache at around the time it is just about to be required. But since the cache line replacement process is random, it is not possible to predict very accurately how this will impinge on the interrupt latency.

▥ 5.6   Exceptions from the application's perspective

Excluding the SWI instruction and the FIQ and IRQ interrupts, each of the exceptions that may occur during the execution of an ARM program is an indication of a potentially serious problem. Some operating systems will use exceptions to implement various types of inter-process protection or virtual memory: data and prefetch aborts, memory management faults and address exceptions are all potentially recoverable if they arise within a well-defined environment.

Undefined instructions and floating-point arithmetic faults are typically handled by floating-point support software, which may or may not be able to take any action to recover: an instruction which is not implemented in hardware may quite correctly be faulted and dealt with by software emulation, but a 'division by zero' exception is hard to do anything about except bring the program in question to a grinding halt.

The precise way in which each kind of exception is dealt with is completely operating system-specific. Operating systems which *do not* provide process protection or virtual memory are likely to treat all kinds of memory aborts as serious errors, since they will usually reflect an attempt to access memory which simply doesn't exist. In those operating system which *do* provide such features a considerable amount of software is required to unravel the cause of an exception and attempt to deal with it. Operating systems such as Unix and its derivatives such as Mach are notable examples of the latter group: both provide sophisticated multi-tasking mechanisms as well as inter-process protection and demand-paged virtual memory.

Programs written in Assembler will usually have to follow the specific guidelines laid down by the operating system in question.

Programs written in high-level languages, notably C, have the benefit of some standardization to define more clearly how exceptions are handled.

5.6.1   Exceptions and C signals

The ANSI C standard defines a class of library function in the header file `signal.h` to support a standardized way of dealing with run-time exceptions. The `armcc` compiler presents exceptions to the application program through the use of signals and allows all types of ARM exception to be propagated to the operating system or application program in a manner which complies with the ANSI standard. So, for example, a signal known as 'SIG_FPE' is raised whenever a floating-point exception occurs, and so forth.

Refer to the ARM Cross Development Toolkit documentation for more information about signals.

▨ 5.7   Summary

In this chapter we have seen how unusual events, both synchronous and asynchronous to the CPU, can cause exceptions which require special processing. In most ARM applications the SWI instruction and IRQ and FIQ interrupts will be sources of 'intentional' exceptions, while other kinds of exception, such as memory aborts, may indicate problems.

It is usually the role of the operating system to provide general-purpose exception handlers, but it is in the nature of exceptions that special treatment may be required in some environments.

The FIQ interrupt in particular is capable of supporting very high bandwidth data transfers, sometimes known as 'software DMA', without the need for external support circuitry. This reduces the cost overheads of data transfers between peripherals and system memory, at the expense of worsened latency for other kinds of exception.

6

ARM architecture extensions

6.1 Introduction

This chapter examines the architectural extensions which enable modular ARM processor variants to be constructed using the ARM QuickDesign service.

Modern computer systems increasingly demand performance and functionality which is not available from a such a simple device as the original ARM processor core, so various commonly required extensions to the ARM architecture have been pre-designed to allow a wide variety of different ARM variants to be constructed. In the past, these architecture extensions have typically been packaged in separate ICs because of the cost penalties of building larger and more complex devices. As the technology of chip fabrication has steadily improved it has become possible to migrate what were previously separate ICs onto the same silicon die, allowing a modular 'building block' approach to be used to assemble highly integrated devices.

The most recent ARM processors, the ARM600 and ARM610, are the result of this kind of evolution. In creating the ARM610 for Apple, ARM Ltd was able to offer 'shrink-wrapped' building blocks including a proven 32-bit RISC processor design, an efficient mixed instruction and data cache and a write buffer custom-made for ARM processor cores; the final component was the design expertise to implement Apple's own patented memory management technology.

The ARM600 includes a coprocessor interface, cache, and memory management unit as well as the ARM processor core (see Figure 8.4).

▓ 6.2   ARM600 system control coprocessor

Those ARM processors that include one or more of the architecture extensions need to have a mechanism for initializing and enabling such things as the cache and the memory management system. Since the introduction of the ARM3 this has been achieved through the use of an on-chip 'system control coprocessor' which exists simply to make the relevant registers easily accessible by means of coprocessor instructions.

The system control coprocessor is always coprocessor number 15 and it has a number of registers which vary according to the type of ARM processor in question. The ARM600/610's system control coprocessor has eight valid registers (0..7), with all the others (8..15) being reserved. A coprocessor register transfer instruction (MCR/MRC) is used to move data between the integer CPU registers and the coprocessor registers, allowing both reading and writing of system control data. Operations on the system control coprocessor's registers may only be performed in a privileged (that is non-User) mode, so they can normally only be exploited by the operating system itself.

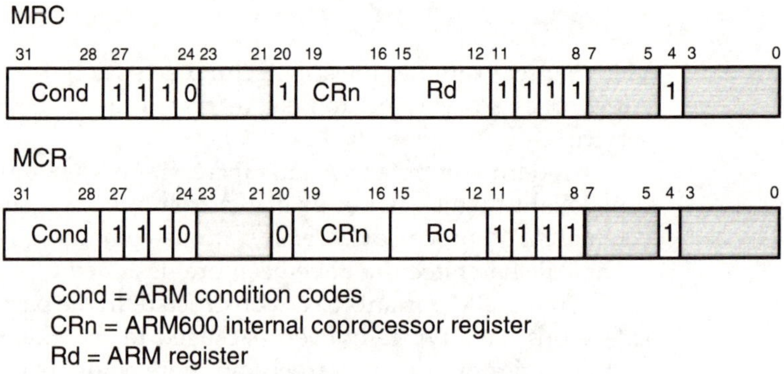

MRC

| 31 | 28 27 | 24 23 | 21 20 19 | 16 15 | 12 11 | 8 7 | 5 4 3 | 0 |

Cond 1 1 1 0   1 CRn Rd 1 1 1 1   1

MCR

| 31 | 28 27 | 24 23 | 21 20 19 | 16 15 | 12 11 | 8 7 | 5 4 3 | 0 |

Cond 1 1 1 0   0 CRn Rd 1 1 1 1   1

Cond = ARM condition codes
CRn = ARM600 internal coprocessor register
Rd = ARM register

Figure 6.1 Internal coprocessor instructions

Table 6.1 summarizes the purpose of each of the ARM600/610 system control coprocessor registers.

Table 6.1 ARM600 system control coprocessor registers

Register #	Read	Write	Comment
0	CPU ID register	Invalid	Revision number
1	Invalid	Control register	Control flags
2	Invalid	Translation table base	MMU pointer
3	Invalid	Domain access control	Domain status
4	Invalid	Invalid	Reserved
5	Fault status register (FSR)	TLB flush control	See text
6	Fault address register (FAR)	TLB purge address	See text
7	Invalid	IDC flush control	Flush cache

6.2.1 System control coprocessor registers

This section considers each of the system control coprocessors in turn; this information is primarily of interest to operating system writers, since these registers may only be accessed in non-User modes. Nevertheless, it is important to understand how overall control of the processor is achieved through these registers in order to understand the sections which follow about the cache, write buffer and memory management unit.

CPU ID register (Register 0)

This read-only register (shown in Figure 6.2) is present in all ARM variants which include a system control coprocessor, including ARM3 and ARM6. It consists of four fields, which are interpreted as follows:

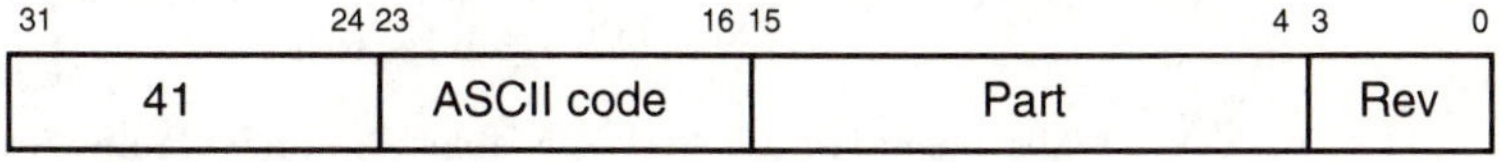

31	24 23	16 15	4 3	0
41	ASCII code	Part		Rev

Figure 6.2 Coprocessor ID register

- Bits [31..24] contain the ASCII code for a capital A
- Bits [23..16] contain the ASCII code for the name of the ARM foun-

dry partner which produced that chip, usually the first initial of the company's name, for example V for VLSI Technology.

- Bits [15..4] contain a 12-bit number representing the processor type, 0x060 for ARM600/10
- Bits [3..0] contain a 4-bit number indicating the processor revision

The revision field, in bits [3..0], is particularly of interest since it reveals which version of the processor is in use; refer to the ARM Data Sheet for the processor in use to determine which revisions are current.

Non-cached 26-bit address bus ARM processors (that is ARM2/250) do not include system control coprocessors and will take the 'Undefined instruction' exception if coprocessor instructions are issued to coprocessor number 15.

Control register (Register 1)

This write-only register contains a number of control bits which determine the precise mode of operation of the processor. Its precise form is shown in Figure 6.3. The interpretation of the valid bits [8..0] is shown in Table 6.2; all other bits are reserved and must be written as zeros.

Table 6.2 Control register bits

Bit	Name	Purpose
S	System	Controls the permission system
B	Big/little endian	B=1 selects big-endian operation, B=0 little-endian
L	Late abort timing	L=1 selects Late abort mode, L=0 selects Early abort mode
D	Data space size	D=1 selects 32-bit data space, D=0 selects 26-bit space
P	Program space size	P=1 selects 32-bit program space, P=0 select 26-bit space
W	Write buffer enable	W=1 enables the write buffer, W=0 disables it, but see text
C	Cache enable	C=1 enables the instruction and data cache, C=0 disables it, but see text
A	Alignment fault enable	A=1 enables alignment faults, A=0 disables them
M	MMU enable	M=1 enables the MMU, M=0 disables it, but see text

The M, C and W bits allow the memory management unit (MMU),

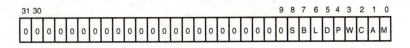

Figure 6.3 Coprocessor control register

instruction and data cache (IDC) and write buffer (WB) to be enabled and disabled independently. However, the internal data cache and the write buffer require the memory management unit to be enabled to operate, so the valid combinations of these control bits are restricted to the subset shown in Table 6.3.

Table 6.3 Valid combinations of M,C and W control bits

MMU	IDC	WB
off	off	off
ON	off	off
ON	ON	off
ON	off	ON
ON	ON	ON

All other combinations are reserved and must not be used since they will give undefined results.

Translation table base (Register 2)

This write-only register, shown in Figure 6.4, stores the starting address of the so-called 'Level One translation table', which is initialized in memory by the operating system for use by the memory management unit. The Level One translation table may only begin on a 16 kbyte boundary, so only bits [31..14] are valid; the rest should be written as zeros.

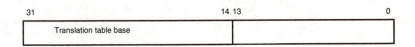

Figure 6.4 Translation table base

Domain access control (Register 3)

This write-only register, shown in Figure 6.5, stores the current access control settings for each of the 16 possible protection domains 0..15. Two bits are used per domain.

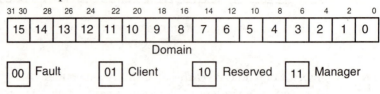

Figure 6.5 Domain access control

Reserved (Register 4)

This register is reserved and no attempt should be made to access it.

Fault Status Register (FSR)/TLB flush control (Register 5)

This register returns the previous data fault status when read and allows the translation look-aside buffer (TLB) to be flushed when written.

Reading from this register, known as the 'Fault Status Register' (FSR) and shown in Figure 6.6, returns the status of the last *data* fault to occur in the format shown below. Prefetch faults do not update this register. Note that only the bottom 12 bits are valid and that the top 20 bits will contain random data which should be masked out and ignored.

Within the 12 least significant bits the information shown in Table 6.4 is returned.

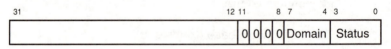

Figure 6.6 Fault status register

Table 6.4 Fault status register bits

Bits	Meaning
11..8	Always zero
7..4	Domain number being accessed when the data fault occurred (one of 15..0)
3..0	Type of access being attempted when the fault occurred

Writing to this register causes all 32 entries of the TLB (see The Translation Look-aside Buffer (TLB) on page 136) to be 'flushed', that is discarded. The data written is ignored, as shown in Figure 6.7; it is the write operation itself which has the effect.

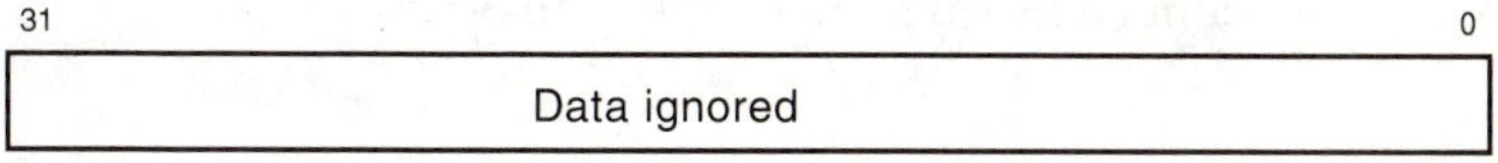

31   0

```
+---------------------------------------------------------------+
|                         Data ignored                          |
+---------------------------------------------------------------+
```

Figure 6.7 Flushing the TLB

Fault Address Register/TLB purge address (Register 6)

This register returns the previous data fault address when read and allows an address to be purged from the translation look-aside buffer when written. Its layout is shown in Figure 6.8.

Reading this register, known as the 'Fault Address Register' (FAR), returns the *virtual* address of the last data fault in all 32 bits of the word. When used in conjunction with the fault status returned by the previous register (FSR) it may be possible for the operating system to accurately locate and re-try faulted data accesses.

31   0

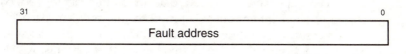

Figure 6.8 Fault address register

Writing to this register causes the memory page whose top 20 bits are those written in bits 31..12 of the data to be searched for in the translation look-aside buffer, as shown in Figure 6.9. If a match is found the corresponding TLB entry is marked invalid and subsequent accesses to that memory region will cause the TLB to be re-loaded.

31	12 11	0
Purge address		

Figure 6.9 TLB purge

IDC flush control (Register 7)

This write-only register allows the instruction and data cache to be completely invalidated ('flushed').

Writing to this register causes the entire IDC to be flushed; the data written is ignored.

System control coprocessor registers 8–15

These registers are not present and any attempt to access them causes the undefined instruction exception to occur.

6.3   Instruction and Data Cache (IDC)

Improvements in CPU performance are usually due to increases in the CPU clock frequency; a higher frequency clock leads to a shorter cycle time and consequent reductions in program execution time. Unfortunately, it is not straightforward simply to increase the clock frequency.

Firstly, the process used to fabricate the CPU may not yield reliable operation at higher frequencies without design changes to the CPU; secondly, the memory to which the CPU is interfaced can itself only operate at a certain frequency and new, faster, RAM chips will undoubtedly be required. It is not uncommon for RAM of the required speed to be prohibitively expensive or to need to be impossibly fast to work correctly.

The contemporary solution to this problem used in many microprocessors, including the ARM family, is to employ a small 'cache' memory on or near the CPU. A small amount of very fast RAM known as the cache maintains a copy of the contents of the most recently accessed memory locations and is able to provide data to the processor very quickly should any address in the cache be accessed again.

Since most programs contain loops, subroutines and references to global variables it is likely that the cache will frequently contain the desired data. Good cache design allows very frequent references to the cache in favour of main memory (known as the cache 'hit rate'), with dramatic peformance improvements as a result. Caches vary widely in size from a few tens of bytes up to several megabytes.

Of course, when a memory access to a location which is not present in the cache occurs the CPU must perform an access to main memory, slowing the CPU down, and copy the data returned into the cache before proceeding. Two CPU clock signals are usually employed: a 'core' clock which determines the operating frequency of the cache and the CPU when a cache hit occurs, and a 'memory' clock which determines the speed of main memory accesses when a cache miss occurs. Switching between these signals requires some synchronization circuitry and usually incurs a performance penalty.

Some extra circuitry is required to control the cache and to ensure that its contents remain consistent with the main system memory: each time a write occurs to main memory the contents of the relevant address must be updated if it occurs in the cache. Some areas of memory may not be suitable for caching (for example memory-mapped peripherals whose register contents may change) and indeed some memory accesses may require the entire cache to be flushed of data and allowed to refill.

Many contemporary CPUs employ caches, either on-chip or off-chip or both. Both the Intel 80486 and the Motorola 68040 have on-chip caches which allow them to operate at significantly higher frequencies than their predecessors. Increasingly common is the use of a 'secondary' off-chip cache to increase the cache hit rate still further. Of course, this also increases the cost of the system by increasing its complexity and the number and size of the components involved.

The first ARM processor to employ a cache was the ARM3; it added a 4 kbyte mixed instruction and data cache to the ARM2 CPU core, while at the same time the entire chip was shrunk to increase its maximum clock frequency. The result was a CPU with an identical instruction set and full backwards code-compatibility which was able to operate some three to four times faster than the ARM2. In fact, the ARM3 was such a good replacement for ARM2 that a number of companies set about producing upgrade products which allowed users of ARM2-based systems to swap processors to take advantage of the new device.

6.3.1   The ARM600 CPU cache

The ARM600 employs the same style of cache as did the earlier ARM3. The cache contains 4 kbytes of storage and is arranged as 256 'lines' of 16 bytes (four words) organized as four blocks of 64 lines. The cache operates on the 'virtual' addresses output by the CPU before the memory management unit has translated them to real 'physical' addresses. Whenever a cache 'miss' occurs a whole cache line (four words) is re-loaded from main memory, improving the chance that the next address will already be cached when it comes to be executed.

Whenever a new line is to be cached it is necessary to ensure that the line it replaces is chosen efficiently. Many studies of cache replacement algorithms have been performed and the designers of the ARM cache conducted extensive simulations before choosing their strategy. The ARM caches chooses lines for replacement using a pseudo-random algorithm; this turns out to give results which are nearly as good as the 'perfect' algorithm of replacing the line which has been least recently accessed, but is considerably simpler to implement.

At 4 kbytes the ARM600 cache is significantly smaller than those of many other contemporary processors. This is an intentional side-effect of the desire for a low-cost device; the use of a six transistor-per-bit RAM cell consumes a significant number of transistors and so the overall size of the device is strongly related to the cache size. Future ARM devices will almost certainly use fewer transistors-per-bit (four is now common) and thus allow larger caches as the fabrication processes become available to support them, with consequent increases in performance.

Despite the small cache size, the ARM600 achieves a higher hit rate than some larger caches because of its relatively high degree of associativity (the number of possible targets for new cache lines). Full associativity (256 ways) was found in simulation not to give significantly better performance than 64-way associativity, but the latter has the greater virtue that only one of the four cache blocks needs to be powered during cache searches, significantly reducing the cache's power consumption.

6.3.2   How the ARM600 IDC works

When the CPU reads data from memory the cache is searched for the relevant address. If the address occurs in the cache its data is fed to the CPU in a single cycle of the core clock, known in ARMs as the fast clock 'FCLK'. If the address doesn't occur in the cache the CPU re-synchronizes to the memory clock 'MCLK' and reads the line of data (four 32-bit words) which includes the address being sought and stores it in a randomly chosen line of the cache.

Write-through strategy

When a write occurs the ARM immediately re-synchronizes to the MCLK and performs a write operation to main memory; this strategy is known as a 'write-through' implementation. If the cache holds a copy of the data at the same address then it is normally updated automatically. However, in some cases it may be desirable to prevent this updating and the ARM cache allows regions of the memory map to be marked 'updateable' or not accordingly.

Virtual addresses and cache flushing

Since the cache works on virtual addresses it is unaware of any remapping of virtual memory addresses to physical addresses that may be performed downstream by the memory management unit. If the virtual to physical mapping of memory is altered then the data in the cache will become invalid and must be flushed out of the cache. The cache may be flushed under software control by performing a write to the cache control coprocessor.

Un-cacheable regions

Certain ranges of addresses may need to be marked as un-cacheable to prevent erroneous data from being used by the CPU. In the case of memory-mapped peripherals, the peripheral device may contain registers whose contents can change between reads by the CPU; in this instance the relevant region must not be cached since the cache contents will be invalid if the peripheral registers change state.

Multi-mapped regions

Because the ARM IDC works on virtual addresses it assumes that every virtual address is mapped by the memory management unit to a different physical address. If the same physical address is mapped to more than one virtual address then the cache will attempt to maintain an entry for both (or as many as there are) mappings. When a CPU write occurs only one of the cache entries will be updated, leaving the other invalid. To avoid such conflicts all multi-mapped virtual addresses must be marked as un-cacheable.

Semaphore SWP instruction (read–lock–write)

The ARM IDC treats the data swap instruction SWP as a special case and never accesses the cache during the read phase of the instruction. The instruction performs a read from external memory, regardless of the cache contents, then writes the new data back to external memory, updating the cache if the region containing the address is marked as cacheable.

6.3.3   Programming the ARM IDC

The ARM IDC uses a pair of control bits to determine its behaviour for each region of memory in the system. In the earlier ARM3 CPU (which has no memory management unit on-chip) a dedicated cache control coprocessor was implemented to allow the system programmer to set up the cache behaviour. In the ARM600 the cache control bits are located within the MMU control tables (for this reason the MMU must be enabled before the instruction and data cache can be used); consult Memory Management Unit (MMU) on page 134 for more information. The IDC is disabled on Reset.

For each memory region supported by the MMU there are two IDC control bits. The 'cacheable' bit (C) determines whether reads from that region are cached, as follows:

- Cacheable (C=1)
  The cache is searched for the relevant address; if it is found in the cache then the cached data at that address is supplied to the CPU in a single FLCK cycle. If the address is not in the cache an external memory access to fetch a cache line (four 32-bit words) is performed and stored in a pseudo-randomly chosen cache line. The data is then passed to the CPU.

- Un-cacheable (C=0)
  The cache is not searched for the address; instead an external memory access to that address alone is performed (not a line fetch) and the cache contents are not updated.

The second IDC control bit for each region, the 'updateable' bit (U), determines the IDC behaviour when writes to that region occur, as follows:

- Updateable (U=1)
  An external memory access is performed and the cache is searched. If the cache holds a copy of the data at that address it is simultaneously updated.

- Non-updateable (U=0)
  An external memory access is performed but the cache is not searched and the contents of the cache are not affected.

6.4   Data Write Buffer (WB)

Where the instruction and data cache improves the performance of ARM600 by increasing the speed with which memory reads take place, the Write Buffer (WB) does the same thing for memory writes. The earlier ARM3 CPU has only the IDC, and although it achieves significant performance improvements as a result, this is offset by the need to slow the CPU down during writes. The data write buffer was introduced in the ARM600 to reduce this effect.

6.4.1   How the ARM write buffer works

The write buffer provides a queue of address/data slot pairs which may be written in a single cycle of the CPU core clock FCLK. As CPU writes occur they fill up slots at the rear of the queue, while the memory interface simultaneously unloads the slots from the front of the queue and performs the 'real' write to memory. Where memory writes are sparsely distributed through a program (frequently the case) the real memory writes will be interleaved with data reads from the IDC and the effective memory bandwidth is increased.

In the ARM600 the write buffer can queue up to eight data words at up to two different initial addresses. A single write requires one data slot and one address slot; a sequential write of n words requires n data slots and one address slot (the address of the first write). So two quad-word writes can be queued, or a single write to one address followed by another write of up to seven words starting at a different address, and so forth.

6.4.2   Programming the write buffer

In the ARM600 the write buffer control bits are located within the memory management unit (MMU) control tables (for this reason the memory management unit must be enabled before the write buffer can be used); consult the section below on the MMU for more information. The write buffer is disabled on Reset.

For each memory region supported by the MMU there is a single WB control bit. The 'bufferable' bit (B) determines whether writes to that region may be buffered in the write buffer or must be written out immediately. When a CPU write occurs the MMU translation tables for the relevant address are consulted and the appropriate action taken according to the state of the B control bit, as follows:

- Bufferable (B=1)
  The data is placed into the write buffer queue in a single FCLK cycle per write and the CPU is allowed to continue. The write buffer performs the external memory write in parallel with subsequent CPU operations. If the write buffer queue is full then the CPU is stalled until there is a free slot in the queue again.

- Unbufferable (B=0)
  The CPU is stalled until the external write is completed; this will require re-synchronization time and possibly several external MCLK cycles.

■ Semaphore (SWP) instruction (read–lock–write)
   In the special case of the data swap instruction SWP all writes are
   treated as unbufferable and cause an external memory write
   regardless of the state of the B bit.

▤ 6.5   Memory Management Unit (MMU)

The ARM600 Memory Management Unit (MMU) is a sophisticated
address translation and memory access control device. All programs executing on the CPU perceive the memory system as a contiguous 4 Gbyte
address space known as the 'virtual' address space. Whenever any access
to an address is attempted with the MMU enabled it intercepts the
address and consults its translation tables, either allowing the access or
'aborting' it and causing the relevant processor exception.

   If the access is allowed the data is transferred and the cache optionally updated to improve retrieval time for subsequent accesses to the
same address. If the access is aborted the CPU branches to one of its abort
exception vectors allowing the operating system to deal with the abort as
appropriate.

   Two separate mechanisms for controlling memory access are provided by the MMU: the first stage involves a view of memory populated
by 'domains' and the second stage involves checking access 'permissions'.

6.5.1   Memory domains

Domains are areas of memory which may be defined to possess individual access rights: each domain has a 'status' associated with it which may
be either 'Manager', 'Client' or 'No Access'. A manager domain is able to
make memory accesses without its access permissions being checked (see
below); a client domain has its access permissions checked and enforced,
resulting in a 'permission fault' if any access violations are encountered.

6.5.2   Access permissions

Permissions determine what sort of memory access is allowed when a
particular domain has 'client' status (remember that manager domains
are unchecked). Permissions indicate which combinations of read and

write access are allowed in each of Supervisor and User modes, as summarized in the Table 6.5.

Table 6.5 Access permissions

Code	System flag	Supervisor mode	User mode	Comment
00	0	No access	No access	Fault all client accesses
00	1	Read only	No access	Read-only in Supervisor mode
01	X	Read/Write	No access	R/W only in Supervisor mode
10	X	Read/Write	Read only	Fault User mode writes
11	X	Read/Write	Read/Write	All types allowed in all modes

The 'System flag' is a bit in the ARM600 control register (coprocessor #15, register 1, bit 8) which allows global control over access permissions; this bit may only be altered in modes other than User mode and will therefore typically be the sole concern of the operating system.

Use of the memory management unit

The combination of domains and permissions in the ARM600 MMU provides the hardware framework for supporting a number of modern operating system memory management strategies including:

- Multi-level memory protection, allowing the operating system to have unrestricted access to the whole memory system while giving user tasks their own protected memory regions
- Memory paging, allowing chunks of memory to be 'moved around' in the virtual address space without any actual copying of the physical data
- Demand paged virtual memory, where fixed disks are used to simulate large amounts of memory when, in fact, only a small amount of real physical memory exists
- 'Object-oriented' memory with support for background garbage collection, through the use of domains.

6.5.3   The theory behind the memory management unit

In order to perform its task the MMU must consist of several logic blocks within the processor and a number of 'translation tables' stored in memory and initialized by the operating system. The MMU control logic interrogates these tables (a process colloquially known as 'table walking') to determine the outcome of each memory access.

To enable the MMU to manage address translation it considers memory to be divided into blocks of one of two types:

- 'Sections' are defined as 1 Mbyte regions of memory and are therefore suitable for the allocation of large regions of the memory map.
- 'Pages' are supported in one of two sizes: 'small' pages consist of 4 kbyte blocks of memory and 'large' pages of 64 kbyte blocks. Pages are further subdivided into 'sub-pages' of a quarter the size, that is 1 kbyte for small pages and 16 kbyte for large pages.

These multiple levels of memory management granularity allow the translation tables to be kept reasonably small while still supporting a good range of memory allocation sizes: 1 Mbyte, 64 kbyte, 16 kbyte, 4 kbyte, and 1 kbyte.

The process of consulting the MMU tables stored in memory is potentially a slow one: in the worst case a memory reference may require two separate memory accesses for table walking before the actual memory access which transfers the first word of data, each access taking 1N and 1S cycle (see Chapter 2) and therefore totalling 3N + 3S cycles. Fortunately, the MMU will usually operate when the IDC is also enabled so that some of the MMU table entries or the actual data required *may* already be cached, but the small size of the cache limits this effect.

The Translation Look-aside Buffer (TLB)

A significant feature of the MMU which reduces the time penalty associated with performing address translation and checking is the Translation Lookaside Buffer (TLB). This consists of a cache of the 32 most recently used translation table entries.

Whenever a memory access is attempted the TLB is consulted to see whether the appropriate table entry is already present; if so, the access control logic determines whether the access is permitted; if not, the translation table walking logic retrieves the appropriate table entry from memory, stores it in the TLB (cyclically overwriting existing entries) and the access control logic then determines whether the access is permitted.

6.5.4   The address translation process

Each virtual memory address generated by the CPU core is translated by the MMU into a physical address and at the same time access permissions are retrieved and checked. The translation and access permissions are stored together in the 'translation table' located in system RAM. The MMU contains the logic necessary to perform these translations and checks without software intervention once the translation table has been initialized by the operating system.

All memory accesses begin in the same way, with the first stage of translation table checking, known as a 'Level One' fetch. According to the contents of the table entry retrieved by the Level One fetch, known as the 'Level One Descriptor', a further Level Two fetch may occur (if the address is mapped as a 'page') or the table lookup process may not complete (if the address is mapped as a 'section').

It is the Level One Descriptors that are cached by the translation look-aside buffer, so a TLB hit shortens the time needed to retrieve this information and thus speeds all accesses to addresses within that page or section.

Level One Descriptor Fetch

To determine where the Level One Descriptor is located the MMU must perform a small amount of indexing arithmetic: the base address of the translation table is stored in system control coprocessor register 2, of which bits 31..14 (18 bits) are considered valid. An index into the translation table must then be added to the base address and this index is taken from bits 31..20 (12 bits) of the virtual address in question, the two least significant bits of the address being zero because this is a word-aligned address (total 32 bits). The resulting physical address is read and the data returned treated as a Level One Descriptor.

The Level One fetch arithmetic is summarised in Figure 6.10.

The Level One Descriptor

The 32-bit Level One Descriptor contains information about the descriptor 'type' (page, section, invalid or reserved), IDC and WB control bits, the domain number of this memory region (four bits) and second-level page table address or section base address as appropriate according to the type.

The format of the Level One Descriptor is shown in Figure 6.11.

The two least significant bits of the descriptor encode the descriptor type as shown in Table 6.5.

The next three bits [4..2] hold the IDC and write buffer control bits U, C and B for sections, or just the U bit for pages. These bits indicate whether the region is Updateable (that is whether the IDC is updated

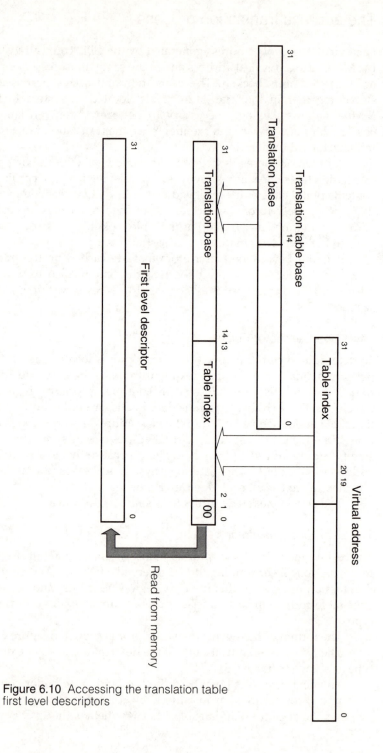

Figure 6.10 Accessing the translation table first level descriptors

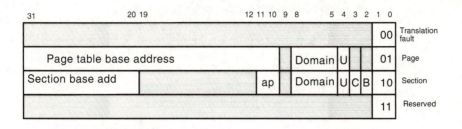

Figure 6.11 Level One Descriptors

Table 6.6 Descriptor types

Bits [1..0]	Type	Comment
00	Invalid	Section Translation Fault always generated
01	Page	Indicates that this is a page descriptor: Level Two lookup required
10	Section	Indicates that this is a section descriptor: no further lookup required
11	Reserved	Reserved for future use. Currently behaves like 'Invalid'.

during writes), Cacheable (that is can be cached by the IDC during reads) or Bufferable (that is can be written through the write buffer), respectively. These bits were discussed earlier in the sections Programming the ARM IDC on page 131 and Programming the write buffer on page 133, above.

Bits [8..5] hold the number of the domain associated with this memory region and whose access permissions are inherited from that domain according to the state of bits in the Domain Access Control register. See the section Memory domains on page 134, above, for more information about domains.

The remaining valid bits of the descriptor [31..10] are treated differently according to whether the descriptor is for a page or a section.

■ For a page descriptor a Level Two lookup will be required so bits [31..10] contain the base address of the Level Two descriptor table. A Level Two fetch is initiated automatically whenever a page descriptor is returned by the Level One fetch. See below for more information on Level Two lookup.

■ For a section descriptor no further lookup is required: Bits [31..20] contain the base address of the section (remember that a section is a 1Mbyte region so the least significant 20 bits are not under consideration) and bits [11..10] contain a two-bit 'access permission' code which is used when accesses are being performed in 'client mode' for this domain. Table 6.7 summarizes the meaning of the access permission bits for client mode access:

Table 6.7 Access permission bits for client mode accesses

Code	System flag (cp#15, r1, b8)	Supervisor mode	User mode	Comment
00	0	No access	No access	Fault all client accesses
00	1	Read only	No access	Read-only in Supervisor mode
01	X	Read/ Write	No access	R/W only in Supervisor mode
10	X	Read/ Write	Read only	Fault User mode writes
11	X	Read/ Write	Read/ Write	All types allowed in all modes

In the case of sections the MMU's work is now almost completed. The domain status register is checked for the specified domain and the access permissions for that domain are then considered: either the access is allowed, in which case the data is transferred as required by the instruction or the access is denied, in which case an 'MMU fault' is raised. Note that if the access is denied by the MMU then this occurs before any external memory access to the data itself; the MMU stores information about the faulting access in its Fault address and Fault Status registers, as described in the section System control coprocessor registers on page 123.

Figure 6.12 summarizes the arithmetic and lookups performed for a section reference.

Level Two fetch

When the Level One fetch from the translation tables returns a Page Descriptor a further sequence of table-walking is needed to retrieve a Level Two descriptor. The Page Descriptor contains the base address of the Level Two descriptor table within which the descriptor for the address in question may be found.

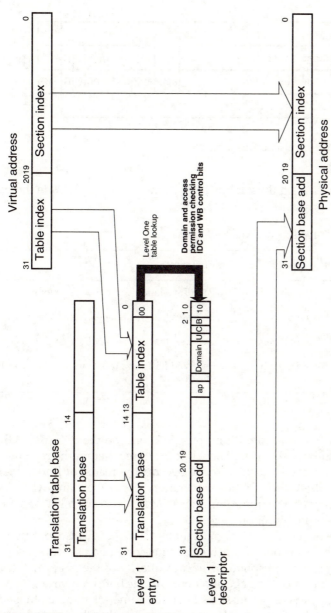

Figure 6.12 Translating section references

The descriptor indicates whether or not the relevant page is valid and, if so, whether the sub-page it represents is a 'small page' (4 kbytes) or a 'large page' (64 kbytes).

The format of the Level Two descriptor is shown in Figure 6.13.

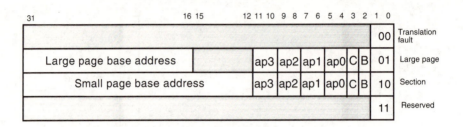

Figure 6.13 Level Two Descriptors

The two least significant bits [1..0] of the descriptor encode the page size or its validity as shown in Table 6.8.

Table 6.8 Page size and validity

Bits [1..0]	Type	Comment
00	Invalid	Page Translation Fault always generated
01	Large page	Indicates that this is a 64K Byte page
10	Small page	Indicates that this is a 4K Byte page
11	Reserved	Reserved for future use. Currently behaves like 'Invalid'.

The next two least significant bits [3..2] encode the IDC and WB control bits C and B for the page. These bits indicate whether the region is Cacheable (that is can be cached by the IDC during reads) or Bufferable (that is can be written through the write buffer) respectively and were discussed in the sections Programming the ARM IDC on page 131 and Programming the write buffer on page 133.

The next eight least significant bits [11..4] comprise four two-bit subfields which encode the access permissions ('access permission fields' ap3..ap0) each corresponding to each quarter of the page. ap3 deals with the top quarter of the page and ap0 with the bottom quarter.

These access permissions have the same meaning as those for sections (see Table 6.6) the only difference being that the fault generated if a permission violation is detected is a 'sub-page permission fault' in this instance.

So, when the MMU translates and checks an address after both a Level One fetch, which returns a Page Descriptor, and a Level Two fetch, which returns a sub-page descriptor, the address is resolved for access permission purposes to a granularity of either 16 kbyte (quarters of a large 64 kbyte page) or 1 kbyte (quarters of a small 4 kbyte page).

It is worth noting that full page mapping of the 4 Gbyte 32-bit memory space requires 16 kbytes of physical RAM for the Level One descriptor table and a further 1 Mbyte of physical RAM for the Level Two tables. It would be exceptional to require this degree of precision in controlling access to memory, so sections are provided to allow a less memory-intensive solution in return for coarser (1 Mbyte) memory mapping. Of course, a combination of sections and pages may be used together as a compromise or a section-mapped region could be switched by the operated system into a page-mapped region dynamically if required.

Figures 6.14 and 6.15 summarize the page mapping process for both large and small pages.

6.5.5   MMU faults and CPU aborts

The memory management unit can generate one of four types of fault during the address-checking process; they are:

- Alignment fault
- Translation fault
- Domain fault
- Permission fault

Furthermore, an external abort (via the processor's 'ABORT' input) may result from an external data access: this might be used to signal a bus error, for example. An external abort will only occur *after* the MMU has tested the address and if it has found no access violations, since otherwise the access will have already been aborted and never reach the system address bus.

When the MMU detects a fault it will abort the access and signal the CPU with the fault condition. The MMU retains status information about the fault (in the FSR) as well as the faulting address itself (in the FAR). Either a data abort or a prefetch abort will be signalled to the CPU according to the nature of the memory access; the MMU treats them differently, as discussed below.

Alignment fault

If the Alignment fault bit [1] of the Control Register (register 1) is enabled (set to 1) the MMU will generate an alignment fault for any data word

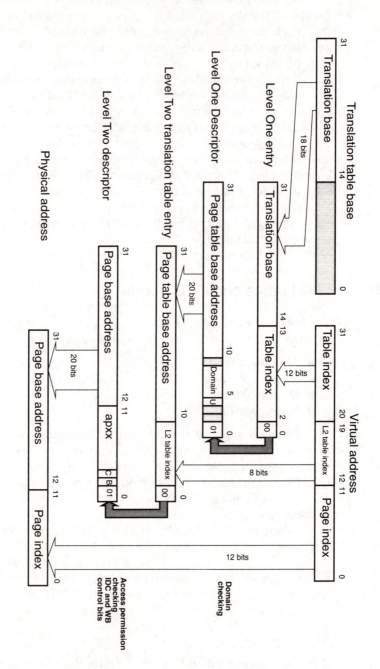

Figure 6.14 Large page translation

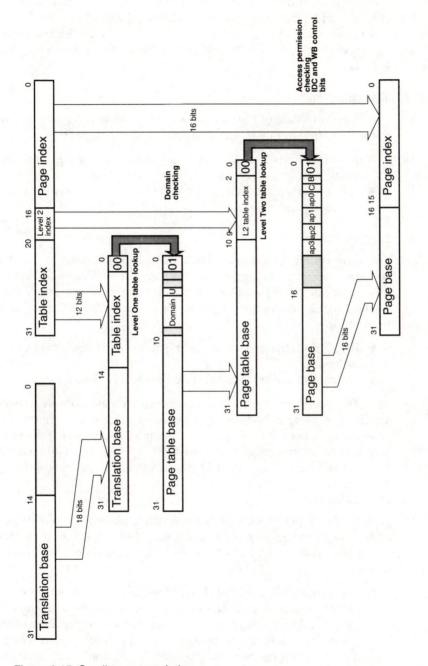

Figure 6.15 Small page translation

access whose address is not word-aligned (that is the two LSBs are not 00). This will occur irrespective of whether the MMU is enabled. Alignment faults will not be generated or any instruction prefetches nor on any byte operations. After an alignment fault no further permission checking will occur.

Translation fault

Two different kinds of translation fault may occur according to whether the address in question is a member of a section or a page:

- A Section translation fault occurs if the Level One descriptor is invalid (descriptor type codes 00 and 11).
- A Page translation fault occurs if the Level Two descriptor is invalid (page size codes 00 and 11).

Domain fault

Two different kinds of domain fault may occur according to whether the address is a member of a section or a page. In both cases the Level One descriptor holds the 4-bit Domain Number which selects one of the 2-bit domain access permission groups in the Domain Access Control Register (register 3):

- For sections the domain number is taken from the Level One descriptor
- For pages the domain is taken from the Level Two descriptor

The two access permission bits for the domain number in question are checked as described earlier. The access permissions are one of: 'No access' (00), 'Client' (01), 'Reserved' (10) or 'Manager' (11). If the resulting access permission is either 'No access' (00) or 'Reserved' (10) then either a Section Domain fault or a Page Domain fault occurs, as appropriate.

Permission fault

Two kinds of permission fault may occur, according to whether the address is a member of a section or a page (see Table 6.9). If the domain access permission group is 'Client' (01) then permissions are checked as follows:

- For sections the 'ap' bits [11..10] of the Level One descriptor determine whether the access is allowed according to the table used earlier and reproduced below. Note that the interpretation of these bits is dependent on the 'System flag' bit [8] of the Control Register. If the access is not allowed a Section Permission fault is generated.
- For sub-pages the Level One descriptor has specified a page and the Level Two descriptor contains four 2-bit domain access permission groups corresponding to the four quarters of the page. The relevant

pair of bits is interpreted just as for sections but if the access is not allowed a Sub-page Permission fault is generated.

Table 6.9 Access permission faults

ap bits Code	System flag (cp#15, r1, b8)	Supervisor mode	User mode	Comment
00	0	No access	No access	Fault all client accesses
00	1	Read only	No access	Read-only in Supervisor mode
01	X	Read/Write	No access	R/W only in Supervisor mode
10	X	Read/Write	Read only	Fault User mode writes
11	X	Read/Write	Read/ Write	All types allowed in all modes

Data, prefetch and external aborts

Data aborts are acted upon immediately by the CPU and the MMU places a fault status code FS[3..0] and a 4-bit Domain number in the FSR, as well as placing the faulting virtual address in the FAR. If more than one type of access violation occurs simultaneously they are prioritized and the fault with the highest priority is retained. Consult the ARM600/610 data sheet for more information on fault priorities.

Prefetch aborts are flagged in the instruction queue when the instructions are fetched. Only if a flagged instruction is actually executed (after testing the condition flags) does it cause an abort. Because the prefetch abort may or may not be acted upon the MMU status information is not preserved for the prefetch abort and the MMU does not update the FSR or FAR.

The ARM600/610 has an external ABORT input (active high) which may be used by external system logic. It is important to recognize that some kinds of external memory access can not be restarted, so the ABORT input must be used with great care. The limitations on restartability are noted below:

- Uncacheable reads
- Unbuffered writes
- Level One descriptor fetch
- Level Two descriptor fetch

- Read–Lock–Write sequence
  These types of memory access can be aborted and restarted safely. When aborted the external memory access will cease on the following cycle. In the case of the Read-Lock-Write sequence the write will never occur.

- Cacheable reads (cache line fetches)
  A line fetch may be aborted safely provided the abort is flagged on the first word (word 0) of the transfer. Otherwise the cache will contain at least one line (four words) of corrupt data and the instruction may not be restartable.

- Buffered writes
  Buffered writes cannot safely be aborted because the instruction execution pipeline within the processor will have moved on by the time the write is aborted, losing the necessary state information which might have allowed the instruction to be restarted. Nevertheless, the FSR does correctly record that such a fault ('Write buffer fault') has occurred; the FAR contains the address of the first operation which was aborted.

Systems should be configured so that buffered writes are *not* performed to areas of memory which are capable of generating an external abort.

 ## 6.6   Summary

The ARM QuickDesign service offers a number of extensions which add functionality to the ARM processor cores and implement options in a building block style. Among these are the memory management unit, which uses patented technology to implement a memory management system aimed at fully object-oriented systems, instruction and data caches, write buffers, and the coprocessor interface which connects coprocessors via a fast 32-bit data bus.

Other architectural extensions will be added to the QuickDesign range as customer requirements dictate.

7

ARM CPU hardware and interfacing

7.1 Introduction

This chapter examines the external hardware interfaces of members of the ARM6 processor family, including the ARM60/61, ARM600 and ARM610 processors.

The ARM6 processors share a common instruction set and support a 32-bit linear address space into which I/O devices are also mapped. Several processor operating modes are supported which form the basis of the memory management and protection systems.

7.1.1 Simple ARM6 family processors

The ARM60 is a single-chip 32-bit RISC processor with a 32-bit address space and support for either big-endian or little-endian operation. It is based on the earlier 26-bit address space ARM2aS core, but it is housed in a new package and has a new pinout. The alterations needed to provide the 32-bit address space mainly affect the design of the processor internally, although it does of course have 32 address pins instead of 26 on the outside. The ARM60 has no cache or other architecture extensions: it is a straightforward 32-bit address/data bus processor which can operate at clock frequencies of up to 25 MHz (Spring 1993).

The ARM61 is a special bond-out variant of the ARM60 which is hard-wired to operate in 26-bit address modes and is pin-compatible with the earlier ARM2.

7.1.2   High-integration ARM6 family processors

The ARM600 and ARM610 include the full range of architectural extensions described in Chapter Six. They differ electrically from each other only in that the ARM610 does not feature the coprocessor interface of the ARM600. This was removed to allow the device to be cost-effectively packaged. As a result the ARM610 is housed in a particularly small carrier, the 144-pin Thin Quad Flat Pack (TQFP), which requires the finished silicon die to be ground down from the underside to reduce its thickness to less than one millimetre before packaging.

The ARM610 in its 144TQFP package is 1.4 mm thick, about the size of a postage stamp and delivers 15 to 20 MIPS at 20 MHz while consuming around 10 µA of static current plus 5 mA per MHz of clock speed.

7.2   The ARM600 bus interface

The ARM600 is the fourth generation of ARM processor and its bus interface reflects this by sharing many signals in common with earlier ARM processors. Central to the ARM600 bus interface are the two major buses: the Address bus (32 bits) and the Data bus (32 bits). The Address bus is only ever an output from the processor, while the Data bus is, of course, bi-directional. Figure 7.1 shows the ARM600 bus interface.

The bus interface can be divided into a number of distinct groups of signals:

- Clock inputs and wait state control
- Address bus and control signals
- Data bus and control signals
- Interrupt inputs and Reset
- Coprocessor interface (not ARM610)
- Bus enables and test inputs

These are discussed in turn below.

7.3   Clock inputs and wait-state control

Two clock inputs, 'FCLK' and 'MCLK' control the frequency of operation

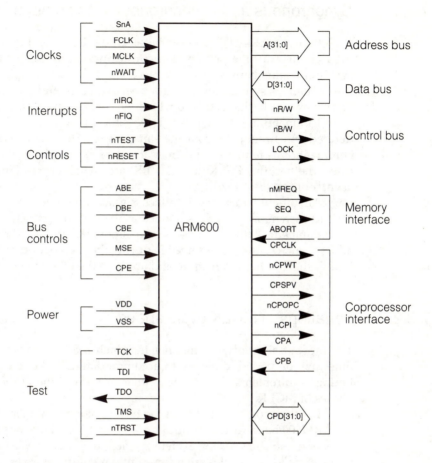

Figure 7.1 The ARM600 bus interface

of the two major parts of the ARM CPU: its processor core and its external memory interface. Typically the core clock will be around twice as fast as the memory clock, for example 24 MHz and 12 MHz.

The core clock signal is known as the Fast clock or FCLK. The CPU core may be clocked at a significantly higher frequency than the memory interface because it communicates only with other parts of the processor, at most a few millimetres away on the chip.

The memory interface, on the other hand, is expected to drive low-cost commercial dynamic RAM (DRAM) devices with limited speed and cycle times; the memory interface clock is known as MCLK. It is possible to build ARM-based systems whose memory runs as fast as the CPU core, but although this performs significantly faster it is prohibitively expensive at present.

7.3.1   Synchronous and asynchronous clock modes

Each time the ARM600 switches between the FCLK and the MCLK during execution a time penalty is incurred in waiting for the appropriate synchronization between the two clock signals before making the switch. This penalty is symmetric and varies between zero and one whole period of the new clock (that is that to which the core is resynchronizing).

To ameliorate this effect it is possible to employ clocks which are derived synchronously from the same source, in which case no re-synchronization is required. The 'SnA' input to the ARM600 is used to indicate whether the FCLK and MCLK are synchronous (SnA high) or asynchronous (SnA low).

All off-chip memory interface signals are timed with respect to MCLK: each memory cycle is defined as the period between two consecutive falling edges (that is high–low transitions) of MCLK. The processor's address and control signals change during the high period of MCLK (that is after the low-high transition) and apply to the following cycle.

7.3.2   Variations in MCLK cycle speed

The most straightforward manner in which the external memory cycle time may be varied, typically to accommodate DRAM access and cycle timing requirements, is to stretch either or both of the LOW and HIGH phases of MCLK.

To allow some flexibility in the timing of external memory accesses the ARM600 has a further control input, 'nWAIT', which may be asserted to extend the duration of a memory access. When nWAIT is asserted (low), extra MCLK cycles are inserted into memory accesses until nWAIT is de-asserted, thus allowing arbitrary timing to be selected by external circuitry (for example memory or peripheral controllers). nWAIT must only change while MCLK is low: it has the effect of stretching the low period of MCLK.

Before the nWAIT input was introduced (on the ARM3 processor) insertion of wait states required external logic to extend the low period of MCLK. In fact, either the low or high periods of MCLK may be stretched but it is usual to stretch the low period as this allows memory management hardware to abort the cycle in time for the next rising edge of MCLK, as the processor specification requires. Dynamic processors such as the ARM3 impose a limit on the maximum hold time for MCLK to ensure reliable data retention; the static ARM600 has no such restrictions.

Refer to the ARM600 Datasheet for more detailed information concerning clocks and the ARM bus interface.

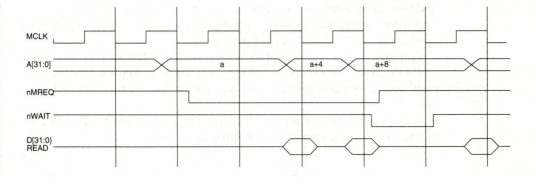

Figure 7.2 Use of the nWAIT pin to stretch timing cycles

7.4   Address bus and control signals

The 32-bit Address bus A[31..0] indicates the address requested for a memory access as the result of an instruction or data fetch by the CPU.

Associated with the address bus are two outputs which indicate the internal state of the processor during bus cycles: Memory Request (written nMREQ) and Sequential (written SEQ). Only two of the possible four combinations of these signals have defined meanings for the ARM6 memory system: bus cycles are flagged as either Active or Latent, that is they do, or do not, access memory. The encodings of these signals are shown in Table 7.1.

Table 7.1 Access bus control signals

Memory cycle type	nMREQ	SEQ
undefined	0	0
Active (A)	0	1
Latent (L)	1	0
undefined	1	1

Chapter 2 showed that some ARM CPU cores use the other two cycle type encodings to represent non-sequential and coprocessor cycles. The ARM600 memory system makes the distinction between sequential and non-sequential memory accesses externally by either driving nMREQ low and then high again (non-sequential access) or keeping nMREQ low (subsequent sequential accesses). Internally, a non-sequential cycle is treated as an L cycle followed by an A cycle.

In effect, the SEQ output is the inverse of nMREQ for the cases currently defined. The existence of SEQ is attributable solely to the needs of earlier memory management hardware and it is now otherwise superfluous.

Figure 7.3 shows the timing of a single-word access to memory: both the case for reading and that for writing are shown.

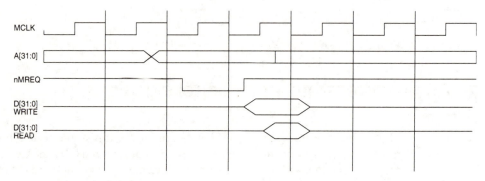

Figure 7.3 One word read or write

Notice that the address bus becomes valid and the nMREQ signal changes state during the cycle *prior* to the data transfer operation itself, a form of 'pipelining' which maximizes the setup time available for the memory management hardware to validate the address before the operation completes.

When more than one word of data is being transferred (for example when a cache line is being loaded or a multiple-register data transfer instruction is executing) it becomes significant to know whether or not the words are at successive addresses: most commercial DRAM supports a fast-access mode, often known as 'paged mode', which can exploit this information to reduce access times. The nMREQ signal remains asserted (low) when subsequent accesses after the first will be at consecutive addresses or the same address; otherwise it is de-asserted for two cycles and then re-asserted again to notify the memory subsystem of the change of address sequence.

Figures 7.4 and 7.5 demonstrate the different effects of sequential and non-sequential memory accesses on the memory interface signals.

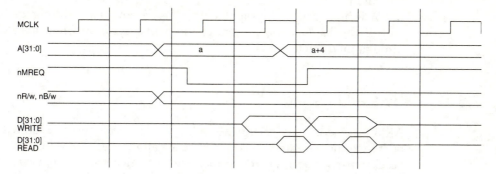

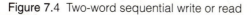

Figure 7.4 Two-word sequential write or read

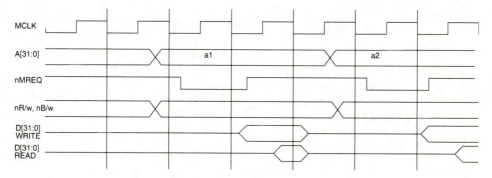

Figure 7.5 Two-word non-sequential read or write

▤ 7.5 Data bus and control signals

The 32-bit data bus (D31..0) carries instructions and data from memory to the processor, and data back to memory, at a width and in a direction specified by the associated control signals nB/W and nR/W. The nB/W signal indicates whether a byte (nB/W low) or word (nB/W high) is to be transferred, while nR/W indicates whether the data is being read (nR/W low) or written (nR/W high). In common with the memory bus these signals are asserted in the cycle prior to the transfer to allow plenty of time for the memory management system to interpret the cycle.

When nR/W is low (during a read cycle) the data must be set up on the data bus before the falling edge of MCLK in the active cycle. When nR/W is high (during a write) the data bus becomes valid during the first half of the latent cycle preceding the active cycle and remains valid throughout the active cycle.

7.5.1   Byte addressing

ARM processors view memory as a linear sequence of bytes upon which both byte and word (4-byte) operations are allowed. All ARM instructions occupy a word and data quantities are also often words. However, the single register data transfer instructions such as LDR, STR and SWP may all be followed by the optional B suffix to reference a single byte at a time.

The two least significant address lines, A0 and A1, encode which byte is being addressed; the ability of the ARM600 processor to be configured to have either a little- or big-endian view of byte ordering makes a tabular approach the only safe way to show this (Tables 7.2 and 7.3).

Table 7.2 Big-endian, from higher address to lower

31..24	23..16	15..8	7..0	Word address
8	9	10	11	8
4	5	6	7	4
0	1	2	3	0

Table 7.3 Little-endian, from higher address to lower

31..24	23..16	15..8	7..0	Word address
11	10	9	8	8
7	6	5	4	4
3	2	1	0	0

7.5.2   Locked bus operations

In common with the earlier ARM3, the ARM600/610 processors support the data swap instruction SWP, which reads the contents of a memory location and exchanges it with that of CPU registers before writing a new value back to memory. The instruction is intended to be performed indivisibly, that is without any danger of the read and write parts of the process being interrupted, to provide for interlocks in multi-processor systems.

To indicate that a bus cycle should be allowed to complete unhindered the 'LOCK' signal is asserted by the CPU throughout the four cycles that are required to complete the instruction. Figure 7.6 shows the process in detail.

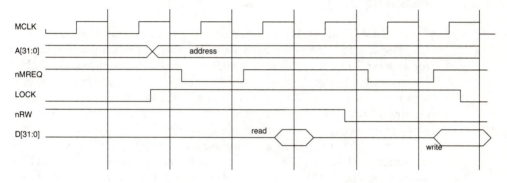

Figure 7.6 Read locked write

▤ 7.6   Interrupt inputs and reset

The ARM600/610 CPUs have two interrupt inputs; nIRQ and nFIQ. Of the two, FIQ has the higher priority and some architectural effort has been put into minimizing the latency (delay) in servicing a FIQ interrupt, for example the large FIQ mode register bank and the placement of the FIQ entry in the vector table. This makes FIQ well-suited to low-latency high-bandwidth data transfers such as those required by disk controllers or other unbuffered peripherals.

Each kind of interrupt may be enabled and disabled under software control by altering the state of the I and F flags in the CPSR (not possible from User mode). When the relevant flag is set then interrupts of that type are disabled. The I and F flags are set automatically upon entry to a FIQ service routine to disable IRQs while the FIQ is being serviced. If an IRQ occurs while I is set then the IRQ will be processed as soon as the I flag is cleared again upon exit from the service routine. I is also set when an IRQ is being serviced.

Both interrupt inputs are asynchronous and level-sensitive (active low) so in order to generate an interrupt successfully the relevant input must be held low, until the processor responds by addressing the interrupt-generating hardware to disable the source. A single-cycle (of FCLK) delay is imposed for synchronization before the flow of execution is affected.

7.6.1   Reset input

The 'nRESET' input is used to restart the processor from a known address; it is an active-low level sensitive input which must remain low for at least 2 FLCK cycles and 5 MCLK cycles to be recognized reliably. Upon recognition of the Reset condition the processor terminates the current instruction and disables the on-chip IDC, WB and MMU before restarting at address &00000000. This address, the 'Reset vector' is the first entry in the vector table discussed in Chapter 5.

Throughout the period during which nRESET is held low the CPU core performs latent (idle) cycles with incrementing addresses: that is address bus pins A31..A2 count upwards as if they were a 30-bit binary counter. Note that the bottom two address bits (A1, A0) used to distinguish between bytes are not involved in this and both remain low. This feature has some attractions during testing as it allows the address bus to show a different signal on every line, very useful in helping to find faults.

7.7   Coprocessor interface

The coprocessor interface is only present externally on some variants of ARM processors, notably the ARM3 and the ARM600. The ARM610, while it has no external coprocessor interface, nevertheless has an on-chip system control coprocessor which is used to control the IDC, WB and MMU. Typically, the external coprocessor interface will be used to add the floating-point support coprocessor known as FPA10 (or its successors) into ARM-based systems: a socket is usually provided into which users requiring high-performance floating-point arithmetic may plug the FPA. Software emulation of the ARM floating-point instruction set allows users of ARM-based computers without the coprocessor socket to execute the same software without modification.

The coprocessor interface allows extra functionality to be added to the processor in a tightly-coupled fashion. It has its own 32-bit data bus, the Coprocessor Data bus CPD[31..0], and control signals, all of which operate at the CPU core frequency, FCLK, imposing tight limits on the maximum separation distance and speed characteristics of any coprocessor devices.

7.7.1   Coprocessor interface clocks

CPCLK (Coprocessor clock) is an output from the ARM that provides the clock against which all coprocessor communication is timed. This clock switches between FCLK and MCLK according to whether the ARM is performing a latent (internal) or active (external) cycle, respectively. Coprocessors must thus be able to work at FCLK speeds to operate correctly.

nCPWT is an output from ARM which is used to qualify the coprocessor clock CPCLK: it must be gated with CPCLK within the coprocessor to time coprocessor operations.

7.7.2   Coprocessor data bus

The coprocessor data bus CPD[31..0] is a bi-directional bus used for all data transfers between the ARM and external coprocessors.

When a coprocessor instruction is being broadcast the ARM outputs the instruction while CPCLK and nCPWT are high. Coprocessor instructions are broadcast unaltered, but non-coprocessor instructions are replaced by the last coprocessor instruction broadcast with CPD[26] forced low (making it invalid as a coprocessor instruction).

When data or registers are being transferred between ARM and a coprocessor the data becomes valid while CPCLK and nCPWT are high. When data is being transferred from coprocessor to ARM the data must be valid at the falling edge of CPCLK.

7.7.3   Coprocessor control signals

The signals CPCLK, nCPOPC, nCPI, CPA, CPB and CPSPV are used to control the handshaking between the ARM and any coprocessors while instructions and data are transferred on CPD[31..0].

CPCLK is the coprocessor clock signal against which all coprocessor bus transactions are timed. Its frequency varies between MCLK and FCLK to track the CPU activity. This means that coprocessors must be able to operate at FCLK speeds.

nCPOPC (Coprocessor opcode fetch) is asserted as each instruction is fetched by the ARM and re-broadcast on the CPD[31..0] bus: valid coprocessor instructions are broadcast unaltered, but non-coprocessor instructions have CPD[26] forced low to signal their invalidity. Note that its name is a little misleading: this signal is for coprocessors, but it is asserted for *all* instruction fetches.

nCPI (Coprocessor instruction) is asserted by the ARM when any coprocessor instruction is executed (that is only if condition codes are satisfied): the ARM then waits for a response from the coprocessor chain (there may be several) signalled on the CPA and CPB lines.

CPA (Coprocessor Absent) is asserted immediately after nCPI by any coprocessor which can execute the instruction. CPA is sampled by ARM on the next occasion that CPCLK is low: if CPA is sampled low ARM will busy-wait until CPB becomes low and then complete the instruction; if it is high when sampled the ARM will abort the coprocessor instruction and take the undefined instruction trap. CPA must be tied high when no (external) coprocessors are present.

CPB (Coprocessor busy) may be asserted by the coprocessor to indicate that the instruction announced by ARM on CPD[31..0] cannot be executed by the coprocessor: CPB is driven high until the coprocessor ceases to be busy; CPB is driven low either immediately or after the coprocessor ceases to be busy. CPB is sampled when CPCLK and nCPI are both low. CPB must be tied high when no (external) coprocessors are present.

CPSPV (Coprocessor supervisor mode) indicates the CPU mode in which instructions broadcast to coprocessors were fetched: CPSPV is high in Supervisor, FIQ and IRQ modes and low for User mode. Coprocessors may use this information to prevent certain instructions from being executed in User mode. CPSPV changes while CPCLK and nCPWT are high.

In summary, when a coprocessor instruction is ready to execute nCPI, CPA and CPB are all sampled by both the ARM and coprocessors at the next rising edge of CPCLK – if all three are low, the instruction is committed for execution.

▤ 7.8   Bus enables and test inputs

The ARM600 and ARM610 have a number of pins devoted to enabling and disable various off-chip interface functions and for testing the device both after fabrication and once the device is in-circuit in a finished design.

7.8.1   The ARM600

The ARM600 has five bus control inputs known as ABE, DBE, CBE, MSE and CPE: these signals are active-high enable inputs for signals generated by ARM. Table 7.4 summarizes the relationship between the enable signals and the system signals they relate to.

Table 7.4 Relationship between enable and system signals

Enable signal	System signal
ABE	Address bus A[31..0]
DBE	Data bus D[31..0]
CBE	Control bus (nB/W, LOCK & nR/W)
MSE	Memory signals (nMREQ and SEQ)
CPE	Coprocessor bus (CPD[31..0], CPCLK, CPSPV, nCPI, nCPOPC and nCPWT)

Any bus enable input which is low will put the relevant ARM outputs into a high-impedance state. These signals may be used to control the presentation of ARM signals to common buses; in simple applications they will simply be strapped high.

A production test mode is supported by the nTEST pin: ARM600 enters a special test mode when this pin is driven low; it must be strapped high when the processor is in-circuit.

Finally, ARM600 supports the IEEE 1149.1-1990 JTAG Boundary Scan standard for in-circuit testing: the five pins TCK, TDI, TDO, TMS and nTRST are used to control the boundary scan circuitry. The IEEE JTAG standard allows devices which implement it to be connected together in a serial daisy-chain to allow both in-circuit device testing and continuity testing between devices. Consult the ARM600 datasheet for further information.

7.8.2   The ARM610

The ARM610 has subtly different bus control and test inputs. Three of the five bus enables are still present: ABE, DBE and MSE. The ARM600 control signal CPE is absent because, of course, there is no coprocessor bus to enable. CBE is also absent and is replaced by 'address latch enable' (ALE) which allows the address bus A[31..0] and nB/W, LOCK, and nR/W to be latched (and prevented from changing) when driven low; presumably this simplifies the design Apple has in mind.

The ARM610 also supports the IEEE JTAG Boundary Scan standard using the associated five pins; it also has a broader test interface for out-of-circuit testing: 17 pins known as TESTIN[16..0] and a further three pins known as TESTOUT[2..0] complete the test complement. The operation of this test interface is beyond the scope of this book.

7.9   Memory management, cache control and multi-processor support

The combination of the many separate bus enable inputs with flexible CPU clock control (including the nWAIT input) and the nMREQ and LOCK outputs provides enough control over the bus interface to allow modern ARM processors (that is ARM3 and later) to be employed in multiprocessor systems in conjunction with external logic.

The nMREQ signals from several processors might serve as inputs to a central bus arbitrator implemented in custom logic. The bus arbitrator would determine which of the processors or other bus claimants should gain control of the bus at any moment and exploit the bus enables and nWAIT inputs to the processors to stall those that were denied the bus. The LOCK signal from each processor must also be considered in order to ensure indivisible memory accesses to allow inter-processor communication.

7.10   Summary

The ARM processor family supports a simple and consistent bus interface for attachment to external memory and peripherals. Particular consideration has been given by the ARM designers to the needs of customers with low-power and low-cost requirements.

Sufficient CPU status signals and bus enables are available to allow ARMs to be connected almost gluelessly to commercial static memories and peripherals. Where dynamic memories must be supported an external DRAM controller will be required to multiplex address signals.

The presence of JTAG boundary scan circuitry in recent ARM processors substantially improves the in-circuit testability of these complex devices.

Multi-processor support is present in the form of the LOCK signal and the individual bus enables for each sub-group of bus signals, allowing an external arbitrator to determine which CPU is active on a shared bus from moment to moment.

8

ARM CPUs, derivatives and support ICs

8.1 Introduction

This chapter lists all the variants of ARM processor and support chips
which have been developed. Not all of these have been available commercially and some were designed for highly specific purposes. However, by examining the many variants of each ARM design it is possible to
see the direction of ARM development.

For each ARM variant a simple block diagram is provided, as well
as a summary of the ARM macrocells used to build each processor.

The chapter concludes with a look at possible future ARM processor
developments, especially the ARM7 processor core and its potential
derivatives.

8.2 Variants of the ARM CPU

The ARM CPUs are effectively divisible into two categories; the original
dynamic processors and the current static processors. In each category
there are both standalone CPUs and processors with other functions, such
as caches, coprocessor interface and memory management hardware,

integrated on to the chip.

8.2.1   The dynamic ARMs: ARM1, ARM2, ARM3

ARM1

The first ARM CPU, the ARM1, was successfully fabricated for the first time and proved to be fully functional in April 1985. A 3 μm fabrication process was used on the 25 000 transistor device. Although designed to operate with a 4 MHz clock, the device was found to still operate reliably at 8 MHz, twice the design speed; a tribute to the care which had gone into the device modelling, all of which was written in BASIC.

ARM2

Before the ARM CPU was employed in a complete computer system design a number of small refinements were undertaken: the multiply unit was added, so too was the coprocessor interface, and finally the device was shrunk to the next smaller fabrication process (2 μm) for good measure. The resulting device, known as ARM2, has been shipped in quantities of hundreds of thousands in Acorn Computer's Archimedes workstations, used mainly in Europe and the UK but also in Australasia. In these workstations it is used with its three support devices, the memory controller MEMC, the video controller VIDC and the I/O controller IOC.

The ARM2 was first shipped running at a clock rate of 8 MHz, but even at this relatively sedate speed still delivered about 4 MIPS when attached to (slow) 120 ns commercial dynamic RAM. Since then, ARM2 has been commercially offered in 10 MHz and 12 MHz speeds, still yielding a performance of about half the clock rate in MIPS.

ARM2 has been used in a number of commercial products besides Acorn's workstations:

- Radius Inc. used ARM2 in one of its first graphics accelerator products for the Apple Macintosh, the QuickColor NuBus card designed to accelerate QuickDraw graphics redrawing on colour Macintosh systems.
- MicroRobotics of Cambridge, England, used ARM2 in its robotics controllers widely used in the animation industry. *Teenage Mutant Ninja Turtles (The Movie)* used animatronic robot turtles which were controlled by an ARM-based real-time processor.

ARM3

The third ARM revision, the ARM3, was a significant upgrade in both design and fabrication technology. It was also the first time that the macrocell approach had been used in the design of an ARM processor. The ARM3 exploits the small size of the ARM2 CPU core and adds to it a 4 kbyte on-chip cache which provides cached data in a single clock cycle (see Figure 8.1). At the same time, the fabrication process was shrunk another couple of steps to allow a significant increase in clock rate.

The ARM3 comprises some 300 000 transistors, more than ten times as many as ARM2 and yet still small by contemporary microprocessor standards (the Intel 80486DX has roughly 1 200 000). ARM3 is capable of operating at 25 MHz when fabricated in a 1.2 μm process and at 33 MHz when fabricated in a 0.8 μm process. At these speeds it typically yields some 13–15 MIPS, yet still requires only relatively slow commercial DRAM.

Even with its transistor-hungry cache the ARM3 is still a compact device: so compact, in fact, that at the point of sealing the finished dies into standard ceramic pin-grid-array packages it was discovered that the die was too *small* to fit. A different package supplier was eventually chosen to resolve this rather unusual problem.

ARM3 has the great attraction that it may be retro-fitted into existing ARM2-based designs. While not pin-compatible (the ARM3 has many more pins to support its coprocessor interface) a simple printed circuit board can adapt the pinout to that of the ARM2 and allow it to be plugged into an ARM2 socket. A number of UK-based companies including Aleph One Ltd of Cambridge, UK offer such upgrades for the machines produced by Acorn Computers.

8.2.2   The first static ARM: ARM2aS

At about the same time as the ARM3 went into production a separate effort was underway to tackle a different aspect of the ARM's design: the use of dynamic logic. Many VLSI devices use dynamic logic for its simplicity, but it does require a minimum level of clock activity to be occuring in order for data not to be lost; this in turn mandates that the device must consume a non-trivial amount of power (related to the minimum clock rate) even when idling.

For modern applications, particularly portable ones, minimizing power consumption is a significant issue and static logic which doesn't require a minimum clock rate is preferred. Static logic may simply be stopped, by stopping the clock, whereupon it only consumes a meagre amount of power until the clock is re-enabled. No data is lost during this process.

The ARM2aS is an ARM2-compatible CPU core macrocell which is entirely static in its implementation: this device has never been commercially available as a standalone part, but a version of it does appear in the

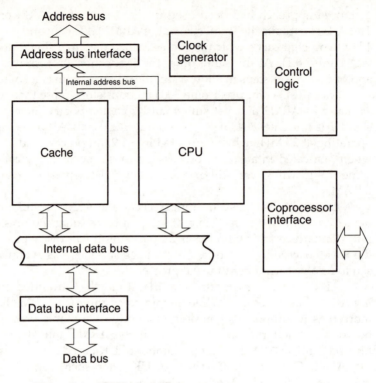

Figure 8.1   ARM3 block diagram

highly-integrated ARM250 device discussed later in this chapter. ARM2aS was intended to be used as the processor core of an integrated device, Hercules, in a handheld computer and communications device, which was never actually produced.

ARM2aS' main contribution to the development of ARMs was to move the devices from dynamic to static technology, and focus both marketing and development efforts on processors suitable for the emergent low-cost consumer and hand-held device market. It also contained a faster ALU unit. Sample ARM2aS devices were produced, using a 2 μm process. All subsequent ARM processors have supported static operation.

In terms of its features ARM2aS is more like ARM2 than subsequent ARMs. Like ARM2 it has a 26-bit address space, and only supports little-endian byte sex.

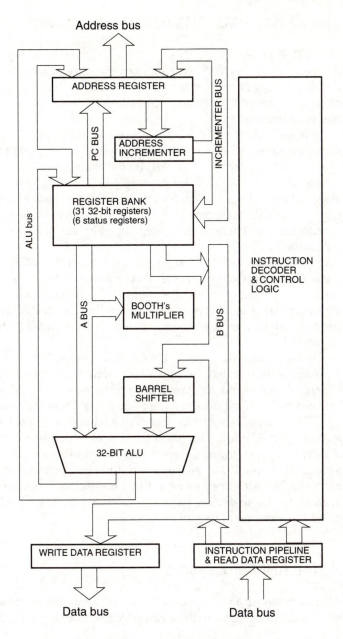

Figure 8.2 ARM6 core block diagram

8.2.3   The 32-bit ARMs: ARM6, ARM60, ARM61

The ARM6 series of RISC CPUs is the fourth generation of ARM devices. All are static ARMs, following on from the development of ARM2aS. The ARM6 processor core was developed before the launch of ARM Limited, although some of the devices incorporating it were completed after ARM had been founded.

When Advanced RISC Machines Ltd. was spun off from Acorn it rationalized the ARM part numbering system at the point of introduction of these devices: single-digit ARMs, for example ARM6, are CPU cores which are not available by themselves; two-digit part numbers are assigned to packaged cores, for example ARM60 and ARM61; and three-digit part numbers are assigned to complete processor designs with many architectural extensions integrated together, for example ARM600 and ARM610.

The ARM6 series differs significantly from the earlier ARMs in having a 32-bit address space rather than a 26-bit address space. This change leads to a number of major alterations to the architecture of the CPU core: condition flag and CPU mode bits can no longer occupy spare bits of the program counter, so new status registers and associated instructions must be created.

At the same time the 32-bit ARMs developed the ability to operate with either little-endian or big-endian memory, a feature which was significantly influenced by Apple Computer, whose traditional Motorola 680x0-based designs assumed the opposite endedness to earlier ARMs.

The standalone ARM6 core is available in two packaged variants: ARM60 and ARM61. The former has a new pinout which straightforwardly brings out the necessary bus and control signals; the latter is packaged in an 84-pin PLCC package with the same pinout and configuration as the earlier ARM2, allowing it to be retro-fitted to existing designs for evaluation. These devices have effectively replaced the ARM2 since they provide a superset of its functionality.

8.2.4   Future ARM processors

Although not yet announced by ARM Ltd, a number of obvious routes for development are open to the ARM processor family:

- Larger integrated caches, possibly with different associativity and/or organization
- Integration of the FPA with the CPU core
- Use of 'self-timed' or 'asynchronous' CPU cores (see below)
- Low-powered versions
- Multiple processors on one device

Larger cache

Since the addition of the 4 kbyte processor cache to the ARM3, such caches have become both larger and more commonplace. The macrocell approach to ARM processor design means that it would be easy for larger caches to be offered in integrated devices based on future ARM processor cores capable of supporting larger caches.

Lower power

Many components, particularly those intended for use in portable and battery-powered designs, are now available in low-power (3.3 V) variants. It is likely that any future ARM processor cores and derivatives will be offered in this lower voltage.

Integration density and fabrication size

The construction of larger caches is really only an issue of fabrication feature size: if the CPU core is smaller then more space is available for cache memory in the same die area, and that cache is in turn more dense. Integration of the FPA is similarly an issue of feature size: both the CPU core and the FPA will be smaller at reduced feature sizes, so a processor which includes both need not have a significantly larger die area.

Self-timed/asynchronous designs

Looking further into the future, advanced research by members of the ARM team provide clues to possible developments which may be incorporated into future ARM processors. Professor Stephen Furber of Manchester University, the original architect of the ARM1, continues to research new developments of the ARM. At the time of writing a 'self-timed' ARM was about to be experimentally fabricated: 'self-timing' means that no clock signal is used to control the flow of data through the CPU core; instead, the data flows through as fast as the fabrication process used allows, so smaller feature sizes directly yield increases in performance without the need to change clock frequencies.

Of course, the CPU must always ultimately be interfaced to memory; although a self-timed cache can easily be constructed to provide the first level of memory, high-density self-timed system memory is not yet commonplace. In the meantime, circuitry must be added to synchronise the core to the external memory clock whenever an off-chip access is required. It will be interesting to see what kind of performance improvements result from the self-timed approach (Pountain, 1993).

▤ 8.3   ARM derivatives and support ICs

This section discusses those ARM processors which comprise ARM processor cores integrated with other controller macrocells.

8.3.1   The ARM250: a highly integrated ARM-based computer

The ARM250 is the result of a design commission from Acorn Computers Ltd to produce a single-chip computer based on the 26-bit ARM2 architecture. It integrates on to a single chip the latest versions of the original four-chip ARM set, along with additional glue logic.

Requirements for the ARM250

During the 1980s Acorn manufactured a variety of desktop personal computers based on a four-chip set comprising ARM2, a memory controller known as MEMC1a, a video and sound controller known as VIDC1 and a glue logic and peripheral I/O device known as IOC. These four devices appeared together in hundreds of thousands of computers; the incentive driving the design of ARM250 was to reduce Acorn's costs in manufacturing such systems by placing all these controllers on the same chip as the CPU.

ARM250 components

The ARM250 integrates the static ARM2aS core, MEMC1a, VIDC1a, IOC and a further glue logic block known as IOEB, which allows cheap PC-compatible peripheral ICs to be attached directly to the IOC bus. The device is fabricated using a 1 μm feature size rather than the 2 μm features used for the previous (separately packaged) versions of these devices; VIDC1 originally appeared in a 2.4 μm process.

ARM2as is described above. The MEMC block acts as an interface between the ARM250 and external ROM and bus RAM. There is a 32-bit data bus and a 20-bit address bus (only 20 of the ARM250's 26 address space bits are brought out to pins). Up to 4 Mbyte of RAM can be addressed directly. MEMC also includes a logical to physical address translator, which allows the implementation of virtual memory and multi-tasking operations.

The VIDC1a video controller generates a high-resolution colour video display with a hardware cursor up to 32 pixels wide, and up to eight channels of stereo sound. A wide range of display formats are supported, with up to 8 bits per pixel and 4096 colours, using three 4-bit digital to analogue converters.

The I/O section of the ARM250 is based on Acorn's original IOC

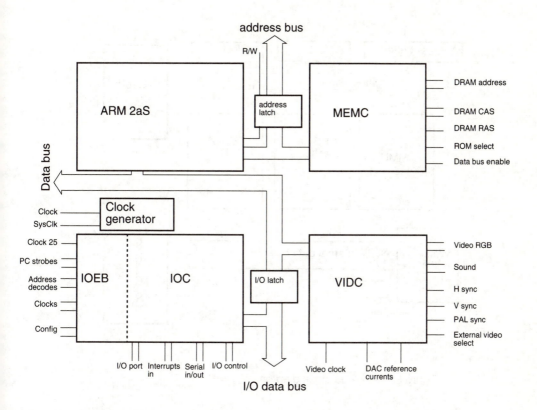

Figure 8.3   ARM250 block diagram

chip, with additional glue logic (IOEB on the block diagram) allowing the ARM250 to be interfaced to PC-compatible peripheral devices through standard ports.

The resulting ARM250 die is housed in a single 160-pin PQFP package and yet has more functionality and operates at higher clock frequencies than the four-chip set it replaces.

ARM250 as an example of the standard cell approach

ARM250 is a classic example of the 'building-block' or 'standard cell' approach to processor construction offered by Advanced RISC Machines, which operates under the name QuickDesign. Several existing devices have been arranged on a new die at a finer feature size and wired together to create the new chip, producing a customized and highly integrated processor offering better performance than the previous non-integrated implementation.

The advantages for Acorn, the customer who requested ARM250,

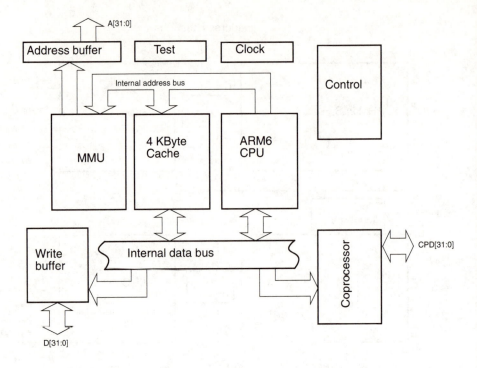

Figure 8.4 ARM600 block diagram

are clear: the single-chip implementation is simpler, more reliable and faster than the previous design while at the same time succeeding in being cheaper to produce. The resulting computer requires only some external ROM, RAM and a single PC-compatible peripheral chip to yield a 6 MIPS RISC workstation, the A3010, which Acorn retails for less than $1000.

8.3.2   The ARM600 and ARM610

As we have seen earlier in this book, the most highly integrated ARMs based on the ARM6 core available at the time of writing are the ARM600-series devices. Their development, in conjunction with Apple Computer, looks set to lead to the wide availability of ARM-based products in the world market. The two current devices differ in their packaging and functionality.

ARM600

The ARM600 comprises an ARM6 core, a 4 kbyte cache, an 8-word write buffer and a memory management unit along with an external coprocessor interface to support the FPA10 floating point coprocessor; it is packaged in a 160-pin Plastic Quad Flat Pack (PQFP). The memory management hardware is intended to facilitate the design of truly object-oriented systems (see Figure 8.4)

ARM610

The ARM610 has the same computational elements as the ARM600 but has no external coprocessor interface. It can therefore be packaged in a much smaller device, saving further space and reducing the cost, both desirable options for its target market of low-cost consumer portable devices. The actual package chosen is the extra-small 144-pin Thin Quad Flat Pack (TQFP) for inclusion in Apple Computer's personal digital assistant (pocket-sized portable computer/organizer) known as Newton.

▤ 8.4   Support devices

This section examines the two ARM support devices currently available as standalone devices, the floating-point accelerator FPA10 and the video controller VIDC20.

8.4.1   The ARM Floating Point Accelerator (FPA10)

The first single-chip coprocessor to be produced for the ARM family was the floating-point accelerator known as FPA10. This device performs IEEE 754-conformant floating-point arithmetic at single, double or extended precision (80 bits) at up to 5 MFLOPs when clocked at 25 MHz; it is housed in a 68-pin PLCC package and is fully static, consuming around 2.5 mA/MHz (that is about 63 mA at 25 MHz).

The FPA10 implements a subset of the ARM floating-point instruction set (discussed in Chapter 4) in silicon. The balance of the floating-point instructions are performed in software through the use of the Undefined Instruction trap, which passes on to support software any instructions obeyed by the CPU which are not implemented in hardware by the FPA10. Together the hardware and software fully implement the IEEE standard for binary floating-point arithmetic.

The design of the FPA10 is intended to maximize the performance/power, performance/cost, and performance/die size ratios while providing balanced floating point versus integer performance for ARM-based

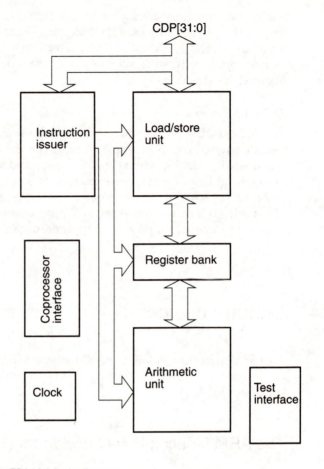

Figure 8.5 FPA10 block diagram

systems, according to ARM Ltd.

RISC principles and the FPA10

RISC principles have been employed to ensure this, along with other advanced design techniques. Firstly, only the core floating point instructions are implemented in the FPA10. These are: basic arithmetic operations, compare, absolute value, round to integral value, floating-point to integer and integer to floating-point conversions, status operations and most load and store operations. Other instructions, including trigonometric instructions and packed loads and stores, are handed to the support code through the Undefined Instruction trap, as are all operations on denormalized numbers, infinities and NaNs (non-numbers), and exceptions other than the inexact exception. By not implementing these less common instructions in hardware a much smaller and less complex chip than would otherwise have been necessary was constructed.

Internal structure of the FPA10

The FPA10 has an 81-bit internal data path between its five main functional blocks. The first block, the coprocessor interface, arbitrates instructions with the CPU and tells the load/store unit when to proceed with data transfers. Like their integer counterparts, all ARM floating-point instructions are conditional. The conditions are evaluated in the CPU and only valid instructions are passed to the FPA.

From the 32-bit coprocessor interface the incoming instruction is transferred to the instruction issuer. This evaluates the instruction to see whether it should be passed to the arithmetic unit or the load/store unit. If an instruction is failed after it has been issued to the load/store or arithmetic units, it is cancelled and the data thrown away; if a prefetched instruction is cancelled after a branch occurs the same happens. The instruction issuer also obviates some data dependency hazards by preventing issue of the instruction until the hazard has been cleared. Instructions are issued in order and one per cycle.

The load/store unit converts data between the 32-bit coprocessor data bus and the FPA's internal 81-bit format. All numbers are checked and those which are found not to be normalized or zero are flagged to be passed to the software FP emulation code.

The register bank contains eight registers which use the FPA's 81-bit format. Control logic deals with data dependencies and further logic supports register-forwarding. An additional 33-bit temporary register is used to transfer intermediate results of FIX, FLT and compare instructions between the load-store and arithmetic units.

The arithmetic unit has a four-stage pipeline, whose stages are Prepare, Calculate, Align and Round. Some instructions can move through the pipeline in half-cycle steps, thus taking only two cycles to complete.

FPA10 compared to other floating point units

At around 130 000 transistors the FPA10 is simple enough to be fabricated cheaply when packaged in its modest 68-pin PLCC package. It is much smaller than CISC floating point accelerators; for example, the Cyrix Fas-Math chip, an Intel 80387 equivalent, has approximately 375 000 transistors.

Using FPA10 with ARM integer processors

The FPA10 is intended to work with all ARM processors with a coprocessor interface, (for example ARM3, ARM600). The ARM60 and ARM2 use their data bus as the corprocessor bus. ARM-based systems wishing to offer optional floating-point performance can simply provide a socket into which this device may be plugged, as Acorn Computers does in some of its more recent RISC workstations.

8.4.2   A second-generation video and audio controller: VIDC20

We saw earlier that the ARM250 integrated a number of devices designed by Acorn Computers for their earlier range of RISC workstations; a second generation of one of these devices, VIDC20, is now in production and offers considerably improved features suited to the next generation of desktop computers.

The second generation video controller, VIDC20, does not itself contain an ARM CPU but instead is designed to be attached to the data bus of an ARM-based system where it can exploit Direct Memory Access (DMA)

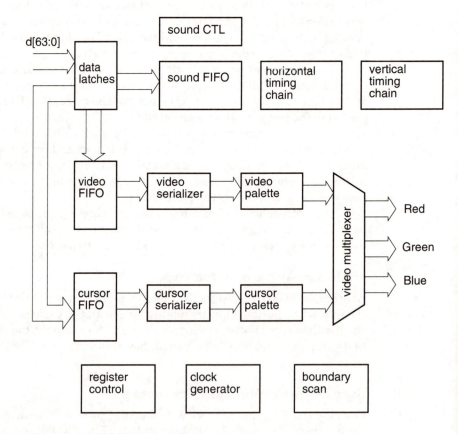

Figure 8.6 VIDC20 block diagram

to read system memory and retrieve graphics and sound data placed there by the CPU. It has a 64-bit data bus which requires two banks of interleaved RAM, although it can also work in 32-bit mode.

VIDC20 is a single-chip video frame buffer controller and RAM-DAC along with a digital audio interface and stereo digital-to-analogue audio playback channels.

VIDC20 can generate high-resolution colour video displays at pixel rates of up to 100 MHz in any of 1, 2, 4, 8, 16 or 32 bits-per-pixel. It can support video modes at a bandwidth of up to 80 Mbytes per second. In 64-bit mode it supports interlaced displays of up to 640 by 512 pixels. Its 8-bit digital-to-analogue converters give a choice from 16 million colours.

At the same time it can play back stereo 16-bit CD-quality digital audio or stereo 8-bit sampled audio through its audio circuitry.

VIDC20 can be interfaced either to commercial DRAM, specialised VRAM video memory or both to allow a variety of cost/performance trade-offs. Only a handful of external components are required to connect the device to a colour monitor or TV modulator.

8.5 Summary

The ARM processor has developed considerably since its humble beginnings. The current range of processors based around the ARM6 processor core offer a wide range of solutions for system designs where the ARM virtues of small size, low power consumption and high size/performance and price/performance ratios are useful.

A range of additional support macrocells which can be built on to the same devices provide flexibility in adding functionality. Further additional functionality is available in the form of the support devices FPA10 and VIDC20 which offer features which have not yet been integrated into any single-device ARM offering.

There are several logical directions ARM's research and development could take; in addition to the prospects for yet smaller or more highly integrated devices, interesting research into areas such as asynchronous computing could provide a further new direction for the company.

9

The ARM floating point instruction set

9.1 Introduction

This chapter examines the ways in which the ARM architecture deals with floating point data types and the arithmetic and data transfer instructions which support them. It examines the development of ARM floating point support, when such operations were performed entirely in software, and the subsequent development of the FPA10 floating point coprocessor device which has recently become available.

Each of the ARM floating point instructions is considered and the floating point Status Register (FPSR) is described in detail. Floating point exceptions are discussed at the end of the chapter.

9.2 Support for floating point arithmetic in the ARM architecture

The ARM CPUs produced to date are not themselves capable of executing floating point instructions; instead the ARM2, ARM3 and ARM600 CPUs all support the idea of 'coprocessors', optional devices which attach to the

CPU and accelerate floating point operations.

Where a coprocessor is not present, the ARM's 'Undefined instruction' trap allows a software program (the 'floating point emulator' or FPE) to simulate the behaviour of the real coprocessor when floating point instructions are encountered during execution. Clearly this results in reduced performance compared to the 'real' coprocessor hardware, but it also results in significantly reduced cost: a compromise which is a foundation of the ARM strategy.

During Spring 1993 the first hardware ARM floating point coprocessor, known as FPA10, became available: this device implements a subset of the ARM floating point instruction set in hardware and uses a simplified floating point emulator package to perform the other operations.

The FPA10 provides a floating point performance of between one and 2.5 MFLOPs at a clock frequency of 25 MHz. FPA10 has an 81-bit internal data path and register bank which allows it to perform floating point arithmetic at IEEE Single, Double, and Extended precisions to conform to the ANSI/IEEE 754-1985 standard when used with the appropriate floating point support software.

Whether software or hardware is used to implement the floating point subsystem in any particular ARM-based design, the programming model remains the same. The only important functional difference between software and hardware implementations is their relative performance.

9.3   Floating point programmer's model

The ARM floating point model comprises eight general-purpose extended precision registers known as f0..f7. The registers provide a working precision of 80 bits, sub-divided into a 64-bit mantissa, a 15-bit exponent and a sign bit.

A floating point status register, FPSR, maintains flags indicating the state of the floating point subsystem. The FPSR contains flags and mask bits for exceptions, a version number, and other control bits. The FPSR can be used to distinguish between different floating point implementations and to enable or disable particular features.

A further register, the floating point control register (FPCR), is present in the FPA10. This register should only be accessed by the floating point emulator support software and not by user programs.

9.4   IEEE arithmetic fundamentals

All floating point operations conforming to the IEEE standard operate as though they were computed to infinite precision and then rounded in one of several ways indicated by the instruction. The following 'rounding modes' are supported:

- Round to nearest (default)
- Round towards $+\infty$ (P)
- Round towards $-\infty$ (M)
- Round towards zero (Z)

In the ARM floating point implementation all computation is performed on the eight general-purpose registers and a limited set of instructions is available for loading and storing values in those registers. It is important to note that the registers are *all* directly addressable by all instructions, as opposed to the stack-like implementations used by Intel, for example.

Floating point values may be stored in ARM memory in one of the five formats shown in Table 9.1.

Table 9.1 Floating point formats

Name	Storage size (bits)	Suffix
IEEE Single Precision	32	(S)
IEEE Double Precision	64	(D)
IEEE Extended Precision	96	(E)
Packed Decimal	96	(P)
Expanded Packed Decimal	128	(EP)

The formats are selected by appending the suffix shown to an instruction mnemonic in front of the rounding mode (see above). The last two formats are mutually exclusive. A control flag in the FPSR is used to determine which sort of BCD format is in use. Figures 9.2–9.6 show the way each format is implemented

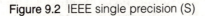

Figure 9.2 IEEE single precision (S)

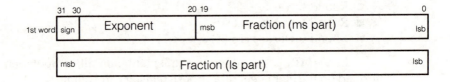

Figure 9.3 IEEE double precision (D)

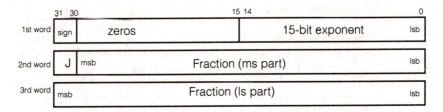

Figure 9.4 Extended precision

Figure 9.5 Packed decimal (P)

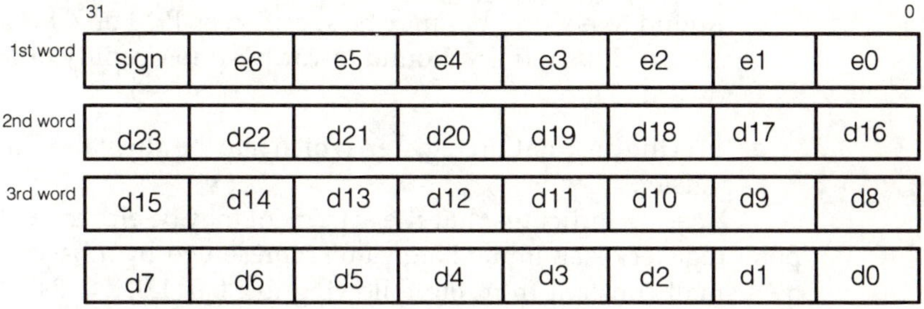

31							0
sign	e6	e5	e4	e3	e2	e1	e0

1st word

d23	d22	d21	d20	d19	d18	d17	d16

2nd word

d15	d14	d13	d12	d11	d10	d9	d8

3rd word

d7	d6	d5	d4	d3	d2	d1	d0

Figure 9.6 Expanded packed decimal (EP)

The ARM floating point model includes instructions to perform a variety of standard arithmetic operations on values stored in the floating point registers with a specified rounding mode and degree of precision. Some implementations may also provide high-speed arithmetic operations at lower than normal precision, but this is not mandatory and should not be assumed.

9.4.1   Floating point data operations

The data operations which form the core of the ARM floating point arithmetic standard are sub-divided into two groups: those which take a single operand, known as 'monadic' operations, and those which take two operands, known as 'dyadic' operations. In all cases the operands are either floating point registers or immediate constants.

The monadic operations supported by the ARM floating point system are summarized in the Table 9.2. The remainder of this section describes each of the instructions in turn.

Floating point data operation syntax

Monadic operations take only one floating point argument and returning a floating point result; they are expressed in Assembly language as follows:

MonadicOpCode{cond}precision{round} Fd, Fm | *#value*

where:

- *MonadicOpCode* is one of MVF, MNF, ABS, RND, SQT, LOG, LGN, EXP, SIN, COS, TAN, ASN, ACS, ATN, URD or NRM
- *{cond}* is an optional integer CPU condition code
- *precision* specifies the destination precision and must be one of

'S', 'D' or 'E' for Single (32-bit), Double (64-bit) or Extended (80-bit)

■ {*round*} optionally specifies the rounding mode, which defaults to 'Round to nearest' but may be specified as P, M or Z for Round towards Plus infinity, Round towards Minus infinity or Round towards Zero.

■ Fd is the destination register, which may be any valid floating point register.

Fm | #*value* indicates that the argument may be either a valid floating point register or an immediate value represented by a hash (#) followed by a small constant from the following list: 0.0, 1.0, 2.0, 3.0, 4.0, 5.0, 0.5, 10.0.

Table 9.2 Monadic operations

Mnemonic	Name	Operation performed
MVF	Move	Fd := Fm
MNF	Move negated	Fd := – Fm
ABS	Absolute value	Fd := ABS(Fm)
RND	Round to integer	Fd := integer value of Fm
SQT	Square root	Fd := square root of Fm
LOG	Logarithm to base 10	Fd := $\log_{10}$ of Fm
LGN	Logarithm to base e	Fd := $\log_e$ of Fm
EXP	Exponent	Fd := e^{Fm}
SIN	Sine	Fd := sine of Fm
COS	Cosine	Fd := cosine of Fm
TAN	Tangent	Fd := tangent of Fm
ASN	ArcSine	Fd := arcsine of Fm
ACS	ArcCosine	Fd := arccosine of Fm
ATN	ArcTangent	Fd := arctangent of Fm
URD	Unnormalized round	Fd := integer value of Fm, unnormalized
NRM	Normalize	Fd := normalized Fm (for results of URD only)

Behaviour of data operations

All data operation instructions, whether monadic or dyadic, accept operands at *any* precision. If executed they largely perform the relevant operation at full working precision (81 bits) and then return the result at a
specified precision, optionally rounded using one of four 'rounding
modes'. A precision for the result must *always* be specified, but the default
rounding mode 'Round to nearest' is likely to need to be overridden only
very infrequently.We now look at each instruction in turn.

MVF   Move

MNF   Move negated

The Move Floating and Move Negated Floating instructions are similar to
their counterparts in the integer instruction set. Values may be moved
from register to register, or constants loaded into registers, with a change
of sign at the same time when MNF is used.

Here are some examples:

```
MVFS        f0, f1 ; f0 := f1

MNFS        f3, f7 ; f3 := -f7

MVFD        f1, # 4.0; f1 := 4.0

MNFE        f2, # 1.0; f2 := -1.0
```

It is important to appreciate that the small constant option is not the
only way to load constants into registers; these constants are specially
optimized for quick loading. Other constants can be initialized by the
Assembler into memory and then loaded using the floating point memory to register instructions discussed below.

ABS   Absolute value

RND   Round to integer

Absolute value and Round to integer both perform simple operations on
the operand:

- ABS makes the sign of the result positive irrespective of the sign of
  the operand.
- RND rounds to an integer using the specified rounding mode, but
  returns the result as a *floating point number.*

For example:

```
ABSS        f2, #5.0      ; f2 := 5.0

RNDD        f7, #0.5      ; f7 := 0.0
```

The default rounding mode (round to nearest) leads to the important distinction shown below:

```
RNDE        f0, f1 ; f0 := nearest integer to f1

RNDEZ       f0, f1 ; f0 := 'integer part' of f1
```

The distinction between the nearest integer and the integer part is frequently significant, but only the former is yielded in the default case.

The combinations RNDEM and RNDEP give what are sometimes known as the 'floor' and 'ceiling' of the second operand.

RND should not to be confused with FIX (see below) which turns a floating point value into a 32-bit integer value.

SQT	Square root	$Fd := $ square root of Fm
LOG	Logarithm to base 10	$Fd := \log_{10}$ of Fm
LGN	Logarithm to base e	$Fd := \log_e$ of Fm
EXP	Exponent	$Fd := e^{Fm}$
SIN	Sine	$Fd := $ sine of Fm
COS	Cosine	$Fd := $ cosine of Fm
TAN	Tangent	$Fd := $ tangent of Fm
ASN	ArcSine	$Fd := $ arcsine of Fm
ACS	ArcCosine	$Fd := $ arccosine of Fm
ATN	ArcTangent	$Fd := $ arctangent of Fm

These are the standard monadic mathematical functions. They accept arguments of any size and attempt range reduction on those which are inappropriate. Here are some examples of these instructions:

```
SQTE        f4, #4.0      ; f4 := 2.0

LOGS        f6, #10.0     ; f6 := 1.0

LGNS        f1, #5.0      ; f1 := LGN(5.0) =
                                1.6094379...

EXPD        f2, #2.0      ; f2 := e² = 7.3890561...

MVFS        f0, # 0.0     ;
SINS        f1, f0        ; f1 := 0.0
COSS        f2, f0        ; f2 := 1.0
ACSS        f3, f2        ; f3 := 0.0
```

```
URD    Unnormalized round        Fd := integer value of
                                    Fm, unnormalized

NRM    Normalize                 Fd := normalized Fm (for
                                    results of URD only)
```

The Unnormalized Round (URD) and Normalize (NRM) instructions together have the same effect as Round (RND); however, implementation issues mean that this operation may be more efficiently performed by breaking it down into two stages. NRM will only produce a meaningful result when supplied with the result of an URD as its argument, and the result of an URD should only be processed by an NRM.

Dyadic floating point data operations

The dyadic operations again include a typical set of common mathematical functions. Some operations mirror their integer counterparts in familiar ways: for example, with 'reverse' instruction forms

Table 9.3 Dyadic operations

Mnemonic	Name	Operation performed
ADF	Add	$Fd := Fn + Fm$
MUF	Multiply	$Fd := Fn * Fm$
SUF	Subtract	$Fd := Fn - Fm$
RSF	Reverse subtract	$Fd := Fm - Fn$
DVF	Divide	$Fd := Fn / Fm$
RDF	Reverse divide	$Fd := Fm / Fn$
POW	Power	$Fd := Fn^{Fm}$
RPW	Reverse power	$Fd := Fm^{Fn}$
RMF	Remainder	$Fd := $ IEEE remainder of Fn / Fm
FML	'Fast' multiply	$Fd := Fn * Fm$ (single precision)
FDV	'Fast' divide	$Fd := Fn / Fm$ (single precision)
FRD	'Fast' reverse divide	$Fd := Fm / Fn$ (single precision)
POL	Polar angle	$Fd := $ ArcTan(Fn/Fm), but see text

Dyadic operations accept two floating point arguments and return a floating point result; they are written in Assembly language as follows:

```
DyadicOpCode{cond}precision{round} Fd, Fn, Fm | #value
```

where:

- *DyadicOpCode* is one of ADF, MUF, SUF, RSF, DVF, RDF, POW, RPW, RMF, FML, FDV, FRD or POL
- {*cond*} is an optional integer CPU condition code
- *precision* specifies the destination precision and must be one of S, D or E for Single (32-bit), Double (64-bit) or Extended (80-bit)
- {*round*} optionally specifies the rounding mode which defaults to Round to nearest but may be specified as P, M or Z for Round towards Plus infinity, Round towards Minus infinity or Round towards Zero.
- Fd, and Fn are any valid floating point register; Fd is the destination, Fn an operand.
- <Fm | #*value*> indicates that the argument may be either a valid floating point register or an immediate value represented by a hash (#) followed by a small constant from the following list: 0.0, 1.0, 2.0, 3.0, 4.0, 5.0, 0.5, 10.0.

The instructions for addition, subtraction, multiplication, division, remainder and power scarcely need any introduction.

The 'reverse' forms of the subtract, divide and power operations exist to allow small constants which are available in place of register Fm to be subtracted from, divided into or raised to a power; this is discussed in more detail below.

The 'fast' forms of multiply, divide and reverse divide are only defined to operate on single-precision arguments; these instructions may or may not execute more quickly on any particular implementation. The FPA10, for example, implements fast multiply (FML) in fewer cycles than Multiply Floating (MUF) but Fast Divide (FDV) and Fast Reverse Divide (FRD) take the same amount of time as Divide Floating (DVF) and Reverse Divide Floating (RDF).

The Polar Angle (POL) instruction computes the Fortran library function ArcTan2, which is the polar angle from the positive *x*-axis to the line joining the origin to (Fn, Fm).

Here are some examples using the monadic and dyadic floating point instructions introduced so far:

- Addition

```
        MVFS        f1, # 2.0;

        ADFS        f2, f1, #1.0; f2 := 3.0
```

- Multiplication

```
        MVFD           f5, # 10.0

        MUFD           f5, f5, f5; f5 := 100.0
```

■ Addition and logarithms

```
        LOGS           f6, #2.0; f6 := log10(2.0)

        LOGS           f7, #5.0; f7 := log10(5.0)

        ADFS           f5, f6, f7; f5 := 1.0 = log10(10)
```

■ Divide and Reverse divide

```
        MVFD           f0, # 2.0;

        DVFD           f2, f0, #3.0; f2 := 0.66666666...

        RDFD           f3, f0, #3.0; f3 := 1.5
```

■ Remainder

```
        MVFS           f4, # 5.0;

        MUFS           f4, f4, f4; f4 := 25.0

        RMFS           f5, f4, # 4.0; f5 := 1.0
```

■ Polar angle

```
        MNFD           f0, #1.0; f0 := -1

        MVFD           f1, #1.0; fo := +1

        POLD           f2, f0, f1; f2 := 3πi/4 = 2.35619
```

9.4.2   Floating point single data transfer instructions

The floating point register transfer instructions exist in single- and multiple-register forms, just like the ARM's integer LDR/LDM and STR/STM instructions. The single-register transfer instructions provide the 'Load floating' and 'Store floating' operations, which allow values to be moved between memory and the coprocessor registers. These instructions are all aliases for 'coprocessor data transfer' instructions and are translated automatically during assembly into LDC/STC instructions.

The instructions in this group are:

```
LDF{cond}format Fd,addressing_mode

STF{cond}format Fd,addressing_mode
```

where:

- {cond} is an optional integer CPU condition code
- format indicates the memory format and must be one of S, D, E or P for Single precision (one 32-bit word), Double precision (two words), Extended precision (three words) or Packed decimal (either three or four words according to the configuration of the EP flag in the FPSR).
- Fd is the destination and may be any valid floating point register.
- addressing_mode determines the source of the address and must be one of the entries in Table 9.4.

Table 9.4 Addressing modes

Style	Type	Offset
[Rn]	Pre-indexed	Zero
[Rn, #expression]{!}	Pre-indexed	± expression
[Rn], #expression	Post-indexed	± expression

where the expression is divisible by four and in the range ±1020.

Post-indexed addressing is always assembled with write-back of the base register without an explicit '!' being required; R15 (PC) must not be used as the base register when post-indexed addressing is used.

Rounding and precision

When a value is stored to memory using STF the value is 'rounded to nearest' to the specified destination precision or is already precise if the destination has sufficient precision. If another rounding mode is required it may be applied with an earlier data operation (including MVFx fp_reg, fp_reg); no additional rounding error is then introduced by this instruction, so the IEEE requirement of rounding only once is not compromised.

9.4.3 Floating point multiple data transfer instructions

The load/store multiple register instructions allow between one and four floating point registers to be transferred from/to memory with a single instruction. These operations are valuable when context-switching obliges many registers to be saved. The limitation on the number of registers which may be transferred is imposed to keep the maximum execution time of the instruction at a par with the longest integer instruction, an integer load/store multiple.

The value is transferred as three words of data per register; the data format is not defined and may change, so the only valid operation is to transfer the data back using the opposite instruction from the same implementation. The data stored in memory must not be used or altered by any user process.

The syntax of these instructions in assembly language takes one of two forms: the first resembles the single-register data transfer instructions, and the second resembles the integer multiple-register instructions and is suitable for stack operations.

Memory address form

```
LDF{cond} Fd, count, addressing_mode

STF{cond} Fd, count, addressing_mode
```

where:

- {cond} is an optional integer CPU condition code.
- count is the number of registers to transfer. Registers are always transferred in ascending order and wrap around at register f7.
- Fd is the destination and may be any valid floating point register.
- addressing_mode determines the source of the address and must be one of the entries in Table 9.5.

Table 9.5 Addressing modes

Style	Type	Offset
[Rn]	Pre-indexed	Zero
[Rn, #expression]{!}	Pre-indexed	±expression
[Rn], #expression	Post-indexed	± expression

where the expression is divisible by four and in the range ±1020 to .

Post-indexed addressing is always assembled with write-back of the base register without an explicit '!' being required; R15 (PC) must not be used as the base register when post-indexed addressing or explicit write-back with pre-indexed addressing is used.

Stack operation form

```
LFM{cond}<FD|EA> Fd, count, [Rn]{!}
```

```
SFM{cond}<FD|EA> Fd, count, [Rn]{!}
```

With this syntax a two-letter suffix of the same style as that for integer instructions must be appended to indicate the type of stack in use; the options are summarized in Table 9.6.

Table 9.6 Stack operation options

Name	Syntax
Post-increment load	LFMFD
Pre-decrement load	LFMEA
Post-increment store	SFMEA
Pre-decrement store	SFMFD

- *count* is the number of registers to transfer. Registers are always transferred in ascending order and wrap around at register f7.
- {!} optionally specifies write-back of the base register Rn. If Rn is R15 (PC) write back must not be specified.

9.4.4   Floating point register transfer instructions

This group of instructions allows registers to be transferred between the CPU and the coprocessor; both the conversion between floating point and integer formats and access to the coprocessor's FPSR and FPCR are supported by this group:

```
FLT{cond}precision{round} Fn, Rd
```

```
FIX{cond}{round} Rd, Fm
```

- {*cond*} is an optional integer CPU condition code
- *precision* specifies the destination precision and must be one of S, D or E for Single (32-bit), Double (64-bit) or Extended (80-bit)
- {*round*} optionally specifies the rounding mode which defaults to Round to nearest but may be specified as P, M or Z for Round towards Plus infinity, Round towards Minus infinity or Round towards Zero.
- Fn and Fm are any valid floating point register.
- Rd is any valid integer register except r15 (PC).

It is *not* legitimate to use constants in place of Fm with the FIX instruction; in any case a MOV instruction loads integer constants much more efficiently.

9.4.5   Floating point compare instructions

The compare instructions allow floating point numbers to be compared either directly or with the second operand negated. Furthermore, they may be compared either with or without exception handling if the operands are 'unordered', that is they are 'Not A Number' (NaN) in the IEEE specification.

The syntax of this group of instructions is as follows:

CMF{*cond*} Fn, Fm

CNF{*cond*} Fn, Fm

CMFE{*cond*} Fn, Fm

CNFE{*cond*} Fn, Fm

Fn and *Fm* are the two operands and may be any valid floating point register (there is no direct result).

The forms with the suffix E enable exception handling.

Results of comparison instructions

The ARM flags N, Z, C, V are set after the comparison, according to the state of the AC bit in the FPSR, as shown in Tables 9.7 and 9.8.

Table 9.7 AC clear

Flag	Meaning
N	Less than, that is Fn less than Fm or –Fm
Z	Equal
C	Greater than or equal, that is Fn greater than or equal to Fm or –Fm
V	Unordered

When testing IEEE predicates the CMF instruction should be used to test for equality (that is when a BEQ or BNE will follow it) or to test for unorderedness. The CMFE instruction should be used for all other tests (that is those followed by BGT, BGE, BLT or BLE). The exception handling

Table 9.8 AC set

Flag	Meaning
N	Less than
Z	Equal
C	Greater than or equal or unordered
V	Unordered

variants CMFE/CNFE produce an exception if the operands are unordered, that is at least one operand is a NaN; the non-exception handling variants only produce an exception when at least one operand is a *signalling* NaN.

Support for exceptions is dependent on the host language and operating system: exceptions are signalled through the 'Undefined instruction' trap and dealt with by the floating point support software. Chapter 5 discusses exceptions in more detail.

9.4.6   A floating point programming example

In order to demonstrate the floating point instructions in action the following example program has been included. It calculates and displays Mandlebrot functions and has been compiled from C. The program assumes direct access to a 640 by 480 display which stores an 8-bit pixel per byte, that is XGA style in PC terminology.

It is interesting to note the particular similarity between the C and Assembler versions of the innermost loop, shown highlighted in bold below. Note also that the C compiler uses the symbols 'a1..a4', 'v1..v4' and others as aliases for registers; this is achieved by means of the RN directive in a header file which is not shown here.

```
/* FPA Mandelbrot */

#include <stdio.h>

#define ZOOM 256
#define TOX -1.252
#define TOY +0.342
#define SIZE 0.01
#define SIZESTEP 0.8
#define BIGNO 1E8

int main( int argc, char *argv[] )
            {
                        /* expect 640 x 480 x 8 XGA-style */
                        unsigned char *screen;
                        double x, y, a, b;
                        double tox, toy;
                        double size;
                        double x2, y2, xy, twoxy, x2addy2,
                                        x2suby2, bigno;
                        int count;
                        int col, row;
                        int zoom;

    if( argc == 3 )
            {
                        sscanf( argv[1], "%f", &tox );
                        sscanf( argv[2], "%f", &toy );

            }
    else
            {
                        tox = TOX;
                        toy = TOY;

            }

    bigno = BIGNO;

    while( 1 )
            {
                        size = SIZE;
                        for( zoom = ZOOM; --zoom >= 0; )
                        {
                        screen = (unsigned char *)((32*1024-
                                320)*1024);
                        b = toy - (double)(240*size);

                        for( col = 480; --col >= 0; )
                        {
                        b = b + size;
```

```
a = tox - (double)(320*size);

for( row = 640; --row >= 0; )
{
a = a + size;
count = 128;

x = a;
y = b;
do
{
x2 = x * x;
y2 = y * y;
xy = x * y;
x2suby2 = x2 - y2;
twoxy = xy + xy;
x = x2suby2 + a;
x2addy2 = x2 + y2;
y = twoxy + b;
}
while( x2addy2 < bigno && --count != 0 );

*(screen++) = (unsigned char)count;
}
}
size = size * SIZESTEP;
}

} /* while */
return 0;
}
```

This is the Assembler output produced by the above program:

```
; generated by Norcroft ARM C vsn 4.41 (Advanced RISC Machines)
[Jan 12 1993]
                AREA  |C$$code|, CODE, READONLY
                        |x$codeseg|

                DCB         &6d,&61,&69,&6e
                DCB         &00,&00,&00,&00
                DCD         &ff000008

                IMPORT      |__rt_stkovf_split_small|
                IMPORT      sscanf
                EXPORT      main
main
                MOV         ip,sp
                STMDB       sp!,{a1,a2,v1-v4,fp,ip,lr,pc}
                SUB         fp,ip,#4
                STFE        f7,[sp,#-&c]!
                STFE        f6,[sp,#-&c]!
                STFE        f5,[sp,#-&c]!
                STFE        f4,[sp,#-&c]!
                CMP         sp,sl
                BLLT        |__rt_stkovf_split_small|
                MOV         v1,a2
                SUB         sp,sp,#&30
                CMP         a1,#3
                BNE         |L000068.J4.main|
                LDR         a1,[v1,#4]
                ADD         a3,sp,#8
                ADD         a2,pc,#L000064-.-8
                BL          sscanf
                LDR         a1,[v1,#8]!
                MOV         a3,sp
                ADD         a2,pc,#L000064-.-8
                BL          sscanf
                B           |L000078.J6.main|
L000064
                DCB         &25,&66,&00,&00
|L000068.J4.main|
                LDFD        f0,[pc,#L0000b8-.-8]
                STFD        f0,[sp,#8]
                LDFD        f0,[pc,#L0000c0-.-8]
                STFD        f0,[sp,#0]
|L000078.J6.main|
                LDFD        f7,[pc,#L0000c8-.-8]
                LDFD        f0,[pc,#L0000d0-.-8]
                STFD        f0,[sp,#&28]
                MOV         v4,#&100
                MOV         v3,#&fb0000
                ADD         v3,v3,#&1000000
```

```
                    LDFD            f0,[pc,#L0000d8-.-8]
                    STFD            f0,[sp,#&20]
                    MOV             v2,#&1e0
                    MOV             v1,#&280
                    MOV             lr,#&80
                    LDFD            f0,[pc,#L0000e0-.-8]
                    STFD            f0,[sp,#&18]
|L0000ac.J7.main|
                    LDFD            f0,[sp,#&28]
                    MOV             a2,v4
                    B               |L00018c.J10.main|
L0000b8
                    DCD             &bff40831,&26e978d5
L0000c0
                    DCD             &3fd5e353,&f7ced917
L0000c8
                    DCFD            1e8
L0000d0
                    DCFD            0.01
L0000d8
                    DCFD            240.0
L0000e0
                    DCFD            0.8
|L0000e8.J9.main|
                    MOV             ip,v3
                    LDFD            f1,[sp,#&20]
                    MUFD            f2,f0,f1
                    LDFD            f1,[sp,#0]
                    SUFD            f1,f1,f2
                    MOV             a4,v2
                    LDFD            f2,[pc,#L000110-.-8]
                    MUFD            f2,f0,f2
                    STFD            f2,[sp,#&10]
                    B               |L00017c.J12.main|
L000110
                    DCFD            320.0
|L000118.J11.main|
                    ADFD            f1,f1,f0
                    LDFD            f3,[sp,#&10]
                    LDFD            f2,[sp,#8]
                    SUFD            f2,f2,f3
                    MOV             a3,v1
                    B               |L000174.J14.main|
|L000130.J13.main|
                    ADFD            f2,f2,f0
                    MOV             a1,lr
                    MVFD            f4,f2
                    MVFD            f3,f1
|L000140.J15.main|
```

```
            MUFD        f6,f4,f4
            MUFD        f5,f3,f3
            MUFD        f3,f4,f3
            SUFD        f4,f6,f5
            ADFD        f3,f3,f3
            ADFD        f4,f4,f2
            ADFD        f5,f6,f5
            ADFD        f3,f3,f1
            CMFE        f5,f7
            BGE         |L000170.J16.main|
            SUBS        a1,a1,#1
            BNE         |L000140.J15.main|
|L000170.J16.main|
            STRB        a1,[ip],#1
|L000174.J14.main|
            SUBS        a3,a3,#1
            BPL         |L000130.J13.main|
|L00017c.J12.main|
            SUBS        a4,a4,#1
            BPL         |L000118.J11.main|
            LDFD        f1,[sp,#&18]
            MUFD        f0,f0,f1
|L00018c.J10.main|
            SUBS        a2,a2,#1
            BMI         |L0000ac.J7.main|
            B           |L0000e8.J9.main|

            AREA        |C$$data|,DATA
|x$dataseg|

            END
```

9.4.7   Floating point status and control (FPSR/FPCR) register transfers

WFS{*cond*} Rd

RFS{*cond*} Rd

These two instructions allow the floating point Status Register (FPSR) to be read and written. Rd is any valid integer register except r15 (PC). The FPSR may be used by applications programs to control the internal formats used for calculations and to configure the handling of floating point exceptions. The format of this register is discussed below.

```
WFC{cond} Rd

RFC{cond} Rd
```

These two instructions were not supported by ARM floating point systems prior to the FPA10. They are intended for use solely by floating point support software and should not be issued in user programs. They are included here only for the sake of completeness.

9.4.8 The floating point Status Register (FPSR)

The floating point Status Register (FPSR) is present in all implementations of the ARM floating point standard and contains status and control bits which allow user programs to determine the precise behaviour of the available floating point system.

The FPSR is a 32-bit word treated as four separate byte fields; a system ID byte, an exception trap enable byte, a system control byte and a cumulative exception flags byte. Note that the FPSR is not cleared on a system reset: it is usually initialized by the floating point support software.

FPSR System ID byte: FPSR[31..24]

The System ID byte, bits 31..24 of the FPSR, allows programs to distinguish between different versions of the floating point system. The values in Table 9.9 were defined at the time of writing.

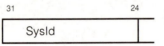

Figure 9.7 System ID byte

Table 9.9 System ID byte values

Value (Hex)	Implementation
00	Floating point emulator software, pre FPA10
01	Floating point emulator software, post FPA10
80	Floating point coprocessor, pre FPA10
81	FPA10 coprocessor

Note that FPSR[31] is set for hardware (that is 'fast') implementations and clear for software (that is 'slow') implementations. This byte of the FPSR is read-only, writes to it are ignored.

FPSR Exception trap enable byte: FPSR[23..16]

The Exception trap enable byte, bits 23..16 of the FPSR, contains a bit field each bit of which enables exception traps of a certain kind or is reserved. Figure 9.8 summarizes the meaning of each of the bits:

Figure 9.8 Exception trap enable byte

If an exception trap enable bit is *clear* when the relevant exception occurs a flag in the cumulative Exception flags byte will be set (see below); if the trap enable bit is *set* an exception trap will occur instead.

Reserved bits should be preserved unaltered by using a read–modify–write strategy in user programs.

FPSR System Control byte: FPSR[15..8]

The System Control byte, bits 15..8 of the FPSR, determine which features of the floating point system are in use. They may be read and written by user programs to allow their preservation during context switches. Figure 9.9 summarizes the meaning of each of the bits:

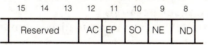

Figure 9.9 System control byte

- AC : Alternative Carry flag interpretation
  When AC is set the ARM Carry flag C is set if the result of a floating point comparison operation is Greater than or equal to or Unordered. This is a new feature of the FPA10 which allows more of the IEEE predicates to be tested for using simple ARM conditional instructions.
  When AC is clear the ARM Carry flag C is set if the result of a floating point comparison is Greater than or equal to. This is the original definition.
- EP : Expanded packed BCD format
  When EP is set the expanded (four-word) format for Packed decimal

(BCD) numbers is used. This allows conversions from Extended precision to Packed decimal values to be performed without loss of accuracy.
When EP is clear the standard (three-word) format for Packed decimal numbers is used.

■ SO : Select synchronous operation of FPA
When SO is set all floating point instructions execute synchronously and the integer CPU will busy-wait until each floating point instruction has completed. This allows exceptions to be reported precisely at the expense of some loss of performance.
When SO is clear then the FPA executes asynchronously any instruction which can proceed without the integer CPU, leading to the possibility of exceptions being reported imprecisely.

■ NE : NaN exception control
When NE is set all conversions between single, double and extended precision will produce an invalid operation exception (see below) if the operand is a signalling NaN.
When NE is clear Extended format is regarded as an internal format as far as conversions of signalling NaNs are concerned: only conversions between single and double precision will produce an invalid operation exception (see below) if the operand is a signalling NaN.

■ ND : No denormalized numbers
When ND is set the floating point support software will force all denormalized numbers to zero to reduce lengthy execution times when dealing with denormalized numbers. This mode is *not* IEEE 754 compliant but may be desirable in some programs for performance reasons.
When ND is clear denormalized numbers are treated in an IEEE 754 compliant way.

Exceptions flags byte FPSR [7..0]

Figure 9.10 Exception flags byte

Whenever a floating point exception occurs and the corresponding trap enable bit is *clear* the appropriate exception flag bit shown above will be *set*. If the corresponding trap enable bit is *set* then an exception is raised to the user program in an implementation-specific manner. Floating point exceptions are discussed in the next section.

9.4.9   Possible causes of floating point exceptions

Unlike other types of exception, such as the interrupts or memory aborts described in Chapter 5, floating point exceptions do not have hardware vectors. Instead, they all start life as an 'Undefined instruction' exception which is trapped by the system's floating point support software or emulator. If it is determined that a floating point exception *has* occurred and the corresponding trap bit is enabled then the exception is passed on to the operating system

The Exception trap enable byte of the FPSR contains bits which determine the fate of floating point faults: if the relevant bit is clear then the relevant cumulative exception flag bit is set(also in the FPSR), otherwise an exception is raised.

Types of floating point exception

There are five kinds of floating point exception, shown in Table 9.10.

Table 9.10 Floating point exceptions

Code	Exception
IO	Invalid operation
DZ	Division by zero
OF	Overflow
UF	Underflow
IX	Inexact

The circumstances which may lead to each of these exceptions are described below.

Invalid operation exception

This exception arises when an operand is invalid for the operation to be performed. When exception trapping is disabled the result of the operation is a 'quiet NaN'. Invalid operations include:

■ Any operation on a signalling NaN except LDF, LFM, SFM, or any of MVF, MNF, ABS or STF without a change of precision.
■ Magnitude subtraction of infinities. Multiplication of zero by an infinity.
■ Division of zero by zero or ∞ by ∞.
■ x REM y where x is ∞ or y is zero.

- Square root of any number less than zero (but SQT(−0) is −0).
- Conversion to an integer when overflow, infinity or NaN make it impossible. If overflow makes a conversion to integer impossible the largest positive or negative integer is returned (depending on the sign of the operand) and an Invalid Operation is signalled.
- CMFE, CNFE when at least one operand is a NaN.
- ACS, ASN when input absolute value is >1.
- SIN, COS, TAN when input is infinite or too large for accurate computation of the function.
- LOG, LGN when input is <0.
- POW when first operand is <0, or first is zero and second is ≤0. On some systems these invalid operations don't occur if the second operand is an integer.
- RPW when second operand is <0, or second is zero and first is ≤0. On some systems these invalid operations do not occur if the second operand is an integer.

Division by zero exception

The division by zero exception occurs if the divisor is zero and the dividend a finite, non-zero number. A correctly signed infinity is returned if the exception trap is disabled. This exception is also raised for LOG(0) and LGN(0), where -∞ is returned, and on some systems for POW with the first operand zero and the second negative or RPW with the second operand zero and the first operand negative.

Overflow exception

The overflow exception occurs when the destination format's largest possible value is exceeded by what would have been the result. A correctly signed infinity or that format's largest possible finite number is returned, depending on the rounding mode.

Underflow exception

Two related events contribute to underflow exceptions:

- Tininess: the creation of a non-zero result smaller than the format's smallest normalized number
- Loss of accuracy: a loss of accuracy due to denormalization that might be greater than would be caused by rounding alone.

If the underflow exception trap enable bit is set then an underflow exception occurs when tininess is detected, regardless of loss of accuracy. If the trap is disabled then both tininess and loss of accuracy must be detected for the underflow flag to be set (and inexactness will also be signalled).

Inexact exception

The inexact exception occurs if the rounded result of an operation is not exact, that is either different from the value computable with infinite precision, or overflow has occured while the overflow trap was disabled or underflow has occurred while the underflow trap was disabled. Overflow and underflow traps take precedence over inexact. Note that except for special cases, such as SIN(0) and COS(0), all transcendental operations are inexact.

9.5 Summary

The ARM floating point system provides a flexible implementation of an IEEE-compliant floating point system which supports arithmetic at Single, Double and Extended precision. The floating point environment can be available to systems both with and without an FPA10 or other hardware coprocessor.

The floating point instruction set includes most traditional monadic and dyadic arithmetic, and transcendental functions. The dense code which results from using this instruction set is particularly efficiently executed by FPA10, yielding floating point performance in the 1–2 MFLOP region when executed on that device.

Floating point exceptions are handled by the floating point support software and upgraded to fatal system errors or high-level language 'signals' as appropriate.

Appendix A

Instruction set mnemonic summary and reference

ADC

Arithmetic add with carry   Rd := Rn + Op2 + Carry

Syntax: ADC{*condition*}{S} Rd, Rn, Op2

Flags affected: N, Z, C, V

Timing: 1 S
                   + 1 S for shift (Rs)
                   +1 S + 1 N if R15 written

If the condition is true ADC adds two 32-bit 2's complement operands. A value of +1 is added to the sum if the Carry was set prior to execution; nothing is added to the sum if the Carry was clear. The flags are set only if the S option is used.

ADC is often used as a step in computing the sums of numbers larger than 32 bits.

For example, to perform a 64-bit signed addition of R0,R1 with R2,R3 giving a result in R0,R1 the following sequence might be employed:

```
ADDS        R0,R0,R2; Add lower words & produce carry
ADC         R1,R1,R3; Add upper words and carry
```

The Op2 operand can be any of the following:

```
Rm, shift Rs
Rm, shift #expression1
Rm, RRX
#expression2
```

where Rd, Rn and Rm are any CPU register (0..15), Rs is a register containing a shift count in the range 0..32, shift is any of ASL, LSL, LSR, ASR, ROR; expression1 is any positive shift count in the range 1..31 and expression2 is any signed expression rotatable by an even amount into an 8-bit value.

If a constant which is not an 8-bit value rotated by an even amount is specified, the Assembler tries generating an SBC instruction with the 1's complement of the constant instead. If this second attempt also fails it produces an error.

The overflow V flag is set if the two operands have the same sign and the result has a different sign.

ADD

Arithmetic Add   Rd := Rn + Op2

Syntax: `ADD{condition}{S} Rd, Rn, Op2`

Flags affected: N, Z, C, V

Timing: 1 S
                   + 1 S for shift (Rs)
                   +1 S + 1 N if R15 written

If the condition is true ADD performs a 32-bit addition of 2's complement operands. The flags are set only if the S option is used.

The state of the carry bit (C) before execution is ignored but will be affected by the result (carry out from bit 31) if the S option is specified in the instruction.

Typical instructions are of the following form:

```
ADD        R0,R0,R2,ASR 2; R0 = R0 + (R2/4)
ADD        R5,R4,#0x8000; R5 = R4 + 32768
```

The Op2 operand can be any of the following:

```
Rm, shift Rs
Rm, shift #expression1
Rm, RRX
#expression2
```

where Rd, Rn and Rm are any CPU register (0..15), Rs is a register containing a shift count in the range 0..32, shift is any of ASL, LSL, LSR, ASR, ROR; expression1 is any positive shift count in the range 1..31 and expression2 is any signed expression rotatable by an even amount into an 8-bit value.

If a constant which is not an 8-bit value rotated by an even amount is specified, the Assembler tries generating a SUB instruction with the 1's complement of the constant instead. If this second attempt also fails it produces an error.

The overflow V flag is set if the two operands have the same sign and the result has a different sign.

ADR

Load address to register   Rd = *expression*

Syntax: ADR Rd, *expression*

Pseudo instruction

This pseudo-instruction exists to allow large constants or addresses to be loaded into a register using a single mnemonic. The assembler will generate the appropriate instructions to load the constant; one of ADD, SUB, MOV, MVN or LDR will be used. Note that it is an address which is produced, so the value at the address must still be loaded using a separate instruction.

For example:

```
ADR        R10, Table+20 ; refer to table
ADR        R0, 0x12345678 ; load constant
```

Where the effective address or constant is within a 256-byte range of the present PC value or is relative to a register a MOV, MVN, ADD or SUB is used. If this is not possible an effective address is generated, stored in a 'long reach' table and an LDR used.

See also: LEA (synonym)

AND

Logical AND   Rd = Rn AND Op2

Syntax: AND{condition}{S} Rd, Rn, Op2

Flags affected: N, Z, C

Timing: 1 S
                    + 1 S for shift (Rs)
                    +1 S + 1 N if R15 written

If the condition is true the destination register receives the 32-bit result of a bitwise logical AND of the two operands. For each bit position in the two sources the bits are compared and if they are both set then the corresponding bit in the destination is set. The flags are set only if the S option is used.

   AND is used to mask bits out or for logical AND operations. To clear the bits specified by a second operand use the BIC (bit clear) instruction.

   No carries are involved in this operation but the Carry flag is set to the shifter carry output.

   For example:

```
AND         R9, R9, #0xFFFFFF00
BIC         R9, R9, #0xFF
```

are both equivalent.

   The Op2 operand can be any of the following:

```
Rm, shift Rs
Rm, shift #expression1
Rm, RRX
#expression2
```

where Rd, Rn and Rm are any CPU register (0..15), Rs is a register containing a shift count in the range 0..32, shift is any of ASL, LSL, LSR, ASR, ROR; expression1 is any positive shift count in the range 1..31 and expression2 is any signed expression rotatable by an even amount into an 8-bit value.

   If a constant which is not an 8-bit value rotated by an even amount is specified, the Assembler tries generating an SBC instruction with the 1's complement of the constant instead. If this second attempt also fails it produces an error.

B

Branch   R15 (PC) = *new address*

Syntax: `B{condition}` *address_expression*

Flags affected: none

Timing: 2 S + 1 N

If the condition is true the Program Counter (PC) in R15 is forced to a new word-aligned address, changing the control flow before the next instruction is fetched. The new PC value is the sum of its present value and the address expression included in the instruction, so a PC-relative branch is caused, not an absolute address branch. However, the assembler will allow absolute branches and calculate the correct offset.

The *address_expression* must be evaluated to a signed 2's complement value and placed in a 24-bit field in the instruction. This is shifted left two bits, sign extended to 32 bits and added to the PC to perform the branch. The instruction can therefore specify a branch of ±32 Mbyte.

The PC always contains a value eight bytes ahead of the current instruction to allow for pre-fetching. This means that offsets for Branch instructions must be (and are) adjusted accordingly by the assembler.

Any of the 15 valid condition code combinations may be used to determine whether the branch takes place. Note that ALways is assumed as the default.

For example:

```
here      BAL         here          ; assembles to &EAFFFFFE

          B           0x2000000     ; branch ALways absolute

          CMP         R1, #0        ; compare R1 with zero
          BEQ         Label         ; branch if equal,
                                    ; to label
```

Computed branches and manually calculated absolute branches may be performed by computing and loading a register and then issuing MOV PC,Rn.

BIC

Bit clear   Rd = Rn AND (1's complement of Op2)

Syntax: BIC{*condition*}{S} Rd, Rn, Op2

Flags affected: N, Z, C

Timing: 1 S
                   + 1 S for shift (Rs)
                   +1 S + 1 N if R15 written

If the condition is true this instruction clears those bits in the first operand indicated by set bits in the second operand. The flags are set only if the S option is used.

For example:

```
BIC        R1, R1, 5; == AND R1, R1, 0xFFFFFFF2
BIC        R0, R0, 1; clear LSB of R0
```

The Op2 operand can be any of the following:

```
Rm, shift Rs
Rm, shift #expression1
Rm, RRX
#expression2
```

where Rd, Rn and Rm are any CPU register (0..15), Rs is a register containing a shift count in the range 0..32, shift is any of ASL, LSL, LSR, ASR, ROR; expression1 is any positive shift count in the range 1..31 and expression2 is any signed expression rotatable by an even amount into an 8-bit value.

If a constant which is not an 8-bit value rotated by an even amount is specified, the Assembler tries generating an AND instruction with the 1's complement of the constant instead. If this second attempt also fails it produces an error.

BL

Branch with link   R14 = PC, PC = <new address>

Syntax: `BL{condition} address_expression`

Flags affected: none

Timing: 2 S + 1 N

If the condition is true the Program Counter (R15) is saved in the Link Register (R14) and the PC is forced to a new word-aligned address supplied by the instruction.

The instruction is used to perform subroutine calls from which a return may be achieved by restoring the contents of R14 to the PC.

The new PC value is the sum of its present value and the address expression included in the instruction, so a PC-relative branch is caused, not an absolute address branch. However, the assembler will allow absolute branches and calculate the correct offset.

`address_expression` is evaluated to a signed 2's complement value and placed in a 24-bit field in the instruction. This is shifted left two bits, sign extended to 32 bits and added to the PC to perform the branch. The instruction can therefore specify a branch of up to ±32 Mbyte.

The PC always contains a value 8 bytes ahead of the current instruction to allow for prefetching. This means that offsets for Branch instructions must be (and are) adjusted accordingly by the assembler.

Any of the 15 valid condition code combinations may be used to determine whether the branch takes place. Note that ALways is assumed as the default.

For example:

```
        BL          RoutineNameHere
```

and to return:

```
        MOV         PC, R14        ; aka MOV PC, LR
```

See also: B

CDP

Coprocessor Data Processing   Coprocessor-specific

Syntax: CDP{*condition*} p*cp_no*, cp_opc, c*Rd*, c*Rn*, c<Rm>
                              {, *expression*}

Flags affected: none

Timing: 1 S + b I (b= no. busy cycles)

If the condition is true a coprocessor data operation is performed. This group of instructions initiate some coprocessor operation specific to the device being addressed. Floating-point coprocessor operations are normally written using dedicated assembler instructions which are assembled into this instruction.

The parameters are: p*cp_no* (a coprocessor number 0..15), cp_opc (an opcode 0..15), cRd/cRn/cRm (coprocessor registers) and an optional expression giving a result 0..7.

Consult the relevant coprocessor data sheet for more information.

For example:

          CDPEQ   p1, 6, c9, c1, c0, 7

See also Appendix B on Floating-Point coprocessor instructions.

CMN

Compare Negative   Flags = Rn + Op2

Syntax: CMN{*condition*}{P} Rn, Op2

Flags affected: N, Z, C, V

Timing: 1 S
                   + 1 S for shift (Rs)

If the condition is true compare negative sets the PSR flags according to the result of comparing the register with a 2's complement number, the result itself being discarded; an S suffix is optional but is always implied. This instruction returns no result but simply sets the flags. It is the inverse of the CMP instruction, which it is preferable to use when Op2 is a constant since the assembler will replace it with CMN if appropriate.

In a 26-bit CPU mode the optional P suffix causes the PSR flags to be set according to the state of bits 28..31 of the result (that is PSR flag bit positions within the result). The P form of this instruction must not be used in 32-bit CPU modes.

For example:

```
CMN         R0, #-23       ; Same as CMP R0, 22

CMN         R10, R2        ; Same as CMP R10, (NOT R2)
```

The Op2 operand can be any of the following:

```
Rm, shift Rs
Rm, shift #expression1
Rm, RRX
#expression2
```

where Rd, Rn and Rm are any CPU register (0..15), Rs is a register containing a shift count in the range 0..32, shift is any of ASL, LSL, LSR, ASR, ROR; expression1 is any positive shift count in the range 1..31 and expression2 is any signed expression rotatable by an even amount into an 8-bit value.

If a constant which is not an 8-bit value rotated by an even amount is specified, the Assembler tries generating an SBC instruction with the 1's complement of the constant instead. If this second attempt also fails it produces an error.

CMP

Arithmetic compare   Flags = Rn – Op2

Syntax: `CMP{condition}{P} Rn, Op2`

Flags affected: N, Z, C, V

Timing: 1 S
            + 1 S for shift (Rs)

If the condition is true a register and a constant or another register are compared, setting the PSR flags and discarding the result; the S suffix is optional and always implied.

The optional P suffix causes the PSR flags to be set according to the state of bits 28..31 of the result (that is PSR flag bit positions within the result). The P form of this instruction must not be used in 32-bit CPU modes.

For example:

```
Hex10      CMP        R2, #"0"        ; test R2 lower bound
           MOVCC      PC, LR          ; return if out of range
           CMP        R2, #"9"        ; test upper bound
           SUBLS      R2, R2, #"0";  convert to decimal
```

The Op2 operand can be any of the following:

```
Rm, shift Rs
Rm, shift #expression1
Rm, RRX
#expression2
```

where Rd, Rn and Rm are any CPU register (0..15), Rs is a register containing a shift count in the range 0..32, shift is any of ASL, LSL, LSR, ASR, ROR; expression1 is any positive shift count in the range 1..31 and expression2 is any signed expression rotatable by an even amount into an 8-bit value.

If a constant which is not an 8-bit value rotated by an even amount is specified, the Assembler tries generating a CMN instruction with the 1's complement of the constant instead. If this second attempt also fails it produces an error.

EOR

Logical exclusive OR   Rd=(Rn AND NOT Op2) OR (Op2
                                         AND NOT Rn)

Syntax: `EOR{condition}{S} Rd, Rn, Op2`

Flags affected: N, Z, C

Timing: 1 S
                   + 1 S for shift (Rn)
                   +1 S + 1 N if R15 written)

If the condition is true a 32-bit logical exclusive OR is performed and the 32-bit
result stored. For each bit in the two operands the destination bit is set if the
source bits differ, otherwise it is cleared. The carry flag is set to the shifter carry
output. The flags are set only if the S option is used.
     The Op2 operand can be any of the following:

```
Rm, shift Rs
Rm, shift #expression1
Rm, RRX
#expression2
```

where `Rd`, `Rn` and `Rm` are any CPU register (0..15), `Rs` is a register containing a shift
count in the range 0..32, `shift` is any of ASL, LSL, LSR, ASR, ROR; `expression1`
is any positive shift count in the range 1..31 and `expression2` is any signed
expression rotatable by an even amount into an 8-bit value.
     For example:

```
EOR         R5, R5, #32; Invert bit 5
EOR         R10, R10, R13
```

LDC

Load coprocessor from memory   Coprocessor load

Syntax: `LDC{condition}{L} pcp_no, cRd, address{!}`

Flags affected: none

Timing: (n-1) S + 2 N + b I (n=no. of words, b=no. of busy cycles)

If the condition is true a coprocessor register is loaded from memory, specifying the coprocessor number, its register number and an address in one of various forms. Pre- and Post-indexing are possible and the address may be register-relative.

For the coprocessor, `pcp_no` is the coprocessor number 0..15, and cRd the coprocessor destination register. The address may take one of the following forms:

```
expression
[Rn]
[Rn, expression]
[[Rn], expression]
```

where `Rn` is a CPU register and `expression` is in the range –1020 to +1020 bytes relative to PC and divisible by four.

For example:

```
LDC         p1, c2, [LK,-4]
```

LDM

Load multiple registers   Stack manipulation (pop)

Syntax: LDM{*condition*}mode Rn{!},{{*reg_list*}}{^}

Flags affected: none, but see below

Timing: n S + 1 N + 1 I (n=no. of words transferred)
                    + 1 S + 1 N if R15 loaded

If the condition is true between one and 16 registers may be loaded from memory using this instruction. Any subset of registers, not necessarily contiguous, may be included in the reg_list. Several instruction variations are allowed, indicating whether the registers are to be loaded in ascending or descending address order and whether the base address register (Rn) is to be incremented or decremented before or after each register load. The lowest numbered register is always loaded with the contents of the lowest address generated.

The instruction mode is chosen from the following list:

Mode	Meaning	Use	Function
IB/ED	Increment Before	Pop upwards	Pre-increment
IA/FD	Increment After	Pop upwards	Post-increment
DB/EA	Decrement Before	Pop downwards	Pre-decrement
DA/FA	Decrement After	Pop downwards	Post-decrement

The mnemonics after the slash are allowed as alternatives; E/F for empty/full, A/D for ascending/descending.

Rn is any register in the range 0..15 and ! controls whether the updated address is written back to the register.

{*reg_list*} (braces mandatory) is the list of registers to be loaded, in any order. The instruction contains a 16-bit field comprising one bit per register so arbitrary lists are permissible.

^ sets the S field of the instruction and affects the behaviour of this instruction differently according to whether or not r15 (PC) is included in the list. If it is, S set causes the SPSR_mode to be transferred to the CPSR at the same time as r15 (PC) is loaded.

If r15 (PC) is not included in reg_list then ^ causes the User mode registers specified to be transferred instead of the registers of the mode in which the instruction is executed, useful for restoring state on process switches. This feature is only available in Supervisor mode (it has no effect in User modes)

LDR

Load register from memory   Rd=[address]

Syntax: LDR{*condition*}{B}{T} Rd, *address* {!}

Flags affected: none, but see below

Timing: 1 S + 1 N + 1 I
                 + 1 S + 1 N if R15 loaded

If the condition is true a register is loaded with the 8-bit or 32-bit value at the specified address. The address of the operand may be relative to any register (including PC) and the register may be auto incremented or decremented. Several register-addressing modes are available (see below). The T option can be used to force address translation in Supervisor mode (simulating User mode).

A 32-bit load is performed unless B is specified, in which case an 8-bit load is performed instead (see also below). If present, T forces address translation (not allowed for pre-indexed forms). Rd can be any register 0..15 and ! causes write-back of the modified register value after use.

address can be any of the following addressing modes:

Mode	Effective address	Indexing
[Rn]	Rn	None
[Rn, #expression]	Rn expression	Pre-indexed
[Rn, +/- Rm]	Rn +/- Rm	Pre-indexed
[Rn, +/- Rm, shift #count]	Rn +/- (Rm shifted by count)	Pre-indexed
[Rn], #expression	Rn	Post-increment
[Rn], +/- Rm	Rn	Post-increment
[Rn], +/- Rm, shift #count	Rn	Post-increment

Rn is any register number 0..15 and holds the base address, Rm is any other register and holds a signed address increment, expression is an expression evaluating to a result in the range –4095 to +4095, shift is one of LSL, LSR, ASR, ROR, RRX and count is a constant in the range 1..31 representing the shift count, which may not come from a register.

The address increment is the value added to the base; it is added to Rn before the transfer when pre-indexing is used (indicated by placing it inside the brackets) and after the transfer when post-indexing is used (indicated by placing it outside the brackets). In pre-indexed modes if the ! follows the] then Rn is

LDR

also incremented, that is post-increment mode.

R15 (PC) must never be used as Rm, nor as Rn if write-back is specified with !. When using R15 as the base (Rn) remember that it contains an address advanced by 8 from the current instruction.

The precise action of this instruction depends on the CPU byte sex configuration; refer to Chapter 7 for further information.

The CPU state after this instruction is affected by the CPU's early/late abort configuration. When configured for early aborts any base register write-back is prevented if an abort occurs. When configured for late aborts the write-back is allowed and the abort handler must correct for this before re-executing the instruction.

MCR

Move CPU register to coprocessor   cRn = rRn {<op> cRm}

Syntax: MCR{condition} pcp_no, cp_opc, rRd, cRn, cRm
{,expression}

Flags affected: none

Timing: 1 S + (b+1) I + 1 C (b=no. busy cycles)

If the condition is true a coprocessor register is loaded with a value from an ARM register, optionally performing an operation before the transfer. This is the form of instruction which is used to provide the floating-point FLT operation, converting an integer from ARM into a floating-point number before the transfer.

The parameters are: pcp_no (a coprocessor number 0..15), cp_opc (an opcode 0..15), rRd (an ARM register), cRn/cRm (coprocessor registers) and an optional expression giving a result 0..7.

For example:

        MCR p5, 0, r1, c3, c5; cR3 := Op0(r1)

MLA

Multiply and accumulate   Rd = (Rm * Rs) + Rn

Syntax: MLA{*condition*}{S} Rd, Rm, Rs, Rn

Flags affected: N, Z, C, V

Timing: 1 S + m I (m=no. mutiplication cycles)

If the condition is true, signed multiply Rm by Rs and add Rn to give a 32-bit result in Rd. The result is the 32 LSBs of the multiplication, so higher-precision results may be calculated using several instructions. Registers Rd and Rm may not be the same and R15 (PC) must not be used in any position. The flags are set only if the S option is used.

The multiplication is performed using a modified Booth's algorithm which will complete in no more than 16 I-cycles; leading zeros will reduce the time still further.

For example:

```
MLA        r1, r2, r3, r4 ; r1:=r2*r3+r4
```

MOV

Move register or constant   Rd = Op2

Syntax: `MOV{condition}{S} Rd, Op2`

Flags affected: N, Z, C

Timing: 1 S
                     + 1 S for shift (Rs)
                     +1 S + 1 N if R15 written

If the condition is true move a 32-bit value from one register to another or move an 8-bit constant, possibly rotated, into a register. If present, S sets the flags after the move.

The Op2 operand can be any of the following:

```
Rm, shift Rs
Rm, shift #expression1
Rm, RRX
#expression2
```

where `Rd`, `Rn` and `Rm` are any CPU register (0..15), `Rs` is a register containing a shift count in the range 0..32, `shift` is any of ASL, LSL, LSR, ASR, ROR; `expression1` is any positive shift count in the range 1..31 and `expression2` is any signed expression rotatable by an even amount into an 8-bit value.

If a constant which is not an 8-bit value rotated by an even amount is specified, the Assembler tries generating a MVN instruction with the 1's complement of the constant instead. If this second attempt also fails it produces an error.

For example:

```
MOV       PC, LK        ; Return

MOV       R1, #0x87654321; load constant

MOVEQ     R8, R6, LSR R3 ; R8:=R6 shifted
```

MRC

Move from coprocessor to CPU registerRn = CRn {<Op> CRm}

Syntax: `MRC{condition} pcp_no, expression1, rRd, cRn,`
`cRm {,expression}`

Flags affected: none

Timing: $1 S + b I + 1 C$ (b=no. of busy cycles)

If the condition is true a CPU register is loaded with a value from a coprocessor register, optionally performing some operation before the transfer.

The parameters are: `pcp_no` (a coprocessor number 0..15), cp_opc (an opcode 0..15), rRd (an ARM register), cRn/cRm (coprocessor registers) and an optional expression giving a result 0..7.

For example:

```
MRC        p2, 5, r3, c5, c6; r3:=Op5(c5,c6)
```

MRS

Move status/flags (PSR) to register   Rn = PSR

Syntax: MRS{*condition*} Rd, *psr*

Flags affected: none

Timing: 1 S

If the condition is true move (copy) the Current Program Status Resgister (CPSR) or Stored Program Status Register (in non-User modes) to a specified register. Only non-User modes have an SPSR, it being the CPSR value stored as a result of the last mode change. The SPSRs for other modes are not accessible except by changing mode.

Rd is the destination CPU register. R15 (PC) may not be used as a destination register.

psr may be one of CPSR/CPSR_all (synonyms), or SPSR/SPSR_all (synonyms).

For example:

            MRS   Rtemp, CPSR; copy current flags

            MRS   Rtemp, SPSR_all; copy stored flags

MSR

Move register to status/flags (PSR)   PSR = Rm

Syntax: MSR{condition} *psr*, Rm

MSR{condition} *psrf*, Rm

MSR{condition} *psrf*, *expression*

Flags affected:

Timing: 1 S

If the condition is true move (copy) a register to the specified Current or Stored Program Status Register (CPSR/SPSR). In User Mode only the CPSR exists to be altered; in other modes the CPSR and the SPSR for the current mode alone are available.

Either the whole PSR or just the flags may be written, according to which variant form of the instruction is used.

Rm is the source CPU register.

psr is one of CPSR/CPSR_all (synonyms) or SPSR/SPSR_all (synonyms)

psrf is one of CPSR_flg or SPSR_flg (flag-only transfers)

expression must be able to be generated from a shifted 8-bit field; the top four bits of the result will be transferred. An error will be generated if the expression value given cannot be generated in this way.

For example, to change processor mode (in a non-User mode):

```
MRS        Rtemp, CPSR    ; copy CPSR
BIC        Rtemp, Rtemp, #&1F; clear mode bits
ORR        Rtemp, Rtemp, #new_mode; select mode
MSR        CPSR, Rtemp    ; write new CPSR
```

To alter only the flags:

```
MSR        CPSR_flg, #&F0000000; set all flags
                             ; no control change
```

MUL

Multiply   Rd = Rm * Rs

Syntax: MUL{condition}{S} Rd, Rm, Rs

Flags affected: N, Z, C

Timing: 1 S + m I (m=no. of multiplication cycles; see Chapter 2)

If the condition is true, signed multiply Rm by Rs to give a 32-bit result in Rd. The result is the 32 LSBs of the multiplication, so higher-precision results may be calculated using several instructions. Registers Rd and Rm may not be the same and R15 (PC) must not be used in any position. The flags are set only if the S option is used.

The multiplication is performed using a modified Booth's algorithm which will complete in no more than 16 I-cycles; leading zeros will reduce the time still further.

For example:

```
        MUL         R1, R2, R3     ; R1:=R2*R3
```

The following code fragment multiplies the two registers r0, r1 containing 32-bit integers to give a 64-bit result in r2, r3. r5 is a temporary register and r0 and r1 are corrupted.

```
mul64      MOV        r5, r0, LSR #16; r5:=top half of r0
           MOV        r3, r1, LSR #16; r3:= top half of r1
           BIC        r0, r0, r5, LSL #16; r0:= bot half of r0
           BIC        r1, r1, r3, LSL #16; r1:= bot half of r1
           MUL        r2, r0, r1     ; partial result
           MUL        r1, r5, r1     ; partial result
           MUL        r0, r3, r0     ; partial result
           MUL        r3, r5, r3     ; partial result
           ADDS       r0, r1, r0     ; add middle parts
           ADDCS      r3, r3, #&10000; carry from above
           ADDS       r2, r2, r0, LSL #16; r2=32 LSB result
           ADC        r3, r3, r0, LSR #16; r3=32 MSB result
```

See also: MLA

MVN

Move negative register   Rd = 0xFFFFFFFF EOR Op2

Syntax: MVN{*condition*}{S} Rd, Op2

Flags affected: N, Z, C

Timing: 1 S
                   + 1 S for shift (Rs)
                   +1 S + 1 N if R15 written

If the condition is true load the 1's complement of Op2 into Rd, optionally setting the flags if S is present.

The Op2 operand can be any of the following:

```
Rm, shift Rs
Rm, shift #expression1
Rm, RRX
#expression2
```

where Rd, Rn and Rm are any CPU register (0..15), Rs is a register containing a shift count in the range 0..32, shift is any of ASL, LSL, LSR, ASR, ROR; expression1 is any positive shift count in the range 1..31 and expression2 is any signed expression rotatable by an even amount into an 8-bit value.

If a constant which is not an 8-bit value rotated by an even amount is specified, the Assembler tries generating an SBC instruction with the 1's complement of the constant instead. If this second attempt also fails it produces an error.

For example:

```
MVN        R12, R5        ; R12:=NOT R5
```

NOP

No-operation

Syntax: NOP

Pseudo-instruction

Timing: 1 S

This pseudo-instruction is not conditional. It is assembled to an instruction which takes a single S-cycle to execute but has no effect other than advancing the program counter.

NOP is assembled to MOV r0, r0.

ORR

Logical OR   Rd = Rn OR Op2

Syntax: ORR{condition}{S} Rd, Rn, Op2

Flags affected: N, Z, C

Timing: 1 S
                   + 1 S for shift (Rs)
                   +1 S + 1 N if R15 written

If the condition is true a 32-bit bitwise logical OR is performed with Rn and Op2 and the result stored in Rd. The flags are set only if the S option is used.

The Op2 operand can be any of the following:

```
Rm, shift Rs
Rm, shift #expression1
Rm, RRX
#expression2
```

where Rd, Rn and Rm are any CPU register (0..15), Rs is a register containing a shift count in the range 0..32, shift is any of ASL, LSL, LSR, ASR, ROR; expression1 is any positive shift count in the range 1..31 and expression2 is any signed expression rotatable by an even amount into an 8-bit value.

For example:

```
ORR        R0, R0, #32; convert ASCII lower case?
```

RSB

Reverse subtract   Rd = Op2 − Rn

Syntax: `RSB{condition}{S} Rd, Rn, Op2`

Flags affected: N, Z, C, V

Timing: 1 S
                     + 1 S for shift (Rs)
                     + 1S + 1 N if R15 written

If the condition is true perform a subtraction, equivalent to SUB except that the operands are reversed. This is attractive since SUB only allows flexible addressing for the second operand (the first must be a register) so this instruction allows the same flexibility for the first operand. The flags are set only if the S option is used.
    The Op2 operand can be any of the following:

```
Rm, shift Rs
Rm, shift #expression1
Rm, RRX
#expression2
```

where `Rd`, `Rn` and `Rm` are any CPU register (0..15), `Rs` is a register containing a shift count in the range 0..32, `shift` is any of ASL, LSL, LSR, ASR, ROR; `expression1` is any positive shift count in the range 1..31 and `expression2` is any signed expression rotatable by an even amount into an 8-bit value.
    For example:

```
RSB        R5, R5, #0xEA000000; R5:= 0xEA000000-R5
```

RSC

Reverse subtract with carry(borrow) Rd = Op2 – Rn – 1 + Carry

Syntax: `RSC{condition}{S} Rd, Rn, Op2`

Flags affected: N, Z, C, V

Timing: 1 S
              + 1 S for shift (Rs)
              + 1S + 1 N if R15 written

If the condition is true perform a subtract with carry (borrow), equivalent to SBC except that the operands are reversed. This is attractive since SBC only allows flexible addressing for the second operand (the first must be a register) so this instruction allows the same flexibility for the first operand. The flags are set only if the S option is used.

The Op2 operand can be any of the following:

```
Rm, shift Rs
Rm, shift #expression1
Rm, RRX
#expression2
```

where `Rd`, `Rn` and `Rm` are any CPU register (0..15), `Rs` is a register containing a shift count in the range 0..32, `shift` is any of ASL, LSL, LSR, ASR, ROR; expression1 is any positive shift count in the range 1..31 and `expression2` is any signed expression rotatable by an even amount into an 8-bit value.

For example:

```
RSC        R1, R2, R3, LSL #3;
```

SBC

Subtract with carry   Rd = Rn – Op2 – 1 + Carry

Syntax: SBC{*condition*}{S} Rd, Rn, Op2

Flags affected: N, Z, C, V

Timing: 1 S
                  + 1 S for shift (Rs)
                  + 1S + 1 N if R15 written

If the condition is true subtract two 32-bit operands storing the result in a register. The value +1 is subtracted from the difference if the Carry flag was clear before the instruction; nothing is subtracted if the Carry flag was set. The flags are set only if the S option is used.

This instruction is well suited to multi-precision calculations; the lowest order words should be subtracted using SUB (possibly generating a Carry) and then the next most significant word pairs subtracted using this instruction until the most significant pair has been subtracted.

Rd is the destination, Rn the first operand.

The Op2 operand can be any of the following:

```
Rm, shift Rs
Rm, shift #expression1
Rm, RRX
#expression2
```

where Rd, Rn and Rm are any CPU register (0..15), Rs is a register containing a shift count in the range 0..32, shift is any of ASL, LSL, LSR, ASR, ROR; expression1 is any positive shift count in the range 1..31 and expression2 is any signed expression rotatable by an even amount into an 8-bit value.

If a constant which is not an 8-bit value rotated by an even amount is specified, the Assembler tries generating an ADC instruction with the 1's complement of the constant instead. If this second attempt also fails it produces an error.

For example, the following sequence performs a 64-bit subtraction of R2,R3 from R0,R1:

```
Sub64        SUB        R0, R0, R2      ; LSBs
             SBC        R1, R1, R3      ; MSBs & borrow
```

STC

Store coprocessor register to memory *address* = CRn

Syntax: STC{*condition*}{L}{T} cp#, CRn, *address*{!}

Flags affected: none

Timing: $(n-1) S + 2 N + b I$ (n=no. of words, b=no. of busy cycles)

If the condition is true store the contents of coprocessor register to memory at the address calculated. This is the equivalent of STR for a coprocessor.

The L option controls a hardware-specific feature of the coprocessor; by convention L=1 implies a long transfer and L=0 a short one. The T option controls whether or not the CPU Trans signal is asserted (T=1 asserts Trans) causing address translation to occur. For the coprocessor, cp# is the coprocessor number, CRn the coprocessor register. The address may take one of the following forms:

```
expression
[Rn]                    T suffix not allowed
[Rn, expression]T suffix not allowed
[[Rn], expression]
```

where Rn is a CPU register and expression is in the range −1023 to +1023 bytes relative to PC.

STM

Store multiple registers   Stack manipulation (push)

Syntax: STM{*condition*}mode Rn{!},{{*reg_list*}}{^}

Flags affected: none

Timing: $(n-1)\,S+2\,N$ (n=no. of words)

If the condition is true between one and sixteen registers may be stored to memory using this instruction. Any subset of registers, not necessarily contiguous, may be included in the reg_list. Several instruction variations are allowed, indicating whether the registers are to be stored in ascending or descending address order and whether the base address register (Rn) is to be incremented or decremented before or after each register store. The lowest address is always loaded with the contents of the lowest register number.

The instruction mode is chosen from the following list:

Mode	Meaning	Use	Function
IB/FA	Increment Before	Pushupwards	Pre-increment
IA/EA	Increment After	Push upwards	Post-increment
DB/FD	Decrement Before	Push downwards	Pre-decrement
DA/ED	Decrement After	Push downwards	Post-decrement

The mnemonics after the slash are allowed as alternatives; E/F for empty/ full, A/D for ascending/descending.

Rn is any register in the range 0..15 and ! controls whether the updated address is written back to the register.

{*reg_list*} (braces mandatory) is the list of registers to be stored, in any order. The instruction contains a 16-bit field comprising one bit per register, so arbitrary lists are permissible.

The optional caret suffix ^ causes sets the S field of the instruction forcing the transfer of the User mode registers listed instead of the registers of the mode in which the instruction is executed.

STR

Store register to memory   <address> = Rd

Syntax: STR{condition}{B}{T} Rd, address {!}

Flags affected: none

Timing: 2 N

If the condition is true store a register with the 8-bit or 32-bit value at the specified address. The address of the operand may be relative to any register (including PC) and the register may be auto incremented or decremented. Several register addressing modes are available (see below). The T option can be used to force address translation in Supervisor mode (simulating User mode).

A 32-bit store is performed unless B is specified, in which case an 8-bit store is performed instead. If present T forces address translation (not allowed for pre-indexed forms). Rd can be any register 0..15 and ! causes write-back of the modified register value after use.

address can be any of the following addressing modes:

Mode	Effective address	Indexing
[Rn]	Rn	None
[Rn, #expression]	Rn expression	Pre-indexed
[Rn, +/- Rm]	Rn +/- Rm	Pre-indexed
[Rn, +/- Rm, shift #count]	Rn +/- (Rm shifted by count)	Pre-indexed
[Rn], #expression	Rn	Post-increment
[Rn], +/- Rm	Rn	Post-increment
[Rn], +/- Rm, shift #count	Rn	Post-increment

Rn is any register number 0..15 and holds the base address, Rm is any other register and holds a signed address increment, expression is an expression evaluating to a result in the range –4095 to +4095, shift is one of LSL, LSR, ASR, ROR, RRX and count is a constant in the range 1..31 representing the shift count.

The address increment is the value added to the base; it is added to Rn before the transfer when pre-indexing is used (indicated by placing it inside the brackets) and after the transfer when post-indexing is used (indicated by placing it outside the brackets). In pre-indexed modes shown above if the ! follows the] then Rn is also incremented, that is post-increment mode.

STR

R15 (PC) must never be used as Rm, nor as Rn if write-back is specified with !. When using R15 as the base (Rn) remember that it contains an address advanced by 8 from the current instruction.

The precise action of this instruction depends on the CPU byte sex configuration; refer to Chapter 7 for further information.

The CPU state after this instruction is affected by the CPU's early/late abort configuration. When configured for early aborts any base register write-back is prevented if an abort occurs. When configured for late aborts the write-back is allowed and the abort handler must correct for this before re-executing the instruction.

SUB

Subtract   Rd = Rn – Op2

Syntax: `SUB{condition}{S} Rd, Rn, Op2`

Flags affected: N, Z, C, V

Timing: 1 S
                  + 1 S for shift (Rs)
                  + 1S + 1 N if R15 written

If the condition is true subtract one 32-bit operand from the other, storing the result in a register. The flags are set only if the S option is used.

Rd is the destination and Rn the first operand.

The Op2 operand can be any of the following:

```
Rm, shift Rs
Rm, shift #expression1
Rm, RRX
#expression2
```

where `Rd`, `Rn` and `Rm` are any CPU register (0..15), `Rs` is a register containing a shift count in the range 0..32, `shift` is any of ASL, LSL, LSR, ASR, ROR; `expression1` is any positive shift count in the range 1..31 and `expression2` is any signed expression rotatable by an even amount into an 8-bit value.

If a constant which is not an 8-bit value rotated by an even amount is specified, the Assembler tries generating an ADD instruction with the 1's complement of the constant instead. If this second attempt also fails it produces an error.

SWI

Software Interrupt   **Operating System call**

Syntax: `SWI{`*condition*`}` *operand*

Flags affected: none

Timing: $2S + 1N$

If the condition is true perform a 'software interrupt', causing the CPU to change to Supervisor mode, passing a 24-bit operand for interpretation by the operating system.

For example:

```
SWI         &0007FC        ; call OS with &7FC
```

SWP

Swap register with memory   Rd:=[Rn], [Rn]:=Rm

Syntax: SWP{cond}{B} Rd, Rm, [Rn]

Flags affected: none

Timing: 1 S + 2 N + 1 I

If the condition is true swap the byte or word between registers and memory. The swap address is given by Rn. The contents of the address given by Rn are read from external memory, ignoring any cached value if present. The source register Rm is then written to the address and the value previously read from the address is placed in the destination register Rd. The same register may be specified for both source and destination.

The processor's LOCK pin is asserted high for the duration of this instruction to signal to the memory system that the operation should be indivisible, ie that the memory should only be addressable by this processor until LOCK returns low. This feature is important in implementing multi-processor systems, but requires external hardware support.

A byte swap (B suffix present) expects to read data on D[7:0] for addresses on a word boundary, bits D[15:8] for addresses on a word boundary plus one etc. The selected byte is placed in the least significant eight bits of the destination register and the remaining bits are filled with zeros. The byte to be written is repeated four times across the data bus, so the external memory system must select the relevant byte according to A[1:0].

R15 shall not be used as an operand (Rd, Rn, Rm) in a SWP instruction.

If a Data Abort occurs during a SWP instruction the processor's state will be prevented from changing, regardless of whether the read or write part of the sequence was aborted. The 'lateabt' configuration has no effect on the behaviour of aborted SWP instructions.

TEQ

Test bitwise equality   Flags = Rn EOR Op2

Syntax: `TEQ{condition}{P} Rn, Op2`

Flags affected: N, Z, C

Timing: 1 S
                   +1 S for shift (Rs)

If the condition is true test the bitwise equivalence of the two 32-bit operands discarding the result but setting the Negative and Zero flags (Carry is cleared and oVerflow unaffected).

An S suffix is optional but is always implied.

The optional P suffix causes the PSR flags to be set according to the state of bits 28..31 of the result (that is PSR flag bit positions within the result). The P form of this instruction must not be used in 32-bit CPU modes.

Rn is the CPU register number for the first operand.

The Op2 operand can be any of the following:

```
Rm, shift Rs
Rm, shift #expression1
Rm RRX
#expression2
```

where `Rd`, `Rn` and `Rm` are any CPU register (0..15), `Rs` is a register containing a shift count in the range 1..32, `shift` is any of ASL, LSL, LSR, ASR, ROR; `expression1` is any positive shift count in the range 1..31 and `expression2` is any signed expression shiftable into an 8-bit value.

For example:

```
CMP r0, #31       ; r0 smaller than 31?
TEQGT r0, #127    ; or r0==127?
MOVLE r0, #"."    ; less than 32 or == 127
```

TST

Test condition codes using AND maskflags = Rn AND Op2

Syntax: `TST{condition}{P} Rn, Op2`

Flags affected: N, Z, C

Timing: 1 S
                     + 1 S for shift (Rs)

If the condition is true test one operand against the other by performing a 32-bit logical AND, discarding the result but setting the flags.

An S suffix is optional but is always implied.

The optional P suffix causes the PSR flags to be set according to the state of bits 28..31 of the result (that is PSR flag bit positions within the result). The P form of this instruction must not be used in 32-bit CPU modes.

Rn is the CPU register number of the first operand.

The Op2 operand can be any of the following:

```
Rm, shift Rs
Rm, shift #expression1
Rm, RRX
#expression2
```

where Rd, Rn and Rm are any CPU register (0..15), Rs is a register containing a shift count in the range 0..32, shift is any of ASL, LSL, LSR, ASR, ROR; expression1 is any positive shift count in the range 1..31 and expression2 is any signed expression rotatable by an even amount into an 8-bit value.

If a constant which is not an 8-bit value rotated by an even amount is specified, the Assembler tries generating an SBC instruction with the 1's complement of the constant instead. If this second attempt also fails it produces an error.

For example:

```
TST       R0, #0x82      ; R0 AND 0x82
BEQ       Both_Zero
BNE       Either_Set
```

Appendix B

Floating point instruction set

ABS

Absolute value   Fd := ABS (Fm)

```
Syntax: ABS{condition}precision{rounding} Fd, <Fm |
                                           #value>
```

If the condition is true this instruction evaluates the absolute value of the operand and stores the rounded result in the specified register.

precision specifies the destination rounding precision: S (single), D (double) or E (extended). A precision *must* be specified.

rounding optionally specifies the rounding mode: the default is round to nearest; otherwise P (round towards Plus infinity), M (round towards Minus infinity) or Z (round towards Zero).

Fd and Fm are any floating point register (0..7) and #*value* is one of the constants 0.0, 1.0, 2.0, 3.0, 4.0, 5.0, 0.5 or 10.0.

Possible exceptions

- Invalid operation: if the operand is a signalling NaN of a different precision to the destination precision of the instruction;
- Overflow: note this can only occur if the operand has a higher precision than the destination precision of the instruction;
- Underflow: note this can only occur if the operand has a higher precision than the destination precision of the instruction;
- Inexact: note this can only occur if the operand has a higher precision than the destination precision of the instruction.

This instruction is assembled to an ARM Coprocessor Data Operation (CDP) instruction; refer to that integer instruction for further information.

ACS

Arc cosine   Fd := arccosine of Fm

Syntax: ACS{*condition*}*precision*{*rounding*} Fd, <Fm |
                                              #value>

If the condition is true this instruction evaluates the arc cosine of the operand and stores the rounded result in the specified register. The rounding mode and precision are only applied to the final result of the calculation; intermediate results are always rounded to nearest at extended precision.

precision specifies the destination rounding precision: S (single), D (double) or E (extended). A precision *must* be specified.

rounding optionally specifies the rounding mode: the default is round to nearest; otherwise P (round towards Plus infinity), M (round towards Minus infinity) or Z (round towards Zero).

Fd and Fm are any floating point register (0..7), and #value is one of the constants: 0.0, 1.0, 2.0, 3.0, 4.0, 5.0, 0.5 or 10.0.

Possible exceptions

- Invalid operation:
  (a) If the operand is a signalling NaN;
  (b) If the operand is an infinity;
  (c) If the operand is a number lying outside the range +1 to −1, both ends included.
- Overflow: cannot occur, since the result always lies in the range 0 to $+\pi$.
- Underflow: cannot occur, since ACS(1) is 0 exactly and the ACS of any representable number less than 1 is more than $2^{(-32)}$ in magnitude.
- Inexact.

This instruction is assembled to an ARM Coprocessor Data Operation (CDP) instruction; refer to that integer instruction for further information.

ADF

Add floating   Fd := Fn + Fm

Syntax: `ADF{`*condition*`}`*precision*`{`*rounding*`} Fd, Fn, <Fm`
`| #`*value*`>`

If the condition is true this instruction adds the operands and stores the rounded result in the specified register.

precision specifies the destination rounding precision: S (single), D (double) or E (extended). A precision *must* be specified.

rounding optionally specifies the rounding mode: the default is round to nearest; otherwise P (round towards Plus infinity), M (round towards Minus infinity) or Z (round towards Zero).

`Fd` and `Fm` are any floating point register (0..7) and `#`*value* is one of the constants 0.0, 1.0, 2.0, 3.0, 4.0, 5.0, 0.5 or 10.0.

Possible exceptions

- Invalid operation:
  (a) If either operand is a signalling NaN
  (b) For $(+\infty) + (-\infty)$
  (c) For $(-\infty) + (+\infty)$
- Overflow
- Underflow
- Inexact

This instruction is assembled to an ARM Coprocessor Data Operation (CDP) instruction; refer to that integer instruction for further information.

ASN

Arc sine   Fd := arcsine of Fm

Syntax: ASN{*condition*}*precision*{*rounding*} Fd, <Fm |
#*value*>

If the condition is true this instruction evaluates the arc sine of the operand and
stores the rounded result in the specified register. The rounding mode and precision are only applied to the final result of the calculation; intermediate results are
always rounded to nearest at extended precision.

   precision specifies the destination rounding precision: S (single), D (double) or E (extended). A precision *must* be specified.

   rounding optionally specifies the rounding mode: the default is round to
nearest; otherwise P (round towards Plus infinity), M (round towards Minus
infinity) or Z (round towards Zero).

   Fd and Fm are any floating point register (0..7) and #*value* is one of the constants 0.0, 1.0, 2.0, 3.0, 4.0, 5.0, 0.5 or 10.0.

Possible exceptions

   ■ Invalid operation:
      (a) If the operand is a signalling NaN
      (b) If the operand is an infinity
      (c) If the operand is a number lying outside the range +1 to –1, both
       ends included.
   ■ Overflow: cannot occur, since the result always lies in the range $-\pi/2$ to
      $+\pi/2$
   ■ Underflow
   ■ Inexact

   This instruction is assembled to an ARM Coprocessor Data Operation
(CDP) instruction; refer to that integer instruction for further information.

ATN

Arc tangent   Fd := arctangent of Fm

Syntax: ATN{*condition*}*precision*{*rounding*} Fd, <Fm |
                                    #*value*>

If the condition is true this instruction evaluates the arc tangent of the operand and stores the result in the specified register. The rounding mode and precision are only applied to the final result of the calculation; intermediate results are always rounded to nearest at extended precision.

   precision specifies the destination rounding precision: S (single), D (double) or E (extended). A precision *must* be specified.

   rounding optionally specifies the rounding mode: the default is round to nearest; otherwise P (round towards Plus infinity), M (round towards Minus infinity) or Z (round towards Zero).

   Fd and Fm are any floating point register (0..7) and #*value* is one of the constants 0.0, 1.0, 2.0, 3.0, 4.0, 5.0, 0.5 or 10.0.

Possible exceptions

- Invalid operation: if the operand is a signalling NaN
- Overflow: cannot occur, since the result always lies in the range $-\pi/2$ to $+\pi/2$
- Underflow
- Inexact

   This instruction is assembled to an ARM Coprocessor Data Operation (CDP) instruction; refer to that integer instruction for further information.

CMF

Compare floating   Flags := (Fn==Fm)

`Syntax: CMF{E}{condition} Fn, <Fm | #value>`

If the condition is true this instruction compares the two operands and sets the flags according to their relation.

If present, the optional E suffix will cause an exception if either operand is a NaN. Otherwise, an exception is only produced if one of the operands is a Signalling NaN. See the section on floating-point exceptions for more details.

Fn and Fm are any floating point register (0..7) and `#value` is one of the constants 0.0, 1.0, 2.0, 3.0, 4.0, 5.0, 0.5 or 10.0.

The ARM CPU flags are set by this instruction in one of two ways according to the state of the AC bit in the FPSR. Refer to the section in Chapter Four on the FPSR for more details. With the FPSR AC bit clear the flags are affected by this instruction as follows:

Flag	Meaning	Example
N	less than	Fn < −Fm
Z	equal	
C	greater than or equal	Fn >= −Fm
V	unordered	

Note that when Fn and Fm are not equal N and C are not necessarily opposites: if the result is unordered they will both be clear. With the FPSR AC bit set:

Flag	Meaning
N	less than
Z	equal
C	greater than or equal, or unordered
V	unordered

Possible exceptions

- Invalid operation:
  (CMF) If either operand is a signalling NaN.
  (CMFE) If either operand is a NaN of any kind.

CNF

Compare negated floating   Flags := (Fn== – Fm)

```
Syntax: CNF{E}{condition} Fn, <Fm | #value>
```

If the condition is true this instruction compares the first operand with the second negated and sets the flags according to their relation.

If present, the optional E suffix will cause an exception if either operand is a NaN. Otherwise, an exception is only produced if one of the operands is a Signalling NaN. See the section on floating-point exceptions for more details.

Fn and Fm are any floating point register (0..7) and #value is one of the constants 0.0, 1.0, 2.0, 3.0, 4.0, 5.0, 0.5 or 10.0.

The ARM CPU flags are set by this instruction in one of two ways according to the state of the AC bit in the FPSR. Refer to the section in Chapter Four on the FPSR for more details. With the FPSR AC bit clear the flags are affected by this instruction as follows:

Flag	Meaning	Example
N	less than	Fn < –Fm
Z	equal	
C	greater than or equal	Fn >= –Fm
V	unordered	

Note that when Fn and Fm are not equal N and C are not necessarily opposites: if the result is unordered they will both be clear. With the FPSR AC bit set:

Flag	Meaning
N	less than
Z	equal
C	greater than or equal, or unordered
V	unordered

Possible exceptions

- Invalid operation:
  (CNF) If either operand is a signalling NaN.
  (CNFE) If either operand is a NaN of any kind.

COS

Cosine   Fd := cosine of Fm

Syntax: COS{*condition*}*precision*{*rounding*} Fd, <Fm |
#*value*>

If the condition is true this instruction evaluates the cosine of the operand and stores the rounded result in the specified register. The rounding mode and precision are only applied to the final result of the calculation; intermediate results are always rounded to nearest at extended precision.

   precision specifies the destination rounding precision: S (single), D (double) or E (extended). A precision *must* be specified.

   rounding optionally specifies the rounding mode: the default is round to nearest; otherwise P (round towards Plus infinity), M (round towards Minus infinity) or Z (round towards Zero).

   Fd and Fm are any floating point register (0..7) and #*value* is one of the constants 0.0, 1.0, 2.0, 3.0, 4.0, 5.0, 0.5 or 10.0.

Possible exceptions

- Invalid operation:
  (a) If the operand is a signalling NaN
  (b) If the operand is an infinity
  (c) If the operand is a number which is so large in magnitude that range-reducing it to a number in the range -π to +π would be very inaccurate (the exact point at which this happens may vary between implementations);
- Overflow: cannot occur, since the result always lies in the range –1 to +1
- Inexact

   This instruction is assembled to an ARM Coprocessor Data Operation (CDP) instruction; refer to that integer instruction for further information.

DVF

Divide floating   Fd := Fn / Fm

Syntax: DVF{*condition*}*precision*{*rounding*} Fd, Fn, <Fm
                                              | #*value*>

If the condition is true this instruction divides the first operand by the second operand and stores the rounded result in the specified register.

   precision specifies the destination rounding precision: S (single), D (double) or E (extended). A precision *must* be specified.

   rounding optionally specifies the rounding mode: the default is round to nearest; otherwise P (round towards Plus infinity), M (round towards Minus infinity) or Z (round towards Zero).

   Fd and Fm are any floating point register (0..7) and #*value* is one of the constants 0.0, 1.0, 2.0, 3.0, 4.0, 5.0, 0.5 or 10.0.

Possible exceptions

- Invalid operation:
  (a) If either operand is a signalling NaN
  (b) For 0 / 0
  (c) For ($\pm\infty$) / ($\pm\infty$)
- Divide-by-zero:
  If the second operand is 0 and the first operand is a non-zero number (if the first operand is 0, an invalid operation exception is produced instead)
- Overflow
- Underflow
- Inexact

   This instruction is assembled to an ARM Coprocessor Data Operation (CDP) instruction; refer to that integer instruction for further information.

EXP

Exponentiation   Fd := e ^{Fm}

Syntax: `EXP{condition}precision{rounding} Fd, <Fm | #value>`

If the condition is true this instruction raises e to the power of the operand and stores the rounded result in the specified register. The rounding mode and precision are only applied to the final result of the calculation; intermediate results are always rounded to nearest at extended precision.

   `precision` specifies the destination rounding precision: S (single), D (double) or E (extended). A precision *must* be specified.

   `rounding` optionally specifies the rounding mode: the default is round to nearest; otherwise P (round towards Plus infinity), M (round towards Minus infinity) or Z (round towards Zero).

   `Fd` and `Fm` are any floating point register (0..7) and `#value` is one of the constants 0.0, 1.0, 2.0, 3.0, 4.0, 5.0, 0.5 or 10.0.

Possible exceptions

   ■ Invalid operation: if the operand is a signalling NaN
   ■ Overflow
   ■ Underflow
   ■ Inexact

   This instruction is assembled to an ARM Coprocessor Data Operation (CDP) instruction; refer to that integer instruction for further information.

FDV (single-prec.)

Fast divide floating   Fd := Fn / Fm

Syntax: `FDV{condition}precision{rounding} Fd, Fn, <Fm`
`                                       | #value>`

If the condition is true this instruction divides the first operand by the second operand and stores the rounded result in the specified register.

This instruction is only defined to yield single-precision results. It is not guaranteed that any particular implementation will execute this 'fast' instruction any faster than its normal counterpart DVF.

precision specifies the destination rounding precision: S (single), D (double) or E (extended). A precision *must* be specified.

rounding optionally specifies the rounding mode: the default is round to nearest; otherwise P (round towards Plus infinity), M (round towards Minus infinity) or Z (round towards Zero).

Fd and Fm are any floating point register (0..7) and #*value* is one of the constants 0.0, 1.0, 2.0, 3.0, 4.0, 5.0, 0.5 or 10.0.

Possible exceptions

- Invalid operation:
  (a) If either operand is a signalling NaN
  (b) For 0 / 0
  (c) For ($\pm\infty$) / ($\pm\infty$)
- Divide-by-zero: if the second operand is 0 and the first operand is a non-zero number (if the first operand is 0, an invalid operation exception is produced instead)
- Overflow
- Underflow
- Inexact

This instruction is assembled to an ARM Coprocessor Data Operation (CDP) instruction; refer to that integer instruction for further information.

FIX

Convert floating to integer   Rd := FIX(Fm)

Syntax: FIX{*condition*}{*rounding*} Rd, Fm

If the condition is true this instruction takes the integer value of the operand and transfers it to the specified CPU integer register.

rounding optionally specifies the rounding mode: the default is round to nearest; otherwise P (round towards Plus infinity), M (round towards Minus infinity) or Z (round towards Zero).

Fm is any floating point register (0..7). Constants cannot be specified in the Fm field for this instruction; it is quicker to load the integer directly into the CPU register using MOV.

If Rd is r15 (PC) the top four bits of the result will be loaded into the CPSR flags N, Z, C, V and the remaining 28 bits will be discarded.

Possible exceptions

- Invalid operation:
    (a) If the operand is a NaN of any kind
    (b) If the operand is $\pm\infty$
    (c) If FIXing the operand (with the specified rounding mode) will overflow the integer range of -2^{31} to $2^{31}-1$
- Overflow cannot occur: if the integer range is exceeded, the instruction produces an invalid operation exception (overflow exceptions are only allowed to occur on instructions with floating point destinations)
- Underflow cannot occur, since the desired result is always an integer
- Inexact: the FIX instruction produces the inexact exception if its result is not exactly equal to its operand, i.e. if the operand was not equal to an integer (and an invalid operation exception did not occur)

This instruction is assembled to an ARM Coprocessor Register Transfer (MRC) instruction; refer to that integer instruction for further information.

FLT

Convert integer to floating   Fd := FLT(Rd)

Syntax: `FLT{`*condition*`}`*precision*`{`*rounding*`} Fn, Rd`

If the condition is true this instruction converts the integer in the CPU register Rd to a floating-point value of specified precision and stores the rounded result in the floating-point register Fd.

precision specifies the destination rounding precision: S (single), D (double) or E (extended). A precision *must* be specified.

rounding optionally specifies the rounding mode: the default is round to nearest; otherwise P (round towards Plus infinity), M (round towards Minus infinity) or Z (round towards Zero).

Rd is any CPU register 0..14. Do not specify R15 (PC) as Rd.

Possible exceptions

- Overflow: cannot occur, since the operand is at most 2^{31} in magnitude
- Underflow: cannot occur, since the operand is always an integer
- Inexact: note this is only possible for FLTS, since double and extended precision numbers can represent all integers in the range -2^{31} to $2^{31}-1$ exactly

This instruction is assembled to an ARM Coprocessor Register Transfer (MCR) instruction; refer to that integer instruction for further information.

FML

Fast multiply floating   Fd := Fn * Fm

`Syntax: FML{`*`condition`*`}`*`precision`*`{`*`rounding`*`} Fd, Fn, <Fm`
`                                     | #`*`value`*`>`

If the condition is true this instruction multiplies the first operand by the second operand and stores the rounded result in the specified register.

This instruction is only defined to work with single-precision source operands. It is not guaranteed that any particular implementation will execute this 'fast' instruction any faster than its normal counterpart MUF.

precision specifies the destination rounding precision: S (single), D (double) or E (extended). A precision *must* be specified.

rounding optionally specifies the rounding mode: the default is round to nearest; otherwise P (round towards Plus infinity), M (round towards Minus infinity) or Z (round towards Zero).

Fd and Fm are any floating point register (0..7) and #*value* is one of the constants 0.0, 1.0, 2.0, 3.0, 4.0, 5.0, 0.5 or 10.0.

Possible exceptions

- Invalid operation:
  (a) If either operand is a signalling NaN
  (b) For (±∞) * 0
  (c) For 0 * (±∞)
- Overflow
- Underflow
- Inexact

This instruction is assembled to an ARM Coprocessor Data Operation (CDP) instruction; refer to that integer instruction for further information.

FRD

Fast reverse divide floating   Fd := Fn/Fm

Syntax: FRD{*condition*}*precision*{*rounding*} Fd, <Fm |
                                               #*value*>

If the condition is true this instruction divides the second operand by the first operand and stores the rounded result in the specified register.

This instruction is only defined to work with single-precision source operands. It is not guaranteed that any particular implementation will execute this 'fast' instruction any faster than its normal counterpart RDF.

precision specifies the destination rounding precision: S (single), D (double) or E (extended). A precision *must* be specified.

rounding optionally specifies the rounding mode: the default is round to nearest; otherwise P (round towards Plus infinity), M (round towards Minus infinity) or Z (round towards Zero).

Fd and Fm are any floating point register (0..7) and #*value* is one of the constants 0.0, 1.0, 2.0, 3.0, 4.0, 5.0, 0.5 or 10.0.

Possible exceptions

- Invalid operation:
  (a) If either operand is a signalling NaN
  (b) For 0 / 0
  (c) For (±∞) / (±∞)
- Divide-by-zero: If the first operand is 0 and the second operand is a non-zero number (if the second operand is 0, an invalid operation exception is produced instead)
- Overflow
- Underflow
- Inexact

This instruction is assembled to an ARM Coprocessor Data Operation (CDP) instruction; refer to that integer instruction for further information.

LDF

Load floating   Fd := *address*

Syntax: LDF{*condition*}*precision* Fd, *address*

If the condition is true this instruction loads the specified floating-point register with a value from memory at the specified precision.

precision determines the size and precision of the value loaded:

Suffix	Precision	Size of value
S	single precision	one 32-bit word
D	double precision	two 32-bit words
E	extended precision	three 32-bit words
P	packed decimal	three 32-bit words

If the EP flag in the FPSR is set then expanded packed decimal format is used when P is specified, occupying four 32-bit words instead of three. This allows conversion between binary and decimal formats with sufficient accuracy to preserve extended precision values.

The address may take one of several forms to allowing indexing variations:

Address	Offset	Indexing
[Rn]	no offset	pre-indexed
[Rn, #expression]{!}	offset of expression	pre-indexed
[Rn], #expression	offset of expression	post-indexed

The address offset is specified in words and must be divisible by four and in the range −1020 to +1020. The offset is added to or subtracted from the base register Rn either before (pre-indexed) or after (post-indexed) being used as the transfer address. The modified base value may either be written back always (in the post-indexed form), or is written back if ! is present in the pre-indexed form, or is preserved.

R15 must not be used as the base register if write-back is specified in pre-indexed modes nor used at all in post-indexed modes.

Possible exceptions

None for unpacked forms (S/D/E suffix).

LDF

Possible exceptions for LDFP:

- Invalid operation: if the operand is a signalling NaN
- Overflow
- Underflow
- Inexact

LFM

Load floating multiple   Pop floating registers

Syntax: LFM{*condition*} Fd, *count*, *address*

LFM{*condition*}<FD|EA> Fd, *count*, [Rn] {!}

If the condition is true this instruction loads a specified number of floating-point registers from memory in a single operation. A variety of addressing modes are supported, allowing stacks to be implemented for efficient context switching.

'Fd, count' indicates which registers will be loaded. 'Fd' stands for the first register to be loaded and 'count' for the total number of registers loaded in the range 1..4. The registers loaded are successive starting with Fd and wrap around from F7 to F0; for example, F6, 4 stands for F6, F7, F0, F1 in that order.

Two alternative syntaxes are allowed, the former having traditional pre- and post-indexing style, the latter having the LDM/STM style supported by integer instructions.

The values are transferred as three 32-bit words per floating-point register. The format of these words is not defined and may change, so the only legitimate operations are to load (LFM) and store (SFM) them.

The address may take one of several forms to allowing indexing variations:

Address	Offset	Indexing
[Rn]	no offset	pre-indexed
[Rn, #expression]{!}	offset of expression	pre-indexed
[Rn], #expression	offset of expression	post-indexed

The address offset is specified in words and must be divisible by four and in the range −1020 to +1020. The offset is added to or subtracted from the base register Rn either before (pre-indexed) or after (post-indexed) being used as the transfer address. The modified base value may either be written back always (in the post-indexed form), or is written back if ! is present in the pre-indexed form, or is preserved.

Note that only EA and FD are permitted: alternative forms available in integer instructions are not permitted for LFM/SFM.

R15 must not be used as the base register if write-back is specified in pre-indexed modes nor used at all in post-indexed modes.

Possible exceptions

■ None

LGN

Logarithm to base e   Fd := log e of Fm

Syntax: LGN{*condition*}*precision*{*rounding*} Fd, <Fm |
                                    #value>

If the condition is true this instruction evaluates log to base e of the operand and stores the rounded result in the specified register. The rounding mode and precision are only applied to the final result of the calculation; intermediate results are always rounded to nearest at extended precision.

   precision specifies the destination rounding precision: S (single), D (double) or E (extended). A precision *must* be specified.

   rounding optionally specifies the rounding mode: the default is round to nearest; otherwise P (round towards Plus infinity), M (round towards Minus infinity) or Z (round towards Zero).

   Fd and Fm are any floating point register (0..7) and #*value* is one of the constants 0.0, 1.0, 2.0, 3.0, 4.0, 5.0, 0.5 or 10.0.

Possible exceptions

- Invalid operation:
  (a) If the operand is a signalling NaN
  (b) If the operand is negative
- Divide-by-zero: if the operand is 0
- Overflow: cannot occur, since the operand lies in the range $2^{(-16446)}$ to 2^{16384} and so the result always lies in the range $-16446 \times LOG(2)$ to $16384 \times LOG(2)$
- Underflow: cannot occur, since LGN(1) is zero exactly and the operand must otherwise lie at least $2^{(-64)}$ away from 1. The LGN of a number which is not 1 is therefore at least $2^{(-65)}$ in magnitude, and so will not underflow even in single precision
- Inexact

   This instruction is assembled to an ARM Coprocessor Data Operation (CDP) instruction; refer to that integer instruction for further information.

LOG

Logarithm to base 10   Fd := log$_{10}$ of Fm

Syntax: LOG{*condition*}*precision*{*rounding*} Fd, <Fm |
                              #*value*>

If the condition is true this instruction evaluates log to base 10 of the operand and stores the rounded result in the specified register. The rounding mode and precision are only applied to the final result of the calculation; intermediate results are always rounded to nearest at extended precision.

   precision specifies the destination rounding precision: S (single), D (double) or E (extended). A precision *must* be specified.

   rounding optionally specifies the rounding mode: the default is round to nearest; otherwise P (round towards Plus infinity), M (round towards Minus infinity) or Z (round towards Zero).

   Fd and Fm are any floating point register (0..7) and #*value* is one of the constants 0.0, 1.0, 2.0, 3.0, 4.0, 5.0, 0.5 or 10.0.

Possible exceptions

- Invalid operation:
  (a) If the operand is a signalling NaN
  (b) If the operand is negative
- Divide-by-zero: if the operand is 0
- Overflow: cannot occur, since the operand lies in the range $2^{\wedge}(-16446)$ to $2^{\wedge}16384$ and so the result always lies in the range $-16446*LOG(2)$ to $16384*LOG(2)$
- Underflow: cannot occur, since LOG(1) is zero exactly and the operand must otherwise lie at least $2^{\wedge}(-64)$ away from 1. The LOG of a number which is not 1 is therefore at least $2^{\wedge}(-66)$ in magnitude, and so will not underflow even in single precision
- Inexact

This instruction is assembled to an ARM Coprocessor Data Operation (CDP) instruction; refer to that integer instruction for further information.

MNF

Move floating negated   Fd := -Fm

Syntax: `MNF{`*condition*`}`*precision*`{`*rounding*`} Fd, <Fm |`
                                              `#`*value*`>`

If the condition is true this instruction negates the operand and stores the
rounded result in the specified register.

   precision specifies the destination rounding precision: S (single), D (double) or E (extended). A precision *must* be specified.

   rounding optionally specifies the rounding mode: the default is round to
nearest; otherwise P (round towards Plus infinity), M (round towards Minus
infinity) or Z (round towards Zero).

   Fd and Fm are any floating point register (0..7) and `#`*value* is one of the constants 0.0, 1.0, 2.0, 3.0, 4.0, 5.0, 0.5 or 10.0.

Possible exceptions

- Invalid operation: if the operand is a signalling NaN of a different precision
  to the destination precision of the instruction
- Overflow: note this can only occur if the operand has a higher precision
  than the destination precision of the instruction
- Underflow: note this can only occur if the operand has a higher precision
  than the destination precision of the instruction
- Inexact: note this can only occur if the operand has a higher precision than
  the destination precision of the instruction

   This instruction is assembled to an ARM Coprocessor Data Operation
(CDP) instruction; refer to that integer instruction for further information.

MUF

Multiply floating   Fd := Fn * Fm

`Syntax: MUF{`*`condition`*`}`*`precision`*`{`*`rounding`*`} Fd, Fn, <Fm`
`| #`*`value`*`>`

If the condition is true this instruction multiplies the first operand by the second and stores the rounded result in the specified register.

precision specifies the destination rounding precision: S (single), D (double) or E (extended). A precision *must* be specified.

rounding optionally specifies the rounding mode: the default is round to nearest; otherwise P (round towards Plus infinity), M (round towards Minus infinity) or Z (round towards Zero).

Fd and Fm are any floating point register (0..7) and #*value* is one of the constants 0.0, 1.0, 2.0, 3.0, 4.0, 5.0, 0.5 or 10.0.

Possible exceptions

- Invalid operation:
  (a) If either operand is a signalling NaN
  (b) For (±∞) * 0
  (c) For 0 * (±∞)
- Overflow
- Underflow
- Inexact

This instruction is assembled to an ARM Coprocessor Data Operation (CDP) instruction; refer to that integer instruction for further information.

MVF

Move floating   Fd := Fm

Syntax: MVF{*condition*}*precision*{*rounding*} Fd, <Fm |
                                               #*value*>

If the condition is true this instruction moves the operand to the specified register; the operand is delivered at the appropriate precision and rounding is performed.

precision specifies the destination rounding precision: S (single), D (double) or E (extended). A precision *must* be specified.

rounding optionally specifies the rounding mode: the default is round to nearest; otherwise P (round towards Plus infinity), M (round towards Minus infinity) or Z (round towards Zero).

Fd and Fm are any floating point register (0..7) and #*value* is one of the constants 0.0, 1.0, 2.0, 3.0, 4.0, 5.0, 0.5 or 10.0.

Possible exceptions

- Invalid operation: if the operand is a signalling NaN of a different precision to the destination precision of the instruction.
- Overflow: note this can only occur if the operand has a higher precision than the destination precision of the instruction.
- Underflow: note this can only occur if the operand has a higher precision than the destination precision of the instruction.
- Inexact: note this can only occur if the operand has a higher precision than the destination precision of the instruction.

This instruction is assembled to an ARM Coprocessor Data Operation (CDP) instruction; refer to that integer instruction for further information.

NRM

Normalize result of URD   Fd := normalized Fm

Syntax: NRM{*condition*}*precision*{*rounding*} Fd, <Fm |
                                          #*value*>

If the condition is true this instruction normalizes the result of a previous URD instruction; the precision and rounding mode of an NRM instruction must match those of the preceding URD instruction, it may deliver meaningless results when applied to any other value. Refer to the URD instruction for further information.

precision specifies the destination rounding precision: S (single), D (double) or E (extended). A precision *must* be specified.

rounding optionally specifies the rounding mode: the default is round to nearest; otherwise P (round towards Plus infinity), M (round towards Minus infinity) or Z (round towards Zero).

Fd and Fm are any floating point register (0..7) and #*value* is one of the constants 0.0, 1.0, 2.0, 3.0, 4.0, 5.0, 0.5 or 10.0.

Possible exceptions

■ Invalid operation: if the operand is a signalling NaN
■ Overflow, underflow and inexact: can only occur when NRM is used in an incorrect way, that is on anything other than the result of an URD instruction with the same destination precision

This instruction is assembled to an ARM Coprocessor Data Operation (CDP) instruction; refer to that integer instruction for further information.

This instruction does not exist in floating-point systems pre-dating the FPA10.

POL

Polar angle (ArcTan2)   Fd := polar angle (Fn, Fm)

Syntax: POL{*condition*}*precision*{*rounding*} Fd, <Fm |
                                            #*value*>

If the condition is true this instruction evaluates the 'polar angle' function
ArcTan2(Fn, Fm), which is closely related to arc tangent(Fm/Fn) and stores the
rounded result in the specified register. The rounding mode and precision are
only applied to the final result of the calculation; intermediate results are always
rounded to nearest at extended precision.

precision specifies the destination rounding precision: S (single), D (double) or E (extended). A precision *must* be specified.

rounding optionally specifies the rounding mode: the default is round to
nearest; otherwise P (round towards Plus infinity), M (round towards Minus
infinity) or Z (round towards Zero).

Fd and Fm are any floating point register (0..7) and #*value* is one of the constants 0.0, 1.0, 2.0, 3.0, 4.0, 5.0, 0.5 or 10.0.

Possible exceptions

- Invalid operation:
  (a) If either operand is a signalling NaN
  (b) If both operands are 0
  (c) If both operands are $\pm\infty$
- Overflow: cannot occur, since the result is always in the range $-\pi$ to $+\pi$
- Underflow
- Inexact.

This instruction is assembled to an ARM Coprocessor Data Operation
(CDP) instruction; refer to that integer instruction for further information.

POW

Power   Fd := Fn raised to Fm

Syntax: POW{*condition*}*precision*{*rounding*} Fd, Fn, <Fm
                                          | #*value*>

If the condition is true this instruction evaluates Fn raised to the power of Fm and
stores the rounded result in the specified register. The rounding mode and precision are only applied to the final result of the calculation; intermediate results are
always rounded to nearest at extended precision.

precision specifies the destination rounding precision: S (single), D (double) or E (extended). A precision *must* be specified.

rounding optionally specifies the rounding mode: the default is Round to
nearest; otherwise P (round towards Plus infinity), M (round towards Minus
infinity) or Z (round towards Zero).

Fd and Fm are any floating point register (0..7) and #*value* is one of the constants 0.0, 1.0, 2.0, 3.0, 4.0, 5.0, 0.5 or 10.0.

Possible exceptions

- Invalid operation:
  (a) If either operand is a signalling NaN
  (b) If the first operand is negative and the second is not a NaN (on some
  systems, this invalid operation won't occur if the second operand is exactly
  equal to an integer)
  (c) If the first operand is 0 and the second is negative or 0 (on some systems,
  this invalid operation won't occur if the second operand is exactly equal to
  an integer)
  (d) If the first operand is +1 and the second is an infinity
  (e) If the first operand is an infinity and the second is 0 (on some systems,
  this invalid operation won't occur)
- Divide-by-zero: If the first operand is 0 and the second is exactly equal to a
  negative integer (on some systems only)
- Overflow
- Underflow
- Inexact

This instruction is assembled to an ARM Coprocessor Data Operation
(CDP) instruction; refer to that integer instruction for further information.

RDF

Reverse divide floating   Fd := Fm / Fn

Syntax: RDF{condition}precision{rounding} Fd, Fn, <Fm
                                    | #value>

If the condition is true this instruction divides the second operand by the first and stores the rounded result in the specified register.

   precision specifies the destination rounding precision: S (single), D (double) or E (extended). A precision *must* be specified.

   rounding optionally specifies the rounding mode: the default is Round to nearest; otherwise P (round towards Plus infinity), M (round towards Minus infinity) or Z (round towards Zero).

   Fd and Fm are any floating point register (0..7) and #value is one of the constants 0.0, 1.0, 2.0, 3.0, 4.0, 5.0, 0.5 or 10.0.

Possible exceptions

   - Invalid operation:
     (a) If either operand is a signalling NaN
     (b) For 0 / 0
     (c) For ($\pm\infty$) / ($\pm\infty$)
   - Divide-by-zero: If the first operand is 0 and the second operand is a non-zero number (if the second operand is 0, an invalid operation exception is produced instead)
   - Overflow
   - Underflow
   - Inexact

   This instruction is assembled to an ARM Coprocessor Data Operation (CDP) instruction; refer to that integer instruction for further information.

RFC

Read floating-point control register   Rd := FPCR

Syntax: RFC{*condition*} Rd

If the condition is true this instruction reads the Floating Point Control Register (FPCR) and stores it in the specified integer CPU register, possibly DESTROYING THE CONTENTS OF FPCR AS IT DOES SO. This instruction may only be executed in Supervisor mode. See the section on the FPCR for more information.

This instruction deals with a register which is implementation-specific.

Possible exceptions

■ None

The use of this instruction outside of floating-point support software is strongly discouraged. Note that this instruction is for internal communication within a floating-point system, for example between the FPA10 and its support software, and may not be implemented in some floating-point systems. Do not use this instruction without referring to the documentation for the floating-point package you are using.

RFS

Read floating-point status register   Rd := FPSR

Syntax: RFS{*condition*} Rd

If the condition is true this instruction reads the Floating Point Status Register (FPSR) and stores it in the specified integer CPU register. Refer to the section in Chapter 9 on the FPSR for more information.

This instruction may be executed freely (unlike RFC/WFC) to allow user programs to interrogate the floating-point system status.

Possible exceptions

- None

RMF

IEEE Remainder   Fd := remainder of Fn/Fm

Syntax: RMF{*condition*}*precision*{*rounding*} Fd, Fn, <FM
                                                    | #*value*>

If the condition is true this instruction evaluates the IEEE remainder when the
first operand is divided by the second operand and stores the rounded result in
the specified register.

    precision specifies the destination rounding precision: S (single), D (dou-
ble) or E (extended). A precision *must* be specified.

    rounding optionally specifies the rounding mode: the default is Round to
nearest; otherwise P (round towards Plus infinity), M (round towards Minus
infinity) or Z (round towards Zero).

    Fd and Fm are any floating point register (0..7) and #*value* is one of the con-
stants 0.0, 1.0, 2.0, 3.0, 4.0, 5.0, 0.5 or 10.0.

Possible exceptions

- Invalid operation:
  (a) If either operand is a signalling NaN
  (b) If the first operand is +/-infinity and the second is not a NaN
  (c) If the first operand is a number and the second is 0
- Overflow: this can only occur if at least one operand has a higher precision
  than the destination precision of the instruction
- Underflow: this can only occur if at least one operand has a higher precision
  than the destination precision of the instruction
- Inexact: this can only occur if at least one operand has a higher precision
  than the destination precision of the instruction

    This instruction is assembled to an ARM Coprocessor Data Operation
(CDP) instruction; refer to that integer instruction for further information.

RND

Round   Fd := integer value of Fm

Syntax: RND{*condition*}*precision*{*rounding*} Fd, <Fm |
                                          #*value*>

If the condition is true this instruction evaluates the integer value of the operand and stores the rounded result in the specified register.

   precision specifies the destination rounding precision: S (single), D (double) or E (extended). A precision *must* be specified.

   rounding optionally specifies the rounding mode: the default is Round to nearest; otherwise P (round towards Plus infinity), M (round towards Minus infinity) or Z (round towards Zero).

   Fd and Fm are any floating point register (0..7) and #*value* is one of the constants 0.0, 1.0, 2.0, 3.0, 4.0, 5.0, 0.5 or 10.0.

Possible exceptions

- Invalid operation: if the operand is a signalling NaN
- Overflow: this can only occur if the operand has a higher precision than the destination precision of the instruction
- Underflow: cannot occur, since the result is always an integer
- Inexact: the RND instruction produces the inexact exception if its result is not exactly equal to its operand; that is if the operand was not equal to an integer, or if overflow occurs

   This instruction is assembled to an ARM Coprocessor Data Operation (CDP) instruction; refer to that integer instruction for further information.

RPW

Reverse power   Fd := Fm raised to Fn

Syntax: RPW{*condition*}*precision*{*rounding*} Fd, Fn, <Fm
                                            | #*value*>

If the condition is true this instruction evaluates Fm raised to the power of Fn and stores the rounded result in the specified register. The rounding mode and precision are only applied to the final result of the calculation; intermediate results are always rounded to nearest at extended precision.

precision specifies the destination rounding precision: S (single), D (double) or E (extended). A precision *must* be specified.

rounding optionally specifies the rounding mode: the default is Round to nearest; otherwise P (round towards Plus infinity), M (round towards Minus infinity) or Z (round towards Zero).

Fd and Fm are any floating point register (0..7, and #*value* is one of the constants 0.0, 1.0, 2.0, 3.0, 4.0, 5.0, 0.5 or 10.0.

Possible exceptions

- Invalid operation:
  (a) If either operand is a signalling NaN
  (b) If the second operand is negative and the first is not a NaN (on some systems, this invalid operation won't occur if the first operand is exactly equal to an integer)
  (c) If the second operand is 0 and the first is negative or 0 (on some systems, this invalid operation won't occur if the first operand is exactly equal to an integer)
  (d) If the second operand is +1 and the first is an infinity
  (e) If the second operand is an infinity and the first is 0 (on some systems, this invalid operation won't occur)
- Divide-by-zero: If the second operand is 0 and the first is exactly equal to a negative integer (on some systems only)
- Overflow
- Underflow
- Inexact

This instruction is assembled to an ARM Coprocessor Data Operation (CDP) instruction; refer to that integer instruction for further information.

RSF

Reverse subtract floating   Fd := Fm – Fn

Syntax: RSF{*condition*}*precision*{*rounding*} Fd, Fn, <Fm
                                              | #*value*>

If the condition is true this instruction subtracts the first operand from the second and stores the rounded result in the specified register.

precision specifies the destination rounding precision: S (single), D (double) or E (extended). A precision *must* be specified.

rounding optionally specifies the rounding mode: the default is Round to nearest; otherwise P (round towards Plus infinity), M (round towards Minus infinity) or Z (round towards Zero).

Fd and Fm are any floating point register (0..7) and #*value* is one of the constants 0.0, 1.0, 2.0, 3.0, 4.0, 5.0, 0.5 or 10.0.

Possible exceptions

■ Invalid operation:
   (a) If either operand is a signalling NaN
   (b) For (+∞) – (+∞)
   (c) For (–∞) – (–∞)
■ Overflow
■ Underflow
■ Inexact

This instruction is assembled to an ARM Coprocessor Data Operation (CDP) instruction; refer to that integer instruction for further information.

SFM

Store floating multiple   Push floating registers

Syntax: `SFM{condition} Fd, count, `*`address`*

`SFM{condition}<FD|EA> Fd, count, [Rn]{!}`

If the condition is true this instruction stores a specified number of floating-point registers to memory in a single operation. A variety of addressing modes are supported, allowing stacks to be implemented for efficient context switching.

Fd, count indicates which registers will be loaded. Fd stands for the first register to be loaded and count for the total number of registers loaded in the range 1..4. The registers loaded are successive starting with Fd and wrap around from F7 to F0; for example, F6, 4 stands for F6, F7, F0, F1 in that order.

Two alternative syntaxes are allowed, the former having traditional pre- and post-indexing style, the latter having the LDM/STM style supported by integer instructions.

The values are transferred as three 32-bit words per floating-point register. The format of these words is not defined and may change, so the only legitimate operations are to load (LFM) and store (SFM) them.

The address may take one of several forms to allowing indexing variations:

Address	Offset	Indexing
[Rn]	no offset	pre-indexed
[Rn, #expression]{!}	offset of expression	pre-indexed
[Rn], #expression	offset of expression	post-indexed

The address offset is specified in words and must be divisible by four and in the range −1020 to +1020. The offset is added to or subtracted from the base register Rn either before (pre-indexed) or after (post-indexed) being used as the transfer address. The modified base value may be written back always (in the post-indexed form), or is written back if ! is present in the pre-indexed form, or is preserved.

Note that only EA and FD are permitted: alternative forms available in integer instructions are not permitted for LFM/SFM.

R15 must not be used as the base register if write-back is specified in pre-indexed modes nor used at all in post-indexed modes.

Possible exceptions

■ None

SIN

Sine   Fd := sine of Fm

Syntax: SIN{condition}precision{rounding} Fd, <Fm |
                                          #value>

If the condition is true this instruction evaluates the sine of the operand and stores the rounded result in the specified register. The rounding mode and precision are only applied to the final result of the calculation; intermediate results are always rounded to nearest at extended precision.

   precision specifies the destination rounding precision: S (single), D (double) or E (extended). A precision *must* be specified.

   rounding optionally specifies the rounding mode: the default is Round to nearest; otherwise P (round towards Plus infinity), M (round towards Minus infinity) or Z (round towards Zero).

   Fd and Fm are any floating point register (0..7) and #*value* is one of the constants 0.0, 1.0, 2.0, 3.0, 4.0, 5.0, 0.5 or 10.0.

Possible exceptions

■ Invalid operation:
   (a) If the operand is a signalling NaN
   (b) If the operand is an infinity
   (c) If the operand is a number which is so large in magnitude that range-
       reducing it to a number in the range -π to +π would be very inaccurate
       (the exact point at which this happens may vary between implementa-
       tions)
■ Overflow: cannot occur, since the result always lies in the range –1 to +1
■ Underflow
■ Inexact

   This instruction is assembled to an ARM Coprocessor Data Operation (CDP) instruction; refer to that integer instruction for further information.

SQT

Square root   Fd := square root of Fm

Syntax: SQT{*condition*}*precision*{*rounding*} Fd, <Fm |
                                    #*value*>

If the condition is true this instruction evaluates the square root of the operand
and stores the rounded result in the specified register.

    precision specifies the destination rounding precision: S (single), D (dou-
ble) or E (extended). A precision *must* be specified.

    rounding optionally specifies the rounding mode: the default is Round to
nearest; otherwise P (round towards Plus infinity), M (round towards Minus
infinity) or Z (round towards Zero).

    Fd and Fm are any floating point register (0..7) and #*value* is one of the con-
stants 0.0, 1.0, 2.0, 3.0, 4.0, 5.0, 0.5 or 10.0.

Possible exceptions

- Invalid operation:
  (a) If the operand is a signalling NaN
  (b) If the operand is negative
- Overflow: note this can only occur if the operand has a higher precision
  than the destination precision of the instruction
- Underflow: note this can only occur if the operand has a higher precision
  than the destination precision of the instruction
- Inexact

    This instruction is assembled to an ARM Coprocessor Data Operation
(CDP) instruction; refer to that integer instruction for further information.

STF

Store floating   <address> := Fd

Syntax: STF{*condition*}*precision* Fd, *address*

If the condition is true this instruction stores the specified floating-point register at the specified address with the specified precision.

   precision determines the size and precision of the value stored:

Suffix	Precision	Size of value
S	single precision	one 32-bit word
D	double precision	two 32-bit words
E	extended precision	three 32-bit words
P	packed decimal	three 32-bit words

   If the EP flag in the FPSR is set then expanded packed decimal format is used when P is specified, occupying four 32-bit words instead of three. This allows conversion between binary and decimal formats with sufficient accuracy to preserve extended precision values.

   The address may take one of several forms to allowing indexing variations:

Address	Offset	Indexing
[Rn]	no offset	pre-indexed
[Rn, #expression]{!}	offset of expression	pre-indexed
[Rn], #expression	offset of expression	post-indexed

   The address offset is specified in words and must be divisible by four and in the range −1020 to +1020. The offset is added to or subtracted from the base register Rn either before (pre-indexed) or after (post-indexed) being used as the transfer address. The modified base value may be written back always (in the post-indexed form), or is written back if ! is present in the pre-indexed form, or is preserved.

   R15 must not be used as the base register if write-back is specified in pre-indexed modes nor used at all in post-indexed modes.

STF

Possible exceptions

STFS/D/E:

- Invalid operation: if the operand is a signalling NaN of a different precision to the destination precision of the instruction
- Overflow: note this can only occur if the operand has a higher precision than the destination precision of the instruction
- Underflow: note this can only occur if the operand has a higher precision than the destination precision of the instruction
- Inexact: note this can only occur if the operand has a higher precision than the destination precision of the instruction

STFP:

- Invalid operation: if the operand is a signalling NaN
- Overflow and underflow: cannot occur, since the range of both packed format exceeds that of single, double or extended precision numbers
- Inexact

SUF

Subtract floating   Fd := Fn – Fm

Syntax: SUF{*condition*}*precision*{*rounding*} Fd, Fn, <Fm
                                  | #*value*>

If the condition is true this instruction subtracts the second operand from the first and stores the rounded result in the specified register.

    precision specifies the destination rounding precision: S (single), D (double) or E (extended). A precision <must> be specified.

    rounding optionally specifies the rounding mode: the default is Round to nearest; otherwise P (round towards Plus infinity), M (round towards Minus infinity) or Z (round towards Zero).

    Fd, Fn and Fm are any floating point register (0..7) and #*value* is one of the constants 0.0, 1.0, 2.0, 3.0, 4.0, 5.0, 0.5 or 10.0.

Possible exceptions

- Invalid operation:
  (a) If either operand is a signalling NaN
  (b) For $(+\infty) - (+\infty)$
  (c) For $(-\infty) - (-\infty)$
- Overflow
- Underflow
- Inexact

    This instruction is assembled to an ARM Coprocessor Data Operation (CDP) instruction; refer to that integer instruction for further information.

TAN

Tangent   Fd := tangent of Fm

Syntax: TAN{*condition*}*precision*{*rounding*} Fd,Fn,Fm|
                                    #*value*

If the condition is true this instruction evaluates the tangent of the operand and stores the rounded result in the specified register. The rounding mode and precision are only applied to the final result of the calculation; intermediate results are always rounded to nearest at extended precision.

   precision specifies the destination rounding precision: S (single), D (double) or E (extended). A precision *must* be specified.

   rounding optionally specifies the rounding mode: the default is Round to nearest; otherwise P (round towards Plus infinity), M (round towards Minus infinity) or Z (round towards Zero).

   Fd and Fm are any floating point register (0..7) and #value is one of the constants 0.0, 1.0, 2.0, 3.0, 4.0, 5.0, 0.5 or 10.0.

Possible exceptions:

   ■ Invalid operation:
      (a) If the operand is a signalling NaN
      (b) If the operand is an infinity
      (c) If the operand is a number which is so large in magnitude that range-reducing it to a number in the range $-\pi/2$ to $+\pi/2$ would be very inaccurate (the exact point at which this happens may vary between implementations)
   ■ Underflow
   ■ Inexact

   This instruction is assembled to an ARM Coprocessor Data Operation (CDP) instruction; refer to that integer instruction for further information.

URD

Unnormalized round   Fd := integer value of Fm

Syntax: URD{*condition*}*precision*{*rounding*} Fd, Fm |
                                    #*value*

If the condition is true this instruction performs an unnormalized round on the operand. This gives a floating-point result whose value is an integer result, possibly in an abnormal form. The NRM instruction must be used on the result of URD before the final result is meaningful. RND should be used in code expected to run on all implementations of the ARM floating-point standard.

precision specifies the destination rounding precision: S (single), D (double) or E (extended). A precision *must* be specified.

rounding optionally specifies the rounding mode: the default is Round to nearest; otherwise P (round towards Plus infinity), M (round towards Minus infinity) or Z (round towards Zero).

Fd and Fm are any floating point register (0..7) and #*value* is one of the constants 0.0, 1.0, 2.0, 3.0, 4.0, 5.0, 0.5 or 10.0.

Possible exceptions:

■ Invalid operation: if the operand is a signalling NaN
■ Overflow: this can only occur if the operand has a higher precision than the destination precision of the instruction
■ Underflow: cannot occur, since the result is always an integer
■ Inexact: the URD instruction produces the inexact exception if its result is not exactly equal to its operand, that is if the operand was not equal to an integer, or if overflow occurs

This instruction is assembled to an ARM Coprocessor Data Operation (CDP) instruction; refer to that integer instruction for further information.

This instruction does not exist in floating-point hardware pre-dating the FPA10. The URD/NRM instruction pair was introduced on the FPA10 to improve implementation efficiency.

WFC

Write floating-point control register   FPCR := Rd

Syntax: `WFC{condition} Rd`

If the condition is true this instruction writes the specified integer CPU register to the Floating Point Control Register (FPCR). This instruction may only be executed in Supervisor mode. See the section on the FPCR for more information.

Possible exceptions

■ None

This instruction deals with a register which is implementation-specific.

The use of this instruction outside of floating-point support software is strongly discouraged. Note that this instruction is for internal communication within a floating-point system, for example between the FPA10 and its support software, and may not be implemented in some floating-point systems. Do not use this instruction without referring to the documentation for the floating-point package you are using.

WFS

Write floating-point status register   FPSR := Rd

Syntax: WFS{*condition*} Rd

If the condition is true this instruction writes the specified integer CPU register to the Floating Point Status Register (FPSR). Refer to the section in Chapter 9 on the FPSR for more information.

This instruction may be executed freely (unlike RFC/WFC) to allow user programs to alter the floating-point system status.

Possible exceptions

- None

Appendix C

Assembler directives

! (Test and assert)

Arithmetic test and assert error   Diagnostic directive

Syntax: ! *arithmetic-expression*, *string_expression*

The ! directive is inspected on both passes of the assembly. The arithmetic expression following the directive is evaluated and its result used to determine whether a user error condition is raised:

If the arithmetic expression evaluates to a non-zero result the string expression is printed as an error message and assembly halts after the first assembly pass.

If the arithmetic expression evaluates to zero no action is taken during the first pass and the string expression is printed as a warning during the second pass.

See also: ASSERT

(Reserve space)

Reserve space in storage map   Store allocation

Syntax: {Label} # *expression*

Reserves the number of bytes specified by the expression in the storage map previously located using the ^ directive.

The label can optionally mark the storage space by name, allowing it to be referred to in future load and store instructions.

See also: ^

& (DCD)

Define constant word   Store initialization

Syntax: *Label & expression-list*

Place word data at the current instruction location and advance the location counter. One or more words are defined by this directive, their expressions being separated by commas.

For example:

```
Wordz        DCD          Word1, Word2, Word3;Define three words
```

See also: DCD, =/DCB, DCW

%

Zero fill/Local label introduction   Store initialization/Local label

Syntax: *Label % numeric-expression*

As a store initialization directive % clears memory (to zero) starting at the current location counter for as many bytes as the expression value indicates.
For example:

```
NullTable    %            &400   ; A 1K table of nulls
```

The % symbol may also be used to introduce a local label. In this case it is employed in the third listing column, in any position where a normal label might have been used. For example:

```
            BNE    %FA16  ; bne to local label 16
```

See also: =/DCB, DCW, &/DCD; ROUT

* (EQU)

Equate   **Symbol definition**

Syntax: *Label * numeric exp|program-relative exp*

Assign a numeric value to a symbol. Program-relative values can also be assigned in this way.

For example:

```
Bell              *              &07
Book              *              &08
Candle            *              &09

Label             *              SWI &1001
Here              *              Label+4
```

See also: EQU (synonym)

= (DCB)

Define constant byte   **Store initialization**

Syntax: *Label = expression-list*

Place byte data at the current instruction location and advance the location counter. One or more bytes are defined by this directive, their expressions being separated by commas.

For example:

```
ErrorZ       =            "Error",&00

Table        =            &00,&FF,&55,&AA
```

See also: DCB, DCD, DCW

[(IF)

IF   Conditional assembly

Syntax: [*logical exp*

              ...instructions executed if expression
                                    true...

              {|

              ...instructions executed if expression
                                    false...}

              ]

Instruction sequences delimited by the IF and ENDIF directives, written [and],
are assembled only if the logical expression evaluates true at the time of assembly.
The optional directive ELSE, written |, allows instructions to be assembled if the
condition is false.

    None of [, | or] may appear as the first character on any line of input to the
Assembler.

    Lines not assembled as a result of these directives are not listed unless the
Assembler's –NOTERSE option is set.

See also:], |, WHILE, WEND

] (ENDIF)

ENDIF   Conditional assembly

Syntax: [*logical exp*

              ...instructions executed if expression
                              true...

              {|

              ...instructions executed if expression
                             false...}

              ]

Instruction sequences delimited by the IF and ENDIF directives, written [and],
are assembled only if the logical expression evaluates true at the time of assembly.
The optional directive ELSE, written |, allows instructions to be assembled if the
condition is false.

      None of [, | or] may appear as the first character on any line of input to the
Assembler.

      Lines not assembled as a result of these directives are not listed either
unless the Assembler's –NOTERSE option is set.

      See also: [, |, WHILE, WEND

| (ELSE)

ELSE   Conditional assembly

Syntax: [*logical exp*

              ...instructions executed if expression
                                    true...

              {|

              ...instructions executed if expression
                                    false...}

              ]

Instruction sequences delimited by the IF and ENDIF directives, written [and],
are assembled only if the logical expression evaluates true at the time of assembly.
The optional directive ELSE, written |, allows instructions to be assembled if the
condition is false.

None of [, | or] may appear as the first character on any line of input to the
Assembler.

Lines not assembled as a result of these directives are not listed unless the
Assembler's –NOTERSE option is set.

See also: [,], WHILE, WEND

^ (Storage map)

Set origin of storage map   Storage allocation

Syntax: `^ expression{, base-reg}`

Sets the origin of a storage reservation map to the address specified by the expression, optionally binding a named base register to simplify the syntax.

For example:

```
                ^              &00010000
Item1       #              4
Item2       #              8
Item3       #              4
Item4a      #              2
Item4b      #              2
```

whereupon references may be made to the items using LDR as follows:

```
        LDR            r0, [r1, #Item1]
```

Since a second register (r1 above) may be used to base the storage map a register binding may be specified when the origin is set, as follows:

```
                ^              0, r12
IO_addr     #              4
BufStart    #              4
BufSize     #              4
CurrPtr     #              4
                . . .
        LDR            r0, IO_addr; use of R12 implied
```

This style of LDR having a clearer syntax.

See also: # (Reserve space)

ALIGN

Align program location counter Storage allocation

Syntax: `ALIGN {power_of_two}{,offset-expression}`

Force the program location counter to be aligned to the specified boundary, advancing it and inserting up to three bytes of zeros if required. Since all ARM instructions must be word-aligned this directive allows correct alignment to be achieved after tables etc.

The default alignment is 4 (that is, word alignment) and the default offset expression is 0.

Larger power-of-two values may be optionally specified to align to a coarser address boundary; the offset expression may also specify a byte offset from that boundary if required.

For example:

```
            ="a string of odd length!" ; 23 chars in fact
            ALIGN                       ; get word boundary
Next        MOV R0,R0                   ; correctly aligned
```

AREA

Define program areas   **Organizational directive**

```
Syntax: AREA name{, attr}{, attr}...{, ALIGN=expres-
                               sion}
```

The AREA directive is used to notify the Assembler and Linker of an indivisible chunk of code or data. AREA takes a name which may be optionally followed by any of the following attributes:

Attribute	Meaning
ABS	Absolute: rooted at a fixed address
REL	Relocateable: may be relocated by the Linker (default)
PIC	Position Independent Code: executes wherever loaded
CODE	Contains machine instructions
DATA	Contains data, not instructions
READONLY	The area will not be written to
COMDEF	Common area definition
COMMON	Common area
NOINIT Data	AREA initialized to zero; must contain no initializations
REENTRANT	The code area is re-entrant
BASED Rn	Static base data area based at Rn; for use with LDR/STR

The optional alignment subdirective forces the start of the area to be aligned on a power-of-two boundary. By default, areas are aligned on word (that is 4-byte) boundaries, but the expression can define any other boundary from 2 to 12 bytes.

See also: ENTRY

ASSERT

Logical test and assert error   **Diagnostic directives**

Syntax: ASSERT *logical-exp*

The logical expression is evaluated and if the result is FALSE the diagnostic message 'Assertion failed' is generated during the second pass of assembly (only).

ASSERT may be used both inside and outside macros.

For example:

```
    ASSERT     1=0     ; always generates an error
```

See also: ! (Test and assert), which differs in being inspected on both assembly passes

CN

Coprocessor register equate   Symbol definition

Syntax: *Label* CN *numeric-exp*

Assign a coprocessor register number to a symbol. The symbol is treated as a constant in an arbitrary expression; however, only coprocessor register names equated using this directive are valid where a coprocessor register name is required.

For example:

```
Scalar1                 CN      0
Scalar2                 CN      1
...
Vector1                 CN      7
```

See also: FN, CP, RN

CP

Coprocessor equate   Symbol definition

Syntax: *Label* CP *numeric-exp*

Assign a coprocessor number to a symbol. Like register names (see RN), coprocessor names are treated as constants in arbitrary expressions, but only a coprocessor name is valid where a coprocessor number is required.

For example:

```
Fuzzy      CP        5      ; Fuzzy logic coprocessor is #5
Octal      CP        6      ; Octal arithmetic coprocessor #6
MMU        CP        15     ; MMU control coprocessor #15
```

See also: CN, RN

DCB (=)

Define constant byte   **Store initialization**

Syntax: *Label* DCB *expression-list*

Place byte data at the current instruction location and advance the location counter. One or more bytes are defined by this directive, their expressions being separated by commas.

For example:

```
ErrorZ       DCB          "Error",&00

Table        DCB          &00,&FF,&55,&AA
```

See also: =, DCD, DCW

DCD (&)

Define constant word   **Store initialization**

Syntax: *Label & expression-list*

Place word data at the current instruction location and advance the location counter. One or more words are defined by this directive, their expressions being separated by commas.

For example:

```
Wordz      DCD         Word1, Word2, Word3;Define three words
```

See also: DCD, =/DCB, DCW

DCFD

Define constant floating-point double-precision   Store initialization

Syntax: *Label* DCFD *fp-const{,fp-const}*

Place a double-precision floating point constant (occupies two 32-bit words) at the current location counter, which must already be word-aligned.

An *fp-const* takes one of the forms:

{-}integerE{-}integer   e.g. 3E8, -1E-3

{-}integer.integer{E{-}integer}   e.g. 1.234E6

See also: DCFS

DCFS

Define constant floating-point single-precision Store initialization

Syntax: *Label* DCFS *fp-const{,fp-const}*

Place a single-precision floating point constant (occupies one 32-bit word) at the current location counter, which must already be word-aligned.

An `fp-const` takes one of the forms:

`{-}integer{-}integer`   for example 3E8, -1e-3

`{-}integer.integer{E{integer`   for example 1.234E6

See also: DCFD

DCW

Define constant half-word   Store initialization

Syntax: *Label* DCW *expression-list*

Place half-word data at the current instruction location and advance the location
counter. One or more half-words are defined by this directive, their expressions
being separated by commas.

For example:

```
A_then_null DCW          "A"      ;stores 65 then 0 in 2 bytes
```

See also: &/DCD, =/DCB

END

Finish assembly source file   Organizational directive

Syntax: END

The END directive tells the Assembler to stop processing a source file.

   If assembly of the file was invoked by a GET directive the Assembler returns to the calling file and re-commences assembly after the calling GET.

   If END is encountered in the top-level source file during the first pass of assembly without any errors, the second pass begins. Reaching the end of a file without encountering an END is an error.

ENTRY

Define AREA entry point   Organizational directive

Syntax: {label} ENTRY

The ENTRY directive declares its offset within the containing AREA to be the unique entry point to any program containing this AREA.

EQU (*)

Equate	Symbol definition

Syntax: *Label * numeric-exp|program-relative-exp*

Assign a numeric value to a symbol. Program-relative values can also be assigned in this way.

For example:

```
Bell            *           &07
Book            *           &08
Candle          *           &09

Label           *           SWI &1001
Here            *           Label+4
```

See also: * (EQU)

EXPORT

Declare symbol for linking   Linking directives

Syntax: EXPORT *symbol*{[FPREGARGS, DATA, LEAF]}

Declare a symbol for use at link time by other separate object files. The optional parameters are as follows:

Parameter	Purpose
FPARGREGS	Symbol expects floating-point arguments in FP registers
DATA	Symbol defines code segment data, not function/procedure
LEAF	Symbol is function which calls no other functions

See also: IMPORT

FN

Floating-point register equate   Symbol definition

Syntax: *Label* FN *numeric-expression*

Assign a floating-point register number to a symbol. The symbol is treated as a constant in an arbitrary expression; however, only register names equated using this directive are valid where a register name is required.

For example:

```
Xdim        FN          f0
Ydim        FN          f1
Area        FN          f2
```

GBLA,GBLL,GBLS

Declare global variable   Symbol definition

Syntax: GBLA *variable-name*

               GBLL *variable-name*

               GBLS *variable-name*

Declare a global variable of type Arithmetic, Logical or String and assign the given variable name to it. Global variables' scope extends across the entire source file (but not beyond). Variables must be declared using either GBLx or LCLx before use; the SETx directives may be used to assign values to them.

For example:

               GBLA   Editor_Mode_Number

               GBLL   File_Auto_Save_Flag

               GBLS   Fatal_Error_String

See also: LCLx, SETx, MACRO

GET

Include file in assembly   File linking directives

Syntax: GET *filename*

Includes the named file into the file being assembled at this point. The included file may in turn employ GET to include other files. All statements up to the END of the included file are assembled and assembly then continues at the line following the GET directive in the the including file.

See also: INCLUDE (synonym)

IMPORT

Announce external symbol   **Linking directives**

Syntax: `IMPORT symbol{[FPREGARGS]}{,WEAK}`

Provides the Assembler with a name (symbol) which is not defined in this assembly but which will be resolved at link time to a symbol defined in another object file assembled separately. The symbol is treated as a program address.

The optional parameters are as follows:

Parameter	Purpose
FPARGREGS	Symbol expects floating-point arguments in FP registers
WEAK	Don't fault unresolved references during linking

See also: EXPORT

INCLUDE

Include file in assembly   **File linking directive**

Syntax: INCLUDE *filename*

Includes the named file into the file being assembled at this point. The included file may in turn employ INCLUDE to include other files. All statements up to the END of the included file are assembled and assembly then continues at the line following the INCLUDE directive in the the including file.

See also: GET (synonym)

KEEP

Maintain local symbol(s) in symbol table   Organizational directive

Syntax: KEEP {symbol}

Retain all symbols (no argument) or the specified symbol in the symbol table for this object file. The Assembler does not normally include local symbols (those not exported using EXPORT) in the object file.

See also: IMPORT, EXPORT

LCLA, LCLL, LCLS

Declare local variable   Symbol definition

Syntax: LCLA *variable-name*

               LCLL *variable-name*

               LCLS *variable-name*

Declare a local variable of type Arithmetic, Logical or String and assign the given variable name to it. Local variables' scope is restricted to a particular instantiation of a macro. Variables must be declared using either GBLx or LCLx before use; the SETx directives may be used to assign values to them.

For example:

```
LCLA        Iteration_Count

LCLL        AddressSpace26
```

See also: GBLx, SETx, MACRO

LTORG

Literal pool origin   **Organizational directive**

Syntax: LTORG *numeric-exp*

Directs that the current literal pool (assembled for use by LDR instructions) be placed immediately following the directive; word alignment is used. This would otherwise occur at the END directive; a typical use is to bring the literal pool in range of the 4 kbyte offset limit for LDR.

MACRO

Begin macro definition   **Macros**

```
Syntax:      MACRO

{$label}     macroname {$parameter1}{,$parameter2}
                               {,$parameter3}...

             ...instructions...

             MEND
```

This directive forms the opening clause of a macro definition: it must be followed by a macro prototype statement (second line of syntax definition above) which states the name of the macro and its parameters. An optional label is permitted if the expanded macro needs to have a label.

The Assembler will replace each occurrence of the macro name in the program source with the instructions defined for that macro, substituting the label and parameters for those values supplied on each macro invocation.

For example, the following macro 'Merge' joins 16-bit half-words from two registers and returns the result in the first:

```
MACRO
MERGE $r0, $r1
MOV $r0, $r0, LSR #16
ORR $r0, $r0, $r1, LSL #16
MEND
```

and to invoke it:

```
MERGE        r4,r5
```

which in turn assembles to:

```
MOV          r4, r5, LSR #16
ORR          r4, r4, r5, LSL #16
```

See also: MEND

MEND

End macro definition   **Macros**

Syntax: MEND

This directive forms the closing clause of a macro definition. Refer to the MACRO directive for more information.

MEXIT

Macro early termination   Macros

This directive allows an early exit from a macro definition.

Normally a macro is closed with MEND; all Assembler constructs, for example WHILE/WEND, must have been closed beforehand. MEXIT allows the macro definition to be finished early and closes all open WHILE/WEND loops or conditional assembly clauses as it exits the macro.

See also: WHILE/WEND, [|], MACRO, MEND

NOFP

No floating-point allowed   Miscellaneous

Syntax: NOFP

Advise the Assembler that the target has no floating-point support and ensure that no floating-point directives or instructions are allowed during the assembly; an error will be generated upon encountering any of the relevant directives or instructions.

OPT

Set assembly options

Listing directives

Syntax: OPT *arithmetic-expression*

The OPT directive is used to control the listing style of the Assembler from within the program being assembled. If listing is turned on when the Assembler is invoked (using the -list command line option) then the value given to OPT affects the style of listing. Permissible values for OPT may be summed together from the following list:

Code	Effect
1	Turn on listing
2	Turn off listing
4	Form feed (starts a fresh page)
8	Reset line counter to zero
16	Turn on listing of SET, GBL and LCL directives
32	Turn off listing of SET, GBL and LCL directives
64	Turn on listing of macro expansions
128	Turn off listing of macro expansions
256	Turn on listing of macro calls
512	Turn off listing of macro calls
1024	Turn on listing during the first assembly pass
2048	Turn off listing during the first assembly pass
4096	Turn on listing of conditional directives
8192	Turn off listing of conditional directives
16384	Turn on listing of MEND directives
32768	Turn off listing of MEND directives

The current OPT setting may be interrogated using the pseudo-variable {OPT} which may be assigned to a variable using SETA, for example:

```
        GBLA    OldOpt
OldOpt  SETA    {OPT}
        OPT     NewValue
        ...
        OPT     OldOpt
```

See also: TTL, SUBT

ORG

Set origin of assembly   **Organizational directive**

Syntax: ORG *numeric-expression*

The program's origin, that is the initial value of the location counter, is determined by the ORG directive.

Only one ORG may ever appear in each assembly and no ARM instructions or store initialization directives may precede it. If no ORG is included the Assembler attempts to generate relocatable output and the location counter is initialized to zero. ORG is best applied to programs with a single AREA.

For example:

```
        ORG         &00080000; starts at &80000

START   =           &00000000; assign START
        ORG         START        ; origin at START
```

RLIST

Define register list   Miscellaneous

Syntax: *Label* RLIST {*list-of-regs*}

Define a label to refer to a list of ARM integer registers (enclosed by mandatory braces) for simplicity when issuing LDM/STM multiple register transfer instructions.

Registers may be listed in any order; register ranges consisting of two valid register numbers joined by a dash are also permitted. Registers are always transferred in the same order regardless of how many or which are included. See LDM/STM.

For example:

```
MyContext    RLIST         {r0,r1,r2,r10-r13}

AllRegs                    RLIST   {r0-r15}
```

RN

Register equate   Symbol definition

Syntax: *Label* RN *numeric-expression*

Assign a register number to a symbol. The symbol is treated as a constant in an arbitrary expression; however, only register names equated using this directive are valid where a register name is required.

For example:

```
AF          RN          0              ; my Z80 emulator regs
BC          RN          1
DE          RN          2
HL          RN          3

...

LK          RN          14
PC          RN          15
```

ROUT

Begin local label region	Local labels
Syntax: {*label*}	ROUT

```
              ...routine instructions here...
```

The ROUT directive is used to demark the scope of a 'routine' within which local labels may be employed; local labels allow many branch references within the same routine without requiring unique label identifiers. Local labels are two-digit numbers in the range 00 to 99.

A local label area begins with the ROUT directive and ends with the next ROUT directive or the end of assembly.

To define a local label enter it at the start of a line, optionally followed by the routine name within which it resides, for example:

```
MyRoutine   ROUT
                          ...
00MyRoutine MOV r0, r1
                          ...
                        CMP r0, #3
                        BNE %BT00MyRoutine
```

To refer to a local label a % symbol introduces the label in a statement whose syntax is of the form:

```
            %{x}{y}<label_number>{routine_name}
```

where the optional x field gives the Assembler a hint about which direction to search for the label (B for backwards, F forwards) and the optional y field indicates whether to look at: A, all macro levels; or T, only this macro level.

See also: %

SETA,SETL,SETS

Assign value to assembly variable   Symbol definition

Syntax:

> variable-name SETA *arithmetic-expression*
>
> variable-name SETL *logical-expression*
>
> variable-name SETS *string-expression*

Assign a value to a local or global variable previously declared using GBLx or
LCLx.

The expression is evaluated and its value assigned to the named variable; an
error or coercion will occur if the types don't match. For example, single ASCII
characters are coerced into their (arithmetic) ASCII value.

The pseudo-values {TRUE} and {FALSE} may be used in assignments to logical variables.

For example:

```
                    GBLA    ArithVar
                    GBLL    BoolVar
                    GBLS    StringVar

ArithVar            SETA    &41560601
Ecstasy             SETA    "E"
BoolVar             SETL    {TRUE}
StringVar    SETS       "ARM600"
```

See also: GBLx, LCLx

SUBT

Set subtitle string   Listing directives

Syntax: SUBT *subtitle-string*

Set a subtitle string to be printed at the top of each page of Assembler listing, assuming listing is turned on. A null string results in a blank subtitle line. Only the most recently encountered subtitle appears on the listing pages.

Listing is controlled both by the Assembler command line option `-list` and by the current OPT directive setting.

See also: TTL, OPT

TTL

Set title string   **Listing directives**

Syntax: TTL *title_string*

Set a title string to be printed at the top of each page of Assembler listing, assuming listing is turned on. A null string results in a blank title line. Only the most recently encountered title appears on the listing pages.

Listing is controlled both by the Assembler command line option -list and by the current OPT directive setting.

See also: SUBT, OPT

WEND

End while   **Conditional assembly**

Syntax: WHILE *logical-expression*

...instructions assembled while expression
is true...

WEND

Instruction sequences delimited by WHILE...WEND are assembled only if the logical expression evaluates true. An assemble-time loop is produced, useful for generating tables etc.

Each WHILE must always be matched by a WEND. It is also permissible to escape from a WHILE inside a macro using MEXIT.

See also: WHILE, MACRO, MEXIT

WHILE

While	Conditional assembly

`Syntax:`

> `WHILE` *logical-expression*
>
> `...instructions assembled while expression`
>   `is true...`

`WEND`

Instruction sequences delimited by WHILE...WEND are assembled only if the logical expression evaluates true. An assemble-time loop is produced, useful for generating tables etc.

Each WHILE must always be matched by a WEND. It is also permissible to escape from a WHILE inside a macro using MEXIT.

See also: WEND, MACRO, MEXIT

Bibliography

ARM Limited (1991). *VIDC20 Data Sheet*. Cambridge: ARM Limited.

ARM Limited (1992). *ARM6 Data Sheet*. Cambridge: ARM Limited.

ARM Limited (1992). *ARM60 Data Sheet*. Cambridge: ARM Limited.

ARM Limited (1992). *ARM600 Data Sheet*. Cambridge: ARM Limited.

ARM Limited (1992). *ARM610 Data Sheet*. Cambridge: ARM Limited.

ARM Limited (1992). *FPA10 Data Sheet*. Cambridge: ARM Limited.

Furber S. B. (1989). *VLSI RISC Architecture and Organization*. New York: Marcel Dekker Inc.

GEC Plessey Semiconductors (1992). *ARM250 Datasheet*. Swindon: GEC Plessey Semiconductors.

Hennessy J.L and Patterson D.A. (1990). *Computer Architecture: a Quantitative Approach*. Palo Alto: Morgan Kaufmann Publishers Inc.

Kane G. (1988). *MIPS RISC Architecture*. New Jersey: Prentice-Hall Inc.

Pountain D. (1992). *A call to ARM*. Byte, November, 293–298.

Pountain D. (1993). *Computing without Clocks*. Byte, January, 145–150.

VLSI Technology, Inc. (1990). *Acorn RISC Machine Data Manual*. New Jersey: Prentice-Hall Inc.

VLSI Technology, Inc. (1992). *ARM Cross-Development Toolkit*. San Jose: VLSI Technology, Inc.

Index